Environmental Studies

Environmental Studies

H.M. SAXENA

RAWAT PUBLICATIONS

Jaipur • New Delhi • Bangalore • Hyderabad • Guwahati • Kolkata

ISBN 978-81-7033-993-9

Reprinted, 2021

Published by
Prem Rawat for **Rawat Publications**
Satyam Apts, Sector 3, Jawahar Nagar, Jaipur 302 004 (India)
Phone: 0141 265 1748 / 7006 Fax: 0141 265 1748
E-mail: info@rawatbooks.com
Website: www.rawatbooks.com

New Delhi Office
4858/24, Ansari Road, Daryaganj, New Delhi 110 002
Phone: 011 2326 3290

Also at *Bangalore, Hyderabad, Guwahati* and *Kolkata*

Typeset by Rawat Computers, Jaipur
Printed at Thomson Press (India) Ltd., New Delhi

Contents

Preface

The United Nations Conference on 'Environment and Development' held in Rio de Janerio in 1992 and World Summit on 'Sustainable Development' held at Johannesburg in 2002 have drawn the attention of people around the globe to the deteriorating condition of our environment. It is clear that no citizen on the earth can afford to be ignorant of environmental issues, therefore, environmental study has become necessary for students. But, in India, adequate attention on environmental studies has not been given. Recognizing this, the Supreme Court of India directed the University Grants Commission (UGC) to introduce a basic course on environment at every level in college education. Accordingly, the UGC has developed a core module syllabus in environmental studies for undergraduate course to be compulsorily implemented in all the universities/colleges of India.

The present book has been designed as per UGC syllabus. The contents of the book have been divided into eight units. Starting from multidisciplinary nature of environmental studies, it deals with natural resources, ecosystems, biodiversity and its conservation, environmental pollution, social issues and the environment, human population and the environment, and finally, fieldwork. Every aspect has been discussed according to the undergraduate standard. Throughout the book, Indian examples have been given, so that students can be able to understand the environmental problems of the country.

Many scholars and friends have had a role, either direct or indirect, in writing this book. I am thankful to all of them as well as all the members of my family. Finally, I am thankful to Rawat Publications for its timely and nicely publication.

H.M. Saxena

List of Figures

1

Introduction: Multidisciplinary Nature of Environmental Studies

Environment is the source of life on earth and it not only directs but also determines the existence, growth and development of mankind and all its activities. Primitive man ate wild fruits—hunted and fished—and relied heavily on nature for his very existence. Even these basic activities damaged nature to some extent. At that time, man did not concern himself with conservation methods, or in other words, there was no need for it because nature was able to cope with whatever damage was inflicted, by quickly restoring its resources.

As society developed, man's impact on environment grew in scope and strength. Until very recently, we adhered to the following dictum: "we cannot expect favours from nature; we must take them". For quite a long time, no thought was given to the possible consequences of such 'taking' from nature. But, the consequences were significant and pervasive. Mankind has long trusted in nature's potential and restorative powers, though there was no reason to believe that these powers were inexhaustible. Only recently, man has come to realize the necessity for conservation. Undoubtedly, this is the result of revolution in science and technology, which has dramatically increased man's ability to use natural environment and its resources. Nature has been increasingly damaged, restorative capabilities have progressively weakened, and human environment is deteriorating day by day to the point of affecting not only the quality of life but even the very existence of life. At this point, man realized the need to preserve and improve his environment, which is now called as the ecological approach.

The human environment is the earth we live on. It includes all the physical parts of the earth, such as air, soil, minerals, rocks and water, as well as all its living organisms, such as animals and plants. Environmental science provides an approach towards understanding the environment of our planet and the impact of human life on that environment. It is also a search for solutions to the environmental problems that confront us. In fact, environmental science is a vast subject, including all those branches of knowledge which deal with ecology as an interdisciplinary science drawing upon subjects like zoology, botany, geography and social and natural sciences. The study of environment basically deals with the study of environment and ecology. Therefore, it is necessary to discuss the various aspects of environment and ecology.

Environment

The term 'environment' etymologically means surroundings. Literally, it is an English term formed by two words, i.e., 'environ' and 'ment' which means 'encircle' or 'all round'. Thus, environment is a complex of many variables which surround man as well as all living organisms. Any external force, substance or condition, which surrounds and affects the life of the organism in any way, becomes a factor of its environment. These factors have been variously called as environmental factors, ecological factors or simply, factors and may be living/biotic as well as non-living/abiotic. The sum of all these living and non-living factors makes the environment of an organism. The place where an organism lives is called 'habitat'. It is also known as 'milieu' which means "total set of surroundings". In fact, habitat is a part of the earth's surface where life originates and develops according to the geographical conditions. Moore, in his book *A Dictionary of Geography* (1967), has defined habitat as "the natural environment of a plant or animal. It is often expressed as one of the main natural regions or one of their sub-divisions, which are recognized in geography as equatorial forests, the tundra". The encyclopaedic definitions of environment are:

> The sum total of all conditions, agencies and influences, which affect the development, growth, life and death of an organism, species or race (*The Universal Encyclopaedia*).
>
> The entire range of external influences acting on an organism, both the physical and biological (in other organisms) forces of nature surrounding an individual (*Encyclopaedia Britannica*).

Environmental Factors

As described, environment is a complex phenomenon of several factors which are the product of the forces and processes of nature, and, according to White and Renners, are universal and inherent all over the earth. These factors are classified into two groups as under:

(i) *Direct factors:* These include light, temperature, soil, air, water, soil nutrients, etc.
(ii) *Indirect factors:* These include soil structure, soil organisms, altitude, wind, slope, etc.

According to Oosting (1948), the environment is a complex of varied factors or causes, which include: (a) substances (soil, water), (b) conditions (temperature, light), (c) forces (wind, gravity), (d) organisms (plants, animals), and (e) time. Another ecologist Daubenmire (1959) classified these factors into seven coordinate headings as: (i) soil, (ii) water, (iii) temperature, (iv) light, (v) atmosphere, (vi) fire, and (vii) biotic factors. Others have grouped these elements as follows:

(i) climatic or aerial factors,
(ii) topographic or physiographic factors,
(iii) edaphic factors, and
(iv) biotic factors.

While studying environment geographers have also considered the above-mentioned factors. These factors are termed as physical factors. The natural environment of any part of the earth's surface can be classified into following fourteen elements:

A. *Abstract Elements*
(i) Location
(ii) Situation
(iii) Geometrical position
(iv) Size or areal space
(v) Form

B. *Physical Elements*
(vi) Physiography/landforms
(vii) Climate
(viii) Rocks and minerals
(ix) Soils
(x) Surface waters of the land
(xi) Underground water
(xii) The ocean and its coasts

C. *Biotic Elements*
(xiii) Natural vegetation
(xiv) Animal life

A brief review of these elements is necessary for proper understanding of environment. *Location* is an environmental factor, which indicates relative occurrence in space or, in other words, it is an indicator of space relationship. Geographical location can be expressed in absolute terms of latitude and longitude relative to the earth's surface as a whole. The latitudinal location also is an indicator of the broad climatic zone in which a specified area/place is located. Whether the place is located in tropical, temperate or cold region, it can easily be ascertained simply by its latitudinal location. Apart from this, location in terms of land and sea is also a factor, which affects the local environment. This is known as *situation* and it means the occurrence of a place with regard to the fixed features of nature. The basic types of situation are: (i) *continental situation*: (a) intermontane situation, (b) midland situation, (c) piedmont situation, and (d) river plain situation; and (ii) *maritime situation*: (a) littoral situation, (b) peninsular situation, (c) insular situation, (d) pelagic situation, and (e) isthmian situation. All these situations have had their impact on the environment in one way or other. Similarly, *size*, i.e., *areal space*, is also an environmental factor, which controls the climate as well as regional environment.

Relief or *landform* is another major physical factor, which affects the environment variously. The impact of relief can be seen not only on climate, natural vegetation and soils but also on the settlement of man and economic development. Because of favourable relief, the river valley civilizations have developed in China, India, Mesopotamia, and even today relief is a controlling environmental factor for all types of economic development. The various geomorphic regions such as hilly, plain, plateau, arid, glacial, coastal, limestone, etc., have had specific natural environment and ecological settings. Mountains are least hospitable to human cultures. The topographical effect on environment can be seen on precipitation, development of snow fields and glaciers, rate of erosion, variations in vegetation types, soils, etc.

Climate of a region is determined by such methodological factors like temperature, pressure, winds, relative humidity, rainfall, evaporation rate, etc. These factors are concerned mainly with the aerial environment of an organism. Climate is not only directed but determines the entire ecological balance of a region. The other environmental factors like natural vegetation, soil, water bodies as well as man's activities are in one way or the other related with climate. The various forms of ecosystem, such as desert, coastal, glacial, are the products of climate. The climate is highly affected by man's activities in the form of pollution, which has now become a global problem. The direct effects of temperature and rainfall can be seen on vegetation and animals.

Soil is also an important environmental factor. Plants depend for their nutrients, water supply and anchorage upon the soil. Soil system is indeed very complex and dynamic, which is undergoing continuous change, and the rate of such change is influenced by a number of environmental factors. For example, soil formation depends upon parent material, climate, vegetation, relief and time. A properly managed soil is an asset, and if it is misused, it can be permanently damaged and will create environmental degradation.

Natural vegetation is an index of other environmental factors such as climate, soil and landforms, while itself it is also a factor of environment. It controls the temperature and helps in rainfall by increasing humidity. It is also a controller of soil erosion. Forests are assets to mankind and a natural resource of national importance. Great damage has been done to forests after the Industrial Revolution and now the world is facing several problems due to deforestation, which has become the main cause of environmental degradation, both in developed as well as developing countries.

Among other environmental factors, water bodies and animals are also important. All these factors of the environment are not independent but are linked with each other in such a way that none can be separated from the other. Therefore, the environment should be taken into consideration in its entirety. The total impact of environment is reflected in all developmental activities—economic, social, political or cultural.

Ecology

Ecology is the science of the relations of all organisms to their environment. The two components of nature—organisms and their environment—are not only complex and dynamic but also interdependent. Ecology is a relatively new science, dealing with the various principles, which govern such relationships between organisms and their environment.

In 1859, St. Hilaire Isodore Geoffory, a French zoologist, proposed the term 'ethology' for "the study of the relations of organisms within the family and society in the aggregate and in the community". Similarly, a British naturalist, St. George Jackson Mivart, used the term 'hexicology', which he defined in 1894 as "devoted to the study of the relations between the organisms and their environment as regards the nature of the locality..." The term 'ecology' was coined by combining two Greek words, viz., 'oikos' (meaning 'house' or 'dwelling place') and 'logos' (meaning "the study of") to denote the relationships between the organisms and their environment. Although, there is some controversy about the original coining of the term but there is consensus that German biologist, Erust Haeckel first gave substance to this term. He used this term first in 1886 but defined for the first time in 1870 as follows: "By ecology we mean the body of knowledge concerning the economy of nature—the investigation of the total relations of the animal both to its inorganic and to its organic environment, including above all, its friendly and inimical relations with those animals and plants with which it comes directly and indirectly into contact."

Today, ecology is a systematic and well-developed science. Some of the definitions of ecology are as follows:

> Ecology is defined as the study of the relations of organisms, or groups of organisms to their environment, or the science of the interrelations between living organisms and their environments (Odum).
>
> Ecology is the science of all the relations of all organisms to their environments (Taylor).
>
> Ecology is the science which treats the organisms in relation to their environment (Moore).
>
> Ecology is the science dealing with the relationship of organisms to one another and to other factors that comprise their environment (*Encyclopaedia Britannica*).
>
> Ecology is the study of plants and animals in relation to their environment (Haggett).
>
> Ecology is the science of the mutual relationship of organisms to their environment (Monkhouse and Small).

It becomes clear from the above definitions that ecology is the study of the interaction of living organisms with their physical, biological and chemical environment. All its components, i.e., energy, air, water, soil, vegetation, animals as well as man have mutual relations, responsible for the development of a particular ecological system. The interrelationship of ecological elements has been depicted in Figure 1.1.

Figure 1.1
Ecological Relationship

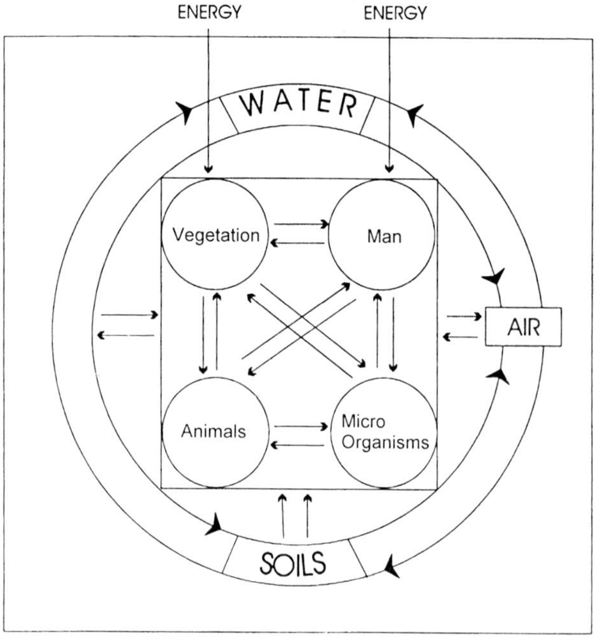

Thus, the elements of environment—biotic and abiotic—not only interrelated but also function in an orderly manner as a definite system. Thus, structure and function provide a base for the study of ecosystem. The spectrum of modern ecology can also be defined in terms of levels of organization. It begins with the groups of organisms, up to ecosystem level. In ecology, the term 'population' is used to include groups of individuals of any one kind of organism. Likewise, community or biotic community in the ecological sense includes all the populations occupying a given area. The community and the non-living environment function together as an ecological system or ecosystem. The present status occupied by ecology is quite evident by its role in the solution of socio-economic and environmental problems of pollution. Besides, its role in managing water, soil, forest and land resources as well as in agricultural development and conservation of resources also become important. The international problem of environmental pollution also needs an ecological approach. In fact, sustainable development is nothing but development within the framework of an ecosystem.

Basic Concepts of Ecology

The basic concepts of ecology are as follows:

(i) All living organisms and their environments are mutually reactive, affecting each other in various ways.

(ii) The environment, which is a complex phenomenon of several interrelated factors, is highly dynamic (i.e., varying with time and space).

(iii) The species puts forth every effort to maintain its uniformity in structure, function, reproduction, growth and development by preservation of its genetic pool.

(iv) Not only does the environment influence the life of organisms, but organisms too modify their environment as a result of their growth, disposal, reproduction, death, decay, etc.

(v) The concept of biome was put forward by Clements and Shelford, who stated that all plants and animals are related to each other by their coaction and reaction on the environment. According to them, under similar climatic conditions, there may simultaneously develop more than one community, some reaching the climax stage, others under different stages of succession. This complex of several communities in any area, represented by an assemblage of different kinds of plants, animals, etc., sharing a common climate, is called biome.

(vi) Each population occupies a specific niche, a unique functional position with respect to other organisms with which it interacts.

(vii) There exist varying degrees of neutral interactions among organisms, at both inter-specific and intra-specific levels.

(viii) The chemical components of the ecosystem move in defined cycles known as biochemical cycles.

(ix) The successful growth of an organism is governed by limiting factors. The minimal and maximal levels of tolerance for all ecological factors of a species vary seasonally, geographically and according to the age of the population.

(x) The exploitation of ecosphere by man's activities is the main cause of the disruption of the ecosphere. It leads to a setback of the state of development and reduction in the stability of the ecosystem.

Multidisciplinary Nature of Environmental Studies

The scope of environmental studies is very vast and related with both natural and social sciences. As we know, environment can be divided into two broad categories, viz.,

(i) physical environment, and
(ii) socio-cultural or man-made environment.

Both these categories are interrelated and interdependent. In fact, socio-cultural environment is the product of physical environment. In a way, physical environment still determines the human environment. Thus, on the one hand, environment is related with physical and biochemical aspects, on the other hand, it not only directs but to some extent determines the human environment, therefore, its study is multidisciplinary in nature.

The environmental studies are very much related with Botany, Zoology, Chemistry, Pedology, Geography, Climatology, Oceanography, Geomorphology, Sociology, Political Science, Economics, Management, etc. Since, environment and man are the primary concerns of environmental studies, all the subjects related with these aspects have relationship with environmental studies.

Botany and environmental study is interrelated with each other. The whole botanical world is the product of environmental conditions. The climate, which comprises of temperature, rainfall and winds, is a controlling factor of natural vegetation. The other factors are relief, soil, water bodies and their congregation. The ecology forms the basis of botany as well as environmental studies. The study of 'biomes' is related with the concept of 'eco-development' or 'sustainable development' is the product of the multidisciplinary nature of environmental studies.

Zoology and environmental studies are also closely related. The growth, development and dispersal of several species in the world are determined by the environment. The question of biodiversity and extinction of several species due to change in climate and other environmental factors now has become a main problem and their protection as well as conservation can be possible only through a habitat study, with multidisciplinary approach.

Relationship between chemistry and environmental studies can be helpful in solving the environmental pollution, ozone depletion, greenhouse effect, etc. The environment pollution is the biggest problem of the world today and it can be properly understood and solved by chemical analysis/chemical engineering. The air, water and soil pollution involve various chemical elements/ gases and their reactions. The studies done by chemical scientists are of full use to the environmentalists. Similarly, physics can help in developing theronal and outset techniques to control the pollution, radioactivity, etc. Pedology is the science of soil and soil is the product of rock structure and its action and reaction with environmental processes. Soil also controls the whole botanical world. The problem of soil degradation has now become one of the main environmental problems, having adversely affected not only natural vegetation but also agriculture.

Apart from the above-mentioned physical sciences, environmental studies are also related with Agricultural Science, Engineering, Climatology, Oceanography, Geomorphology and all other sciences.

Geography and environmental studies are very much related to each other. Geography, in its broad spectrum, is a group of sciences concerned with the surface of the earth, including the distribution of life upon it, its physical features, the evolution of landforms and life, present and the past climate and the human intervention which has changed the physical and cultural landscape over the years. Similarly, the study of environment is a primary concern of geography. Geographers not only analyze the environment and its various components in isolation but also deal with environmental impact on man and his activities and vice versa. Man is an integral part of the biosphere today. With a myriad of activities, born out of the intellect of the human race, man radically changed the natural environment and the ecosystem existing therein.

The spatial aspect is associated with geographical studies of environment. In fact, every ecosystem has its own geographical conditions, which need complete analysis and this aspect provides a base for geography of environment. Today, terms such as 'human ecology', 'social ecology', 'ecological technology' and 'ecological equilibrium in the environment' have sprung into existence to connote man's relation with environment and conservation of nature, which is also a primary objective of the geography of environment. Moore (1967) has observed that "ecology lies on the frontiers of so many other subjects, including various branches of geography".

Geography is a science, analyzing spatial distribution based on 'cause and effect'. The geographical data are very useful for effective analysis of the environmental and ecological aspect (now GIS or Geographical Information System, which provides detailed information for any part of the world). Gerasimov, a Russian geographer, in his *Geography and Ecology* (1983), has observed: "Geography has accumulated a huge volume of information on the natural conditions and resources of the entire world and on the degree and forms of their development and economic use. It is no less important that handling these new formidable tasks geography can rely on the complex system of its branches."

Strahlers have discussed the geographical aspects and its relationship with environment in their book *Geography and Man's Environment* (1976) and have observed: "The phrase 'man and the land' is often used to convey the essence of geography. While the relationship of human to their earthly environment is a core concept in geography, an equally important idea is that the relationship has a certain distribution in space. Geographers recognize of richness or poverty of life forms capable of being supported."

Social sciences like sociology and political science also have indirect relationship with environmental studies. In sociology, all the social aspects, including social problems, are discussed. Nowadays, problems related with environment have become social problems. The society is playing a vital role in environmental awareness and many social organizations are doing very good work in this field. Similarly, various issues related with environment have become political issues. The politics of environment, role of world and national organization and environmental legislations are some of the issues related both with political science and environment studies.

It thus becomes clear from above analysis that environmental studies are of 'multidisciplinary' nature.

Importance of Environmental Studies

Environmental studies are necessary to understand the environment, ecology and their impact on man. Environment is a controller of life on earth. It is not only necessary for the growth but also for existence of life on the earth. Kevin R. Cox (1972) has pointed out that a good environment should be:

(i) pollution free,
(ii) healthy,
(iii) having prospects of employment,
(iv) having entertainment facility,
(v) having good housing facilities,
(vi) having educational facilities, etc.

The quality of the life of the people is very much dependent upon good environment. The main objectives of the environmental studies are:

- to develop awareness about environment,
- to explain man-environmental relationship,
- to explain the causes and effects of environmental degradation,
- to explain the causes and effects of the air, water, land, soil, noise and radioactive pollution,
- to study the natural hazards and their impact on environment,

— to discuss the development vis-à-vis environment,
— to discuss the population explosion and its impact on environment,
— to study the conservation of natural resources,
— to study global, national, regional and local environmental problems,
— to explain the problems related to biodiversity, climatic change, global warming, extinction of species, ozone depletion, acid rain, deforestation, desertification, etc.,
— to protect man and animals from pollution,
— to educate people at all levels about environment,
— to develop long-term and short-term plans for conservation of the environment, and
— to develop strategies for sustainable development.

In brief, environmental studies are the need of the hour. These are not only necessary for understanding the environment, its various facets and problems but also for its planning. The environmental education will create an atmosphere in which all the people of the society will not only protect environment for themselves but also for their future generations.

2

Natural Resources

The modern economy is a resource-based economy and the development of a country or a region is based on its resources, especially natural resources. Nature has given us abundant resources in the form of water, air, heat, natural vegetation, soil, wild animals, metals, fossil fuels, etc., and man by his technical skill and knowledge is using all these resources in some way or the other right from the dawn of civilization. 'Resource' is a wide term and its dictionary definitions are:

- that upon which one relies for aid, support, or supply;
- means to attain given ends; and
- the capacity to take advantage of opportunities or to extricate oneself from difficulties.

According to Zimmermann (1951), "the word 'resource' does not refer to a thing or a substance but to a function, which a thing or a substance may perform or to an operation in which it may take part". In fact, resource is an abstraction reflecting human appraisal and relating to a function or operation. In the process of the utilization of natural resources man often misuses its availability, thus affecting the natural ecosystem. Earlier, this aspect was not considered properly by man, which resulted in the overexploitation of natural resources, but soon he realized that these resources are not unlimited and unless properly used the day is not far off when he will not only be deprived of some of these natural resources but will also have to face ecological consequences. This apprehension has propounded the concept of 'conservation'. Prior to a detailed discussion on the concept, it is necessary to know the types of resources.

Natural Resources: Classification

Any element of our natural environment such as soil, water, forest, wildlife, minerals, etc., that man can utilize to promote his welfare, may be identified as a natural resource. Since natural resources vary greatly in quantity, mutability and re-usability, these can be classified into two major categories, namely, inexhaustible and exhaustible.

Inexhaustible

(a) *Immutable*: Seemingly incapable of much adverse change through man's activities, such as:
(i) wind power
(ii) precipitation
(iii) tidal power
(iv) atomic energy

(b) *Misusable*: Little danger of complete exhaustion, but when improperly used, their resource quality may be impaired, such as:
(i) solar power
(ii) atmosphere
(iii) ocean
(iv) water power of flowing streams

Exhaustible

Maintainable: Those resources in which their permanency is dependent upon method of use by man. These are:
(a) *Renewable*: The living or dynamic resources whose perpetual harvest is dependent upon proper planning and management of man. These are:
(i) water in place
(ii) soil fertility

(iii) products of the land—agricultural products, forests, forage land, wild animals
(iv) products of lakes, streams and ponds—freshwater fish, black bass, lake trout, catfish
(v) products of oceans—marine fish, marine mammals
(vi) human resources

(b) *Non-renewable*: Once gone, there is no hope of replacement. These are:
(i) mineral resources
(ii) fossil fuels
(iii) species of wildlife

In general, the concept of conservation was started for non-renewable resources but for renewable resources also proper management is necessary, which is a part of conservation.

Concept of Resource Conservation

The word 'conservation' is derived from two Latin words, '*con*' meaning "together" and '*servare*', meaning "to keep or guard". Literally, therefore, conservation means "to keep together". The word was coined by Gifford Pinchot shortly after the White House Conference of 1908. Some of the definitions of resource conservation are:

> Resource conservation is the scheduling of resource use so as to provide the greatest yield for the greatest number over the longest time period (P. Haggett).

> Conservation means a sacrifice of the present generation to future generations, whenever it is carried for, this conflict beginning far before the ideal is reached which conservationists are inclined to advocate (S.R. Eyre).

> The optimum allocation of natural, human and cultural resources in the scheme of national development, whereby maximum economic and social security will be assured (Harold M. Rose).

The US President John F. Kennedy, in a special message to the Congress in 1962, interpreted conservation as "the wise use of our natural environment, the prevention of waste and despoilment while preserving, improving and renewing the quality and usefulness of all our resources".

The conservation of natural resources is a concept that deals with the rational use of resources so that a harmony between man's resource requirements and its availability can be established. While renewable resources need a proper resource management system (a part of conservation), the non-renewable resources require a long-term strategy for their proper use. This is not only necessary to assure long-term resource use but also to protect the ecosystem. Nowadays, every country is very particular about its natural resources and tries to genuinely adopt conservation policies. During the colonial period, from 18th century to mid-20th century, most of the countries of Asia, Africa and Latin America have suffered a lot due to their resource exploitation by colonial powers. Gradually, all these countries got their freedom but either for economic needs or for political adjustment, their natural resources have been exploited unwisely, resulting in not only the loss of several resources but also many problems of environmental degradation.

The conservation movement, in its present form, was first started in USA under the guidance of Gifford Pinchot, head of the US Forest Service from 1898 to 1910, with active support from the then President Franklin D. Roosevelt. The first wave of conservation was actually started when Roosevelt called the White House Conference on Natural Resources in 1908, followed by a number of important events in several subsequent decades, and the enactment of several laws which regulated the manner in which the natural resources of the country can be protected. As a result of the conference, a fifty-men National Conservation Commission comprising scientists, statesmen and businessmen was formed. After 1930, in USA, several agencies have been established and several acts have been passed to protect forests, soils, wildlife and other natural resources. This tradition was followed by other US Presidents like John. F. Kennedy, Lyndon B. Johnson, Richard M. Nixon, Bill Clinton and George Bush too and these are still in force. In 1970, Nixon set up the National Environmental Protection Agency.

The conservation wave was not limited to the US only but also started in European countries as well as in Russia and soon all the countries of the world realized the need to conserve natural resources. Therefore, apart from national efforts by each country, efforts on global level have also been started under the United Nations. Different agencies of the UN are now playing a key role in setting the world on the long road towards conservation of natural resources and protection of the environment. The increase in public support for conservation measures, both at international and local levels, has given this movement a new life, but still there is a long way to go in this direction.

Forest Resources

Where geographical conditions permit vegetation to take the form of trees, the forest is one of the major forms of the natural landscape. The forest resources are valuable as an integral part of the ecosystem, from the commercial point of view, and as providers of shelter to wildlife. Today, forests provide raw materials for over 5,000 products worth about 23 million dollars. They support industry, which employs 1.3 million people. In fact, forests are still the natural habitat of several species of plants and animals, as well as of several tribal groups of the world. But, the most unfortunate setback came in the form of commercial exploitation, which resulted in mass destruction of forest cover year after year. Originally, over two-fifths of the land area of the earth, exclusive of the polar regions, or about 1,200 million hectares, was covered with natural forests. But, now, more than one-third of this area has been robbed by man of its natural protective cover and has been turned into barren land.

The history of the exploitation of forests is as old as man himself, but during earlier times it was balanced through a natural growth process because at that time forest cutting was done for personal or community use only. But, with the expansion of agriculture, forest lands have been cleared. More destruction has been done after industrial revolution and urbanization. During the colonial period commercial exploitation began and this was the main cause of the depletion of forests. The commercial use of forests nowadays has reached such an extent that it has become a threat to the environment in the form of:

(i) increase in temperature,
(ii) lesser precipitation,
(iii) increased rate of soil erosion,
(iv) increase in frequency and volume of floods,
(v) loss of soil productivity,
(vi) extinction of several species,
(vii) non-availability of several essential forest products, and
(viii) imbalance in ecosystem.

The harmful effects of deforestation are so much that all over the world people and authorities have realized that forest resources must be conserved properly in order to protect the ecosystem.

The forest is a national resource as well as a social asset. It yields a great social profit which lies wholly outside the realm of business. But, at present, most of the forests of the world are so used that experts predict dire calamities in the not-too-distant future and irreparable damage on a catastrophic scale. If properly used and put on a sustained-yield basis, it will be one of man's greatest resources and for this, conservation of forest is the only alternative.

Deforestation

The herculean feat of economic gains and development have been at the cost of deforestation. Deforestation is one of the outcomes of various developmental activities having the character of extensional development and it is true that deforestation is a havoc wreaked by thoughtless destructive activities of development. Forest clearings were made not only for village settlements but also for cultivation and pastures. As the population increased more forests began to be cleared for various uses. Apart from this, the commercial exploitation of forests is the main cause of deforestation. There was a time when 70 per cent of the land area was covered with forests and now the total forest cover has shrunk to 16 per cent only. Nowadays, tropical deforestation has become a concern of all and its impact is not only limited to the region itself, but the climatic conditions of the whole world are alarming. The annual decline in forest cover in tropical countries has been depicted in Figure 2.1. It is clear that in countries like Brazil, India,

Figure 2.1

Area of Closed Forests Cleared Annually in Selected Tropical Countries

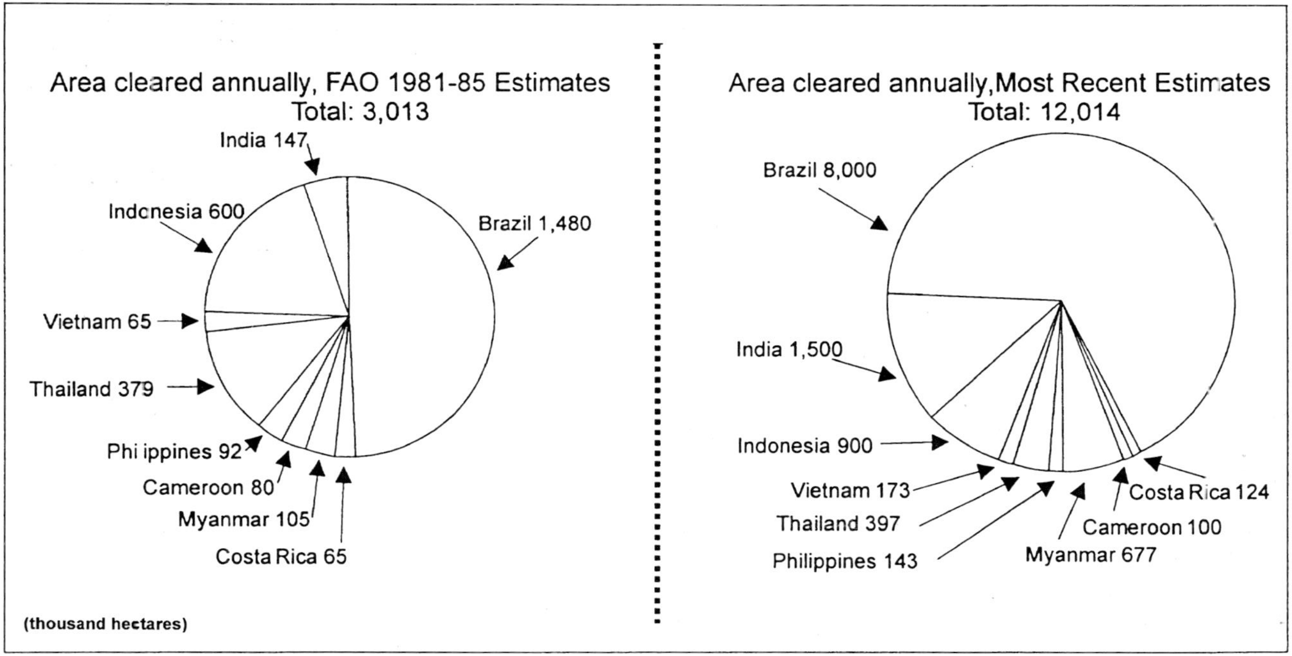

Indonesia, Thailand, etc., the rate of annual cutting of forests is very high and has become a great problem to the environment and ecosystem.

In India, deforestation is going on at a very fast pace. The story of overexploitation of forests dates back to World War II, when the British started clearing forests to meet their needs. In the post-independence period, the process of exploitation has been accelerated to meet developmental projects of railways, industries, mining, river valleys, defence, etc. The urbanization and expansion of agricultural activity have also contributed to the exploitation of forests. During the 1951-75 period, 43.28 lakh hectares of forest land has been lost to different developmental works. The commercial exploitation of forests is still going on in spite of several legal provisions to restrict it. Maximum deforestation has occurred in Madhya Pradesh, where loss of forest is about 2 million hectares, while in Maharashtra, Orissa, Andhra Pradesh, and Jammu and Kashmir over a million hectares and in Rajasthan and Himachal Pradesh over half-a-million hectares of forest land has been cleared. But, in terms of proportion, Rajasthan, Haryana and Punjab lost over half of the forest cover and states like Himachal Pradesh and Jammu and Kashmir lost over a third of their forest cover. In Tripura, Manipur, Meghalaya and Mizoram, the loss of forest cover was minimum during the 1970-90 period.

The impact of deforestation on the environment can be seen in the form of micro-climatic change, increase in temperature and decrease in humidity/rainfall, soil erosion in the form of sheet, rill and gully erosion, increase in frequency of floods and landslides, loss of soil fertility, etc. All these lead to unaccountable destruction and also pose serious ecological problems. Serious efforts will have to be made to protect and conserve forests both at government as well as public levels. Due attention should be given to forest management. Some useful steps in this direction are:

(i) a proper ratio between forest cutting and plantation of trees should be maintained;
(ii) actual growth of trees be supervised;
(iii) strict prohibition of the cutting of trees for fuel be imposed;

(iv) alternative media for wood such as moulded plastic, etc., be developed for furniture and other domestic articles;
(v) protection from forest fires;
(vi) development of national parks and game sanctuaries;
(vii) social forestry be developed;
(viii) plantation of trees according to local ecological conditions;
(xi) forest survey be conducted and classification be done accordingly; and
(x) long-term master plan for forest conservation and development be prepared.

In fact, forests can be protected through public movements like '*Chipko*'.

Methods of Forest Conservation

The following methods should be adopted for the conservation of forests:

Regulated and Planned Cutting of Trees

One of the main reasons of deforestation is commercial felling of trees. According to an estimate, about 1,600 million cubic metres of wood have been used for various purposes in the world. Although trees are considered as perennial resource, when exploited on a very large scale, their revival cannot be possible. Therefore, cutting should be regulated by adopting methods like:
(i) clear cutting,
(ii) selective cutting, and
(iii) shelter wood cutting.

The clear cutting method is useful for those areas where the same type of trees are available over a large area. In that case, trees of same age group can be cut down in a selected area and then marked for replantation. In selective cutting only mature trees are selected for cutting. This process is to be followed in rotation. Shelter wood cutting is where first of all useless trees have been cut down followed by medium and best quality timber trees. The time gap between these cuttings is helpful in the re-growth of trees. In regulated cutting only one-tenth of the forest area is selected for use and rotational system is always followed for their protection.

The forest can be managed in such away that a timber crop may be harvested indefinitely year after year without being depleted. This technique is called the 'sustained yield' method adopted by many countries of the world.

Control over Forest Fires

Destruction or loss of forest by fire is fairly common, because trees are highly exposed to fire and once started it becomes difficult to control. Sometimes, the fire starts by natural process, i.e., by lightning or by friction between trees during speedy winds, while in most cases it is caused by man, either intentionally or unintentionally. According to an estimate, during the period from 1940 to 1950, in the US alone, fires consumed an average of 21.5 million acres of timber yearly and as many as 1,175,664 cases of forest fires occurred between 1955 and 1964. Throughout the world, forest fires are common and in most cases the man is behind it. As John D. Guthrie, former fire inspector of US Forest Service, has written: "To stage a forest fire you need only few things—a forest, the right atmospheric conditions, and a spark either from a lightning bolt or a match in the hands of a fool or a knave. The formula is simple—the larger the forest, the drier the air, the bigger the fool, the bigger the fire you will have."

In order to save forests from fire, it is necessary to adopt latest techniques of fire-fighting. Some of the fire suppression techniques are to develop three metre-wide fire lanes around the periphery of the fire, back fires, arrangement of water spray, fire retardant chemicals should be sprayed from back tank and if possible by helicopters. There must be a trained staff of fire-fighters to control the fire.

Reforestation and Afforestation

The sustained yield concept dictates that whenever timber is removed, either by block cutting or by selective cutting, the denuded area must be reforested. This may be done by natural or artificial methods. Similarly, any forested land, which has been destroyed by fire or mining activities, should be reforested. In rugged terrain aerial seeding can be the ideal method.

Besides all this, fresh afforestation programmes should be started. New plantations will not only increase the forest cover but also help in making up the eco-balance. For afforestation, selection of trees should be done according to local geographical conditions and care must be taken during initial growth of the trees.

Check over Forest Clearance for Agricultural and Habitation Purposes

Most of the present-day agricultural land was once forested and then cleared for the use of agriculture. But, now, it has reached the stage where further clearance will be dangerous for the entire ecosystem. There are tribals in some parts of Asia, Africa and South America, where shifting cultivation is still a part of their system of land procurement. According to an estimate, about 40 million sq km of land is used for this purpose by 200 million tribals of the world. For the conservation of forests, this should be checked and an alternative system should be suggested to them. Similarly, for the development of villages, towns and cities, forest lands have been cleared and this process continues to this day causing loss of forest cover. This also should be checked and green belts around cities be developed.

Protection of Forest

The existing forests must be protected in every situation. Apart from commercial cutting, unorganized grazing is also one of the reasons. There are several forest diseases resulting from parasitic fungi, rusts, mistletoes, viruses and nematodes, which cause the destruction of trees. The forests should be protected either by use of chemical spray, antibiotics or by development of disease-resistant strains of trees.

Proper Utilization of Forest Products and Forests

Generally, forests are cut for logs and rest of the tree—stump, limbs, branches and foliage, etc., is left out as worthless debris. Further waste occurs at the sawmill. There is thus need to utilize all this waste material. Now several uses have been developed and products like waterproof glues, boards, etc., can be obtained from this material.

Similarly, forests can be developed as tourist centres. Such forests-turned-tourist centres can earn substantial foreign exchange for the country. This practice has been adopted by many countries—both developed and developing. The concepts of 'national park' and 'game sanctuary' have now become popular and every country has developed its unique forest area as a 'national park'. In India alone, there are as many as 20 national parks. This is a good method of forest conservation.

Role of Government in Forest Conservation

Although the government in every country is very particular about conservation of its forest resources and frames several rules and laws for the protection of forests, but their effective implementation is not done. Both national and provincial governments can take some steps in this direction, such as:

(i) enact acts for the conservation of forests,
(ii) survey of the forest resources,
(iii) categorization of forest areas and proper delimitation of reserved forest areas,
(iv) find out the areas where reforestation can be done,
(v) regulate the commercial use of forest products,
(vi) protect forests from fire, mining and other natural calamities,
(vii) develop national parks,
(viii) encourage forests developmental activities like social forestry, agro-forestry, etc., and
(ix) prepare master plans, both for long-term and short-term periods, etc.

Forest Management

Management of forest resources is the key to all conservation efforts. In forest management, the following aspects should be taken into consideration:

(i) survey of forests,
(ii) categorization of forests,
(iii) economic use of forests,

(iv) administrative setting for forest management,
(v) training programmes for persons engaged in forest conservation activities,
(vi) use of forest land as tourist centres,
(vii) social and agro-forestry,
(viii) development of new techniques for the conservation of forests,
(ix) research for efficient use and conservation of forest, and
(x) policy decisions and their proper implementation.

In brief, conservation of forest resources can be done by cooperative efforts of the government, non-government organizations and the public through a proper management system.

Water Resources

Water is an indispensible component of our ecosystem and the essence of our life. On an average, each individual uses 50 litres of water per day in rural areas and 150 litres in urban areas. Wherever available, about 12,000 m^3 to 14,000 m^3 water is used annually to irrigate one hectare of land. The main source of water is rainfall occurring through 'hydrological cycle', while other sources include underground water and water from melting of snow. The oceans are full of water but because of salinity it cannot be used. There are many areas in the world where water is a scare commodity.

Water is the source of life and right from the origin, it is being used by humankind for various purposes. The ancient civilizations have developed in river valleys. This is also true about medieval townships and other developments, and even all modern developments are related directly or indirectly to water. The main concern is that by using water, humans have influenced both its quantity and quality. Earlier, the influence of human activity on water resources was limited but now this has become a major problem of environmental degradation throughout the world. However, there are many ways in which humans influence water, for example, by direct channel manipulation, modification of watershed characteristics, urbanization and pollution.

The construction of dams and reservoirs is widespread throughout the world for irrigation purpose, to generate power or to provide a reliable source of water. More than 700 dams have been built worldwide and their number is increasing year after year. In countries like Brazil, Argentina, Canada, India, Japan, Turkey, Spain and China, run-off of water has been regulated by water reservoirs. The impact of human activities is especially marked in Africa and North America where about 20 per cent of total run-off is now controlled. The impact of dam construction is apparent in the form of change in ecosystem and environmental conditions. Bigger the dam, more will be its impact. Dams like Hoover (USA), Kiev (Russia), Aswan (Egypt), Akosombo (Ghana), and Bhakra Nangal, Gandhi Sagar, Damodar and Rihand (India) have had their impact on regional ecology. The recent environmental controversy over Tehri and Sardar Sarovar dams reflects people's awareness against construction of dams and their possible damaging environmental impact. The environmental consequences of dams include subsidence, earthquake triggering, transmission and expansion in the range of organism, the build-up of soil salinity, changes in groundwater levels, waterlogging, deforestation, etc.

The process of urbanization has too a considerable impact, both in terms of controlling not only rates of erosion but also the delivery of pollutants into rivers and in influencing the nature of run-off and other hydrological characteristics. The impact of urbanization can be summarized as follows:

(i) removal of trees or vegetation,
(ii) construction of houses and sewerage lines,
(iii) construction of septic tanks,
(iv) diversion of nearby streams for public supply,
(v) accelerated land erosion,
(vi) larger quantities of untreated waste into local streams,
(vii) pollution of streams and wells,
(viii) drilling of deeper, large capacity industrial wells, and
(ix) increased use of water for domestic and commercial purposes.

Deforestation is a human activity that gives rise to floods, annual run-off levels and also affects on-stream flow. In many parts of the world, humans obtain water supplies by pumping from groundwater. This has two main effects, i.e., the reduction in the level of water table and the replacement of freshwater by saline water. Environmental consequences of these two phenomena include ground subsidence and soil salinization.

Conservation of Water

Proper Distribution System of Water

The water distribution system should be such that loss of water should be minimum and remain free from pollutants. The distribution system should be developed according to local/regional conditions. A few general steps for distribution of water are:

(i) As far as possible water distribution should be done through pipes.

(ii) If water storage place is small, it should be cemented and if its size is big, it should be located where non-porous rocks exist.

(iii) The channels and distributaries of canals should be cemented, and in fields also either pipes be used or cemented channels (*nalahs*) be constructed.

(iv) For irrigation, sprinkle and drip system should be used.

(v) If possible, water tanks should be covered to avoid evaporation and also for cleanliness.

Rational Use of Underground Water

Underground water is also a main source of water, especially in arid and semi-arid regions. The overexploitation of underground water often results in the lowering of water table, intrusion of saline water, subsidence of land, etc. The prime need is the proper and limited use of water and also geological and hydrological survey of the region for assessment of water availability.

Purification of Waste Water

Through recycling of waste water it can be used for irrigation purposes. There are several mechanical devices for the waste water treatment, some of them are expensive also. The government agencies and industrial establishments should establish treatment plants, which will help in containing water pollution.

Control over Deforestation

The loss of vegetation is the main reason of drought and reduction in rainfall activity, thus lowering the water table. In order to maintain humidity in the atmosphere, which helps in rainfall, and to minimize evaporation rate, forest cover should be protected.

Protection of Water from Pollution

Apart from availability of water, quality of water is also important; in other words, water should be free from pollution. Nowadays, several techniques, such as physico-chemical purification methods, which include—hydrolysis, electrolysis, ion-exchange, absorption, congutation, chlorination, ozonization, etc., are in use. Similarly, biological purification method is also employed. But, the conservation of water can be done only by a proper water management system.

Floods, Droughts and Famines

Both floods and droughts are natural hazards and are related with rainfall. If there is heavy rain in the catchment area of a river, floods will occur. On the other hand, if there is less rain or failure of monsoon, droughts will occur. In both the situations, their impact on environment creates problems and also affects the regional ecosystem adversely.

Flood is a hydrological phenomenon, which occur in any drainage basin. Its magnitude and frequency varies primarily on the precipitation conditions in the catchment area. Most of the river valleys are subjected to varying degrees of flood incidences, either creating minor damages or devastating havoc at times. Such calamities pose a serious threat to the whole environmental set-up of the region, bringing about phenomenal changes in the physical environment ushering in accelerated erosional, transportational and depositional activities of the river with the consequent effects on soil. The devastating effects of floods can be seen on vegetation, agriculture, industry, settlements, causing loss of human and animal lives as well as infrastructures.

The main cause of flood is excessive rainfall but it might also occur due to earthquake, deforestation in the upper catchment areas, failure of dams, excessive snow melting, etc. The beneficial effects of floods have been established beyond doubt in the form of fertilization of soil. But its devastating effects far exceed the benefits.

In India, the problem of floods and challenge to the environmental setting is of gigantic magnitude, mainly because of (i) typical seasonal rainfall, and (ii) erratic nature of tropical cyclones and rainstorms. The following are the areas, which may be termed as flood-prone areas:

(a) Upper catchment and piedmont zone of the Himalayan river basins.
(b) Ganga river valley—upper, middle and lower deltaic zones.
(c) Brahmaputra valley and its tributaries.
(d) Deltaic region of Mahanadi, Godavari, Cauvery and Krishna rivers.
(e) Narmada and Tapti basins.

The common measures of the flood control are as follows:

(i) Control of erosion in upper catchment areas.
(ii) Construction of dams and reservoirs at suitable sites.
(iii) Prevention of overflow in channels.
(iv) Construction of multiple channels for distribution of the excess river water.
(v) Development of shelters in flood-prone areas.

The flood problem should be taken up with more intensive preventive measures, in order to avoid environmental problems.

Drought is also a natural hazard, which has its impact on the regional ecosystem. The areas, which get less rainfall, i.e., amount of rain is too less to support agricultural production or even grasslands, are usually called drought-prone areas. When droughts become severe, they cause famines, which are devastating for men, animals and also environment. Generally, droughts occur when rainfall is less than 25 to 50 per cent of the average. If it is below 50 per cent of the average, famines occur. In 1899, India faced the severest famine known as *Chappan-ka-Akal*. A similar famine also occurred in 1917. In both these famines several lakhs of people lost their lives. In 1992-93, Ethiopia also suffered from the grips of a bad famine, in which more than 30 lakh people died. In India, famine conditions are common in states like Rajasthan, Gujarat, Haryana, Madhya Pradesh, Orissa and Andhra Pradesh. In Rajasthan, famine has become a regular phenomenon. During 1985-95, as many as 21 to 28 districts remained under famine in Rajasthan. Similar situation also existed from 1998 to 2002. During this period, whole of Rajasthan was under the grip of famine due to failure of monsoon in successive years.

The impact of droughts and famines on vegetation, soil, water resources, animals and climatic conditions is far-reaching. Therefore, preventive measures should be taken.

Environmental Impact of Big Dams

As stated earlier, throughout the world, big dams have been constructed to fulfil the growing needs of power and water for irrigation and other purposes. There is no doubt that these dams have become an indicator of the level of development and have boosted the regional economy of the respective areas. But, during the last twenty years, environmentalists of the world have suspected the suitability of these dams from the point of view of the environment. In other words, the ecosystem has been disturbed by these dams due to (i) submergence of large areas under water, (ii) destruction of vegetation, wildlife and other animals, (iii) instability may provide sustainability to earthquakes, (iv) silting, and (v) large-scale human migration, etc. In spite of these problems, dams are being constructed unabatedly and the process will continue in future too. But, at this point, it is necessary to review the sustainability of big dam projects from the point of view of degradation of environment and then only implementation be done. As far as possible, emphasis should be placed on small dams. Similarly, selection of dam site be done properly so that there is minimum impact on the environment.

In India, during post-independence period, several dams have been constructed. Certainly, these dams have changed the entire scenario of power supply and agricultural development. Notwithstanding their negative impact on environment these are considered vital. However, a controversy has emerged regarding the Tehri dam and Sardar Sarovar projects.

The Tehri dam project has gained significance because of the dimensions of the project and the multitude of the issues. The salient features of the Tehri dam are:

Location	-	Tehri, District Tehrigarhwal, Uttranchal
Rivers	-	Bhagirathi, Jil Ganga
Height	-	260.5m
Catchment Area	-	6921.25 sq. km.
Submergence	-	112 villages and Tehri township, 36,000 ha. forests, 1,600 ha. agricultural land
Power Generation	-	1000 mw (1981), 2000 mw (1989)
Irrigation	-	2.7 lakh ha.
Cost	-	Rs.126.8 crores (1967), Rs.197.9 crores (1977), Rs. 3,000 crores (1989)

The points raised by environmental activists are:

(i) The ecology will suffer, invaluable forests will be destroyed because of submergence of forest lands. The wildlife and birds, etc., living in these areas, would face extinction.

(ii) The possibility of earthquakes would be more in view of the large size of the dam.

(iii) The deposition of silt in the base of dam may restrict flow of huge quantum of water.

(iv) The stagnant waters of the reservoir would spread water-borne diseases in adjoining areas.

(v) The rehabilitation of tribals and other people may not be proper.

All these issues have been raised not only for big dam projects but for other projects also and experts are of the opinion that for sustainable development it is necessary to construct small dams.

That will not only save cost and energy but also not harmful for the environment. Whenever there is national necessity, the decision should be taken after considering the environmental issues also.

In case of the Tehri dam, doubts about its safety have been expressed by many on account of the fact that the it is located in a region of high seismocity and is, therefore, potentially unsafe. This has, however, been denied by experts. There is no doubt about the fact that Tehri dam will change the entire ecosystem of the region, but looking at the benefits in the form of power generation and water supply, this project has not only been approved by the government but its work is near completion. In fact, issues raised regarding environmental degradation are present, but what is not generally pointed out is that environmental degradation is already there.

Similarly, the Sardar Sarovar project has been designed to provide irrigation water to drought-hit areas of Gujarat, Madhya Pradesh, Rajasthan and Maharashtra. This project, which is estimated to cost over Rs.6,400 crores, will, on completion, provide irrigation facilities in about 18 lakh hectares of land and create installed capacity of power of 1,450 MW. It will benefit about 25 lakh people in 3,340 villages. It will also provide drinking water for 295 lakh people residing in 131 towns and 4,720 villages in Gujarat. But, it will create serious environmental problems, for which proper steps should be taken in advance in order to maintain the regional eco-balance.

Land Resources

Soil is the uppermost layer of earth's surface, which supports all forms of life and considered as the primary land resource. It is in the soil that all plants have their roots and from which they absorb life-sustaining moisture and nutrients. Man, in turn, feeds directly upon these plants or upon plant eating animals. Thus, virtually, all terrestrial life ultimately derives from the soil. If a nation's soil resources are fertile and abundant, in like measure, that state will have vigour and stability. When this resource is exhausted because of mounting demands of a swelling population or long mismanagement, the nation's survival is in jeopardy. Some authorities believe that one of the causes of the decline of the Roman Empire was deterioration of soils. The loss of soil, either by natural process or mismanagement, is harmful not only for agricultural development but to the whole ecosystem also. Therefore, its conservation has now become a matter of grave concern.

Soil Erosion

Soil is usually defined as "any part of earth's crust in which plants root" and is formed as a result of long-term process of complex interactions between climatic, topographic and biological factors. Bare rock surfaces are exposed to various types of physical, chemical and biological processes, which lead to physical and chemical disruption. Physical processes of weathering include action of water, temperature, glaciers and gravity, which cause weathering of rocks through such processes as wetting drying, heating, cooling, freezing, glaciation, solution and sand blast, etc. The chemical processes of weathering include hydration, hydrolysis, oxidation-reduction, carbonation, etc. All these processes disintegrate the soil but their impact on the environment is limited. On the other hand, soil erosion leads to the degradation of the environment. Apart from these natural processes, soil erosion is also caused by human actions. The main types of soil erosion are as follows:

(i) normal or natural erosion,
(ii) fluvial erosion,
(iii) aeolian or wind erosion,
(iv) marine erosion, and
(v) accelerated soil erosion by human actions.

Actually, normal or natural soil erosion is a continuous and ongoing process and its impact on environment is also limited, but when it occurs on a large scale due to water or wind erosion, it not only degrades the environment but is also responsible for the expansion of wasteland due to gullies and ravines, as has been the case of the Chambal region of Madhya Pradesh and Rajasthan. Four types of soil erosion due to water have been identified. These are:

(i) sheet erosion,
(ii) rill erosion,
(iii) gully erosion, and
(iv) riparian erosion.

Soil erosion due to wind is a common phenomenon in arid and semi-arid regions and is often a cause of desertification or desert expansion. The process of soil erosion is always accelerated by man either by overgrazing, faulty land practices or deforestation.

Figure 2.2 shows the areas of soil degradation in the world affected by deforestation, overgrazing and overexploitation of vegetation.

There are certain phenomena associated with the process of soil erosion, such as soil creep, earthflow and mudflow, mass wasting, landslides, etc. The slow downslope movement of soil and regolith is known as soilcreep. It is a process in which particles slowly move down the hill slope. In humid climatic regions where slopes are steep, a mass of water-saturated soil may slide downslope during a period of a few hours in the form of an earthflow. When it takes place in the form of mass wasting, it becomes mudflow, a mud stream that pours down canyons in mountainous region and poses a serious environmental hazard. It also occurs in desert regions during a cloud burst. Earthflow and mudflow are a common cause of blockage of highways and railroad lines, supply of irrigation water and also damage property and cause loss of life.

The impact of soil erosion on the environment is both local as well as regional. The following are the general impacts:

(i) formation of gullies and ravines and the whole region becomes an undulating area not suitable for human activities;
(ii) washout of the upper layer of the soil, specially along hillside slope;
(iii) uprooting of plants due to soil cutting, thus responsible for deforestation;
(iv) loss of soil fertility;
(v) loss of pastures;

Figure 2.2

Soil Degradation: The Hot Spots

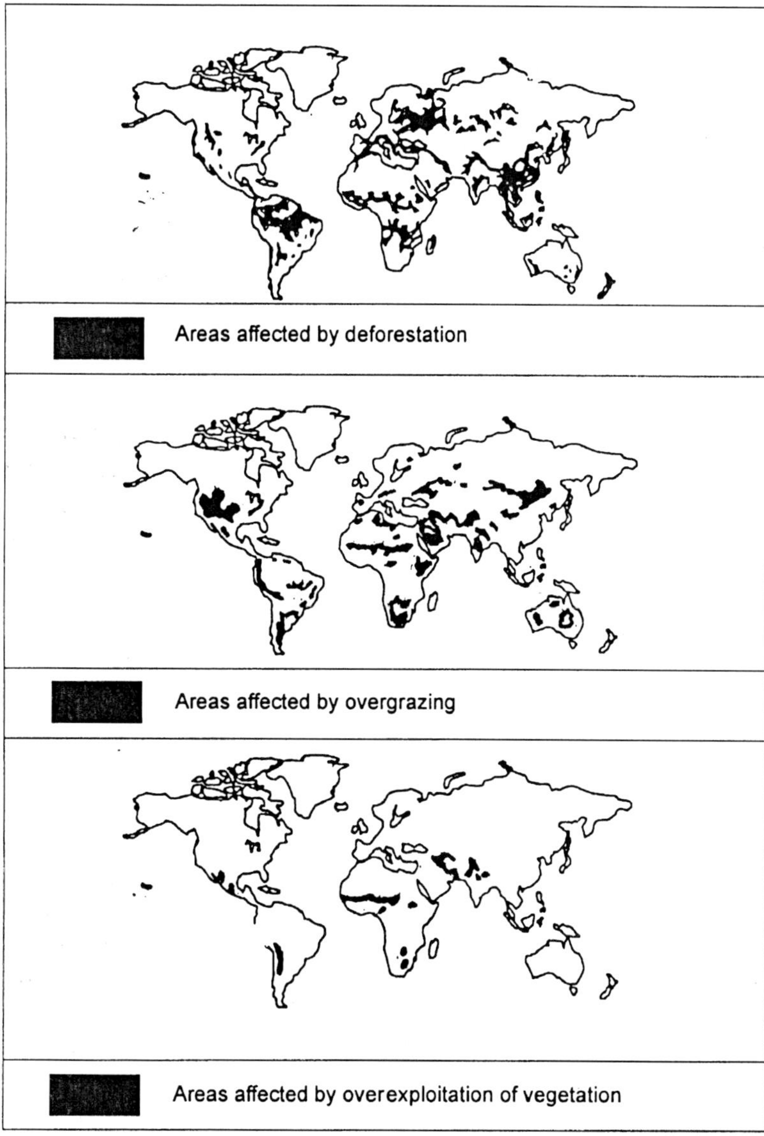

(vi) expansion of deserts; and
(vii) increase in frequency of droughts and floods.

In fact, large-scale soil erosion is one of the major causes of eco-imbalance. In India, the problem of soil erosion can be seen in Jammu & Kashmir, Himachal Pradesh, Uttar Pradesh, Bihar, Assam, Arunachal Pradesh, Sikkim as well as in areas of Rajasthan and Madhya Pradesh. It has been estimated that in our country about 53 per cent of the area is suffering from the problem of soil erosion. Indian rivers use to carry about 600 million tons of soil every year to the sea. Soil erosion can be checked by adopting the following measures:

(a) Biological methods
 (i) Strip cropping
 (ii) Crop rotation
 (iii) Application of manure
 (iv) Shelter belt
 (v) Vegetation cover
(b) Mechanical methods
 (i) Contouring
 (ii) Terracing
 (iii) Control of gully through retention of run-off, diversion of run-off, new structures
(c) By maintaining soil fertility through proper soil management system

Landslides

Landslide is another event, which may cause disruption in the general ecosystem. It is a natural hazard and means any downslope movement of mass of regolith or bedrock under the influence of gravity. It is a rapid sliding of large rock masses beginning their descent as unit of blocks, without internal flowage. When a landslide occurs in the form of huge blocks, it is known as rock avalanche. In Switzerland, Norway or Canadian Rockies, villages built on the floors of steep-sided valleys have been destroyed by the sliding of rock masses. In India, reports of rockslides often appear in the news in hilly states like Jammu & Kashmir,

Himachal Pradesh as well as north-east states. The environmental hazard of rockslides is extremely high for towns located on the floors of glacial troughs and at heads of fiords. The blockage of roads by landslide is a common phenomenon but sometimes it also blocks the course of the small rivers, thus, causing much damage.

Desertification

Desertification is a complex process affecting more than six hundred million people and approximately one-third of the earth's land surface. Desertification, to an ecologist or environmental scientist, is a systematic phenomenon involving deterioration of the ecosystem due to change in the presence of human adaptation or use system. It is a process through which fertile or non-desertic land is converted into dry, infertile or desertic land.

According to Mann (1977), "desertification can be defined as a package of processes which brings about certain basic changes in a particular ecosystem and converts it from a relatively non-desertic to desertic terrain. This involves an interplay of climatic, adaphic and biotic factors, which may (a) work through time starting with a climatic accident and ultimately resulting in the formation of a desert, or (b) lead to accentuation of the arid conditions within an already desertic terrain, or (c) cause a creep of the desertic conditions within a desertic tract towards its adjoining areas".

According to the United Nations Environmental Programme (UNEP), about 900 million people are threatened by desertification, which affects more than 6.1 billion hectares, or about 35 per cent of the earth's land area (Figure 2.3). Each of the 16 years that have passed since the UN Conference on Desertification (UNCOD) in 1977 has seen approximately 6 million hectares of previously productive land rendered infertile. In terms of income, on an average, this is an annual loss of about 45 billion dollars.

In India, the arid zone covers about 12 per cent of the country's geographical area and occupies over 3,20,000 sq km of hot desert located in parts of Rajasthan (62%), Gujarat (19%), Punjab and Haryana (9%), and Andhra Pradesh and Karnataka (10%). In these regions, as well as in other arid regions of the

Figure 2.3
Threat from Desertification

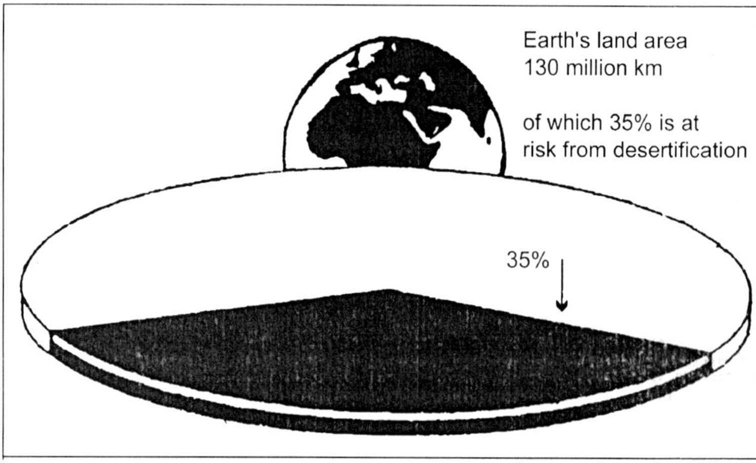

world, due to the high pressure on grazing lands and overexploitation of resources, degradation of environment is growing day by day. Increased desertification problems are also evident in the form of salinity hazard, seepage and waterlogging problems in irrigated areas of the desert. The increased pressure of livestock results in overexploitation of resources leading to soil erosion and removal of surface vegetation. The monitoring of deserts is necessary and should by done by remote sensing methods, both orbital and aerial. In order to control desertification, the following steps should be taken:

(i) ban on cutting of desert vegetation,
(ii) plantation of ecologically suitable plants,
(iii) development of pasture lands,
(iv) control overgrazing,
(v) stabilization of sand dunes,
(vi) proper use of available groundwater resources,
(vii) management of landuse and farming practices,
(viii) National Watershed Programme should be intensified, and
(ix) public awareness should be generated.

Mineral Resources

Possession of mineral resources is a positive factor for a nation because industrial development or, in other words, national strength depends on the internal supply of mineral resources. Mineral resources being stock resources are fixed in supply and concentrated in a relatively small number of places on the earth's surface and this gives each of these areas a certain importance. A handful of countries account for the greater part of the world's production of each of the important minerals.

Minerals are of two types:

(i) *Metallic minerals*: Iron ore, copper, lead, zinc, tungeston, beryllium, mangenese, gold, silver, etc.

(ii) *Non-metallic minerals*: Mica, uranium, gypsum, phosphate, pyrites, diamond and other gem stones, barytes, salt, fluorite, limestone, soapstone, calcite, building stones like sandstone, marble, granite, slate, asbestos, etc.

Another category of minerals comprises of energy resources, such as coal and petroleum.

There is a great variation in production and area of minerals. For example, iron ore is widely distributed but its major reserve are concentrated in countries like Russia, USA, India, Brazil, France, Canada, China, UK, Sweden, etc. Copper is found in USA, Kzakistan, Uzbekistan, Russia, Chile, Kango, Zambia, Peru, Canada, etc. Forty per cent bauxite is produced only in Australia, while Malaysia is the largest producer of tin. South Africa is the largest gold producer country in the world. Similar is the story of other mineral resources. But, our main concern here is not the production of minerals but their impact on environment. In fact, mining has had direct impact on environment and it is one of the main causes of environmental degradation in most areas where it is carried out.

Mining and Environmental Degradation

Mining is one of the most important economic activities in the world. With growing knowledge of the mineral resources as well as due to technological and scientific developments, nowadays, mining is performed on a very large scale. The extraction of minerals is done not only to fulfil regional or national needs but also for trade. With the result that large scale mining operations have become a threat to the environment and is responsible for environmental degradation.

Mineral resources are the product of geological structure and their formation may take a very protracted period, extending over several thousands of years. Therefore, any mineral extracted cannot be formed again for use. There are three types of mineral resources, viz., non-metallic minerals, metallic minerals and mineral fuels. All these are useful to man in some way or the other. Therefore, mining operations are expanding day by day without taking into consideration its impact on the environment. Digging of land is carried out on a very large scale, and has affected the environment in the following ways:

(i) In mining areas, destruction of land due to deep and surface mining is a common feature. In USA alone, about 1,50,000 acres of land has become wasteland due to mining. In areas of coal, iron ore, building material and other ores, etc., one sees no signs of the original relief. In India, in mining areas of Bihar, Orissa, MP and Rajasthan, one can also see the destruction of land.

(ii) Heaps of unused material is also a great problem. Generally, mine owners do not care for this waste material, therefore, it becomes the cause of environmental degradation.

(iii) Large-scale destruction of natural vegetation and wildlife creates ecological problems.

(iv) Pollution due to dust spreading all over the area is not only a threat to the environment but also the cause of many diseases among the workers as well as the residents of nearby areas.

The other impacts of mining include:

(i) expansion of barren land,

(ii) creation of 'ghost town' after mining, and

(iii) ecological crisis due to air, water, land and noise pollution.

Unplanned and unorganized mining is a danger to the environment and this should be checked. Other measures in this direction may be:

(i) levelling of mining areas,
(ii) re-use of waste material,
(iii) plantation in mining areas,
(iv) rehabilitation of people in mining,
(v) measures to check air and land pollution,
(vi) improvement in mining areas,
(vii) health and safety measures should be taken,
(viii) policy of resource conservation should be adopted and alternative material should be developed, and
(ix) proper management and planned regulated mining can solve many problems.

Pesticides and Environmental Degradation

The problem of contamination through pesticides in our food, dairy products, vegetables, fruits or in our living environment as a whole has been visualized very well. Pesticides have been used in farming to: (i) minimize the loss of food caused by pests and ensure a more bountiful harvest, and (ii) decrease the extent of vector-borne diseases. Contrary to these benefits, it has seriously degraded environmental quality and altered the ecological balance, as shown in Figure 2.4.

Figure 2.4
Pesticide Impact Cycle

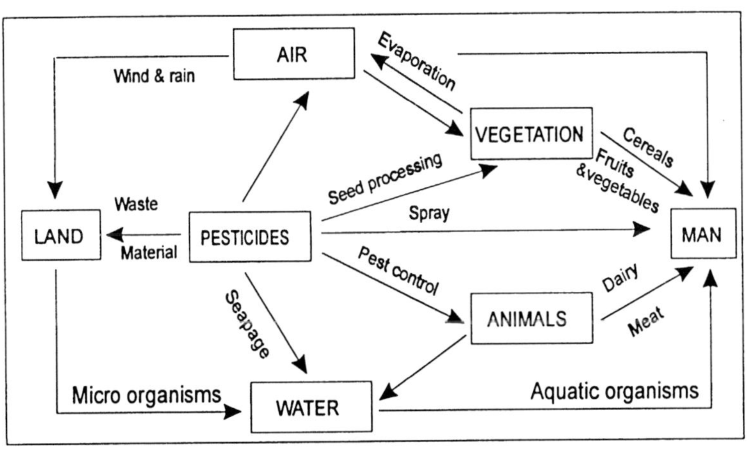

The pesticides, which have been widely applied throughout the world, are carried forth by wind and water and distributed elsewhere. It was found that the some pesticides slowly decomposed into compounds that were toxic to fish and wildlife species in recent years. Worldwide, today, more than 70,000 chemicals are in use.

Energy Resources

Almost 90 per cent of the world's current energy supply is based on fossil or mineral sources, oil, coal, gas and uranium. Only 10 per cent comes from renewable sources, especially hydropower and biomass, while the share of solar and wind energy is below 1 per cent. The following table indicates the pattern of energy consumption in the world:

Table 2.1
Energy Consumption in the World

Energy Source	*Consumption*	*Percentage*
Oil	21678.10^6 barrels	34.2
Coal	4765.10^6 tons	30.2
Gas	1923.10^9 cbm	19.1
Nuclear	1670 TWH	5.0
Hydropower	2050 TWH	6.1
Wood/biomass	1219.10^6 tons	5.3
Wind	3 TWH	1.10^{-2}
Solar	0.1 TWH	1.10^{-3}
Geo-thermal energy	76 TWH	0.1

It is undisputed that this structure of supply involves three problems: (i) if consumption rates do not change, reserves of non-renewable energy will largely run out in one or two generations; (ii) the waste products caused by consumption in the water, the earth and in the atmosphere threaten mankind and the environment, and finally (iii) the cost of this shortage and the effects on consumption will be too much. The use of energy is increasing day by day and according to an estimate the oil and gas will be in shortage after 2000 AD and coal reserves will also fall short after 2200 AD. Even today, there are problems in coal mining. The world supply of natural gas is also limited.

Nuclear power, which amounted to over 5 per cent of global energy production, accounts for very limited use and after the Chernobyl accident, more technological precautions are needed. At present, there is a need for adopting methods for conservation of energy resources and also to develop and use more and more renewable energy sources.

The conservation methods should be applied for coal, petroleum and natural gas in order to preserve these resources, so that their use may be possible for a longer period and their environmental effects can be minimized. The coal mines have become deeper in most of the countries, therefore, new techniques should be applied. The new methods like gasification may help in deeper mining operations. The coal should be classified and cleared at production centres itself. The use of secondary coal products like coaltar, ammonium sulphate, gas, light oil, benzol, sulphur, etc., should be increased. A better transportation and marketing system as well as research in use and mining of coal may also prove beneficial.

The conservation of petroleum or mineral oil is the need of hour because the availability of petro-reserves is limited and the use of oil is increasing day by day, especially in the field of transportation. The following steps may help in conservation of petroleum:

(i) reduction in the consumption of petroleum and petroleum products,
(ii) development of such engines, which consume lesser petroleum,
(iii) intensive survey for new resources,
(iv) exploitation of oil resources from ocean floors,
(v) correct estimation of available resources,
(vi) developing new techniques for oil drilling and refining,
(vii) reducing petroleum consumption in certain areas such as for military purposes,

(viii) developing alternative sources of energy for automobiles, etc., and

(ix) research institutes working in this field should intensify their work.

The energy crisis can be solved to some extent by proper use of renewable sources of energy. These include solar energy, wind energy, tidal energy, hydropower, ocean energy and geo-thermal energy. Renewable energies are also called the energies of the future, because they are inexhaustible and neutral in terms of CO_2. The renewable energy sources mainly come from three primary sources:

- isotopic disintegration in the earth's interior,
- thermo-nuclear conversion (fusion) in the sun, and
- the movement of planets, combined with mass attraction.

The greatest of the renewable energy sources is solar energy or solar radiation reaching the earth's atmosphere. Every 29 seconds the solar energy that falls on our planet is equivalent to human energy needs for one day at the 1980 consumption level. In case of solar-thermal utilization, the solar energy is converted to heat through absorption. This can occur through passive systems, i.e., through constructional measures for collecting, storing and distributing solar energy, which renounce thermal installations to a considerable degree or through active system, i.e., collectors or absorbers. The advantages of using solar energy are: limitless supply, no air pollution, no water pollution, no harmful wastes, no possibility of a large scale explosion or disaster. There is a need to evolve cheaper technology to harvest solar energy. At least for tropical regions it is the greatest source of energy.

There is no need to stress the importance of *water energy* or *hydropower*. Water energy is already in use in developed countries, but in developing countries vast energy potentials exist.

There is enough *wind energy* available to meet the world's energy needs, and it is technically feasible to build windmills capable of producing electricity, either as small home-sized units or as large central generators. Besides the conversion of rotation energy into electrical energy, the conversion of rotation energy into mechanical energy also finds application in pumping of water, etc.

Ocean energy refers to a number of different renewable energy sources, e.g., tidal energy, wave energy, ocean currents and ocean heat. Today, the significant attempts at harnessing the energy of the ocean have been related to tidal power. In many coastal regions, the flow of the tide naturally funnels through narrow entrances into bays and estuaries, and strong currents can be used to generate power.

Energy derived from the heat of the earth's crust is called *geo-thermal energy*. In various places on the globe, hot springs, geysers and underground steams are available, which can be used for power generation.

Bio-energy can be produced by organic compounds through chemical and biological processes. The combustion, gasification and liquification help in production of gas, which can be used as a source of energy. The bio-gas plant has now become a common feature in rural India.

Viewed in the long-term perspective, the utilization of renewable energy sources is of major significance, in terms of both the conservation of the reserves of fossil fuels and the reduction of pollutant emissions caused by the conversion of energy from coal, oil and gas. The renewable energy sources have good chances for the future energy supply. How large their contribution will be, depends upon the question of how safe, economical and environment-friendly each particular 'new' energy is.

Food Resources

Food is probably the most important of the economic elements. Lack of an adequate food supply results in undernourishment and finally in starvation. An adequate supply of foodstuffs is a common condition of human welfare. If a food supply is not assured in time, it may result in the form of unrest. Many nations in the world are not completely self-sufficient in food resources and they have to depend on imports from other countries. while countries like USA, Canada, China, Russia, etc., are self-sufficient, UK and Japan import about half the total food requirements of their populations. India, which was once not able to provide food to its growing population, is now in a position to produce sufficient foodstuffs on its own. Many African countries are also not having proper and enough food supply.

Food is a common denominator of life. But, for many people on the earth, it is not available. Thousands of people are dying of hunger and millions are suffering from malnutrition. There is a close relationship between population, food supply and environment. The production of food, not only of farm products but also marine and others, depends on suitable climatic conditions. The non-availability or limited supply of food is a cause of tension and conflict on the one hand, and overexploitation of resources, on the other.

The world food supply, like population, is unevenly distributed. Most of the developed countries either have less population and surplus food supply or are endowed with enough resources to obtain food from outside. On the other hand, in developing countries, food supply is limited and population is more, resulting in hunger and insufficiency of essential nutrients causing infant mortality, impaired development and disease.

The most important question related with population and food supply is the nutritional value of the food measured in terms of caloric intake. The UN World Food Survey has pointed out that 2,550 to 2,650 calories is the minimum requirement for each individual. A balanced meal means:

(a) 1,200 to 1,800 calories from cereals,
(b) 100 to 200 calories from starch,
(c) 100 to 150 or 200 calories from fats,
(d) 250 to 300 calories from meat and pulses,
(e) 100 calories from fruits, and
(f) 300 to 400 calories from milk and milk products.

If we look at the pattern of the world calorie intake status (as shown in Figure 2.5), it becomes clear that most of the countries of Asia, Africa and Latin America have very low intake, i.e., less than 2,500 calories per day per person. Some of the countries have a medium level intake (2,500 to 2,900 calories) and only USA, Canada, countries of Europe and Russian Federation, Australia

Figure 2.5

World Pattern of Calorie Status

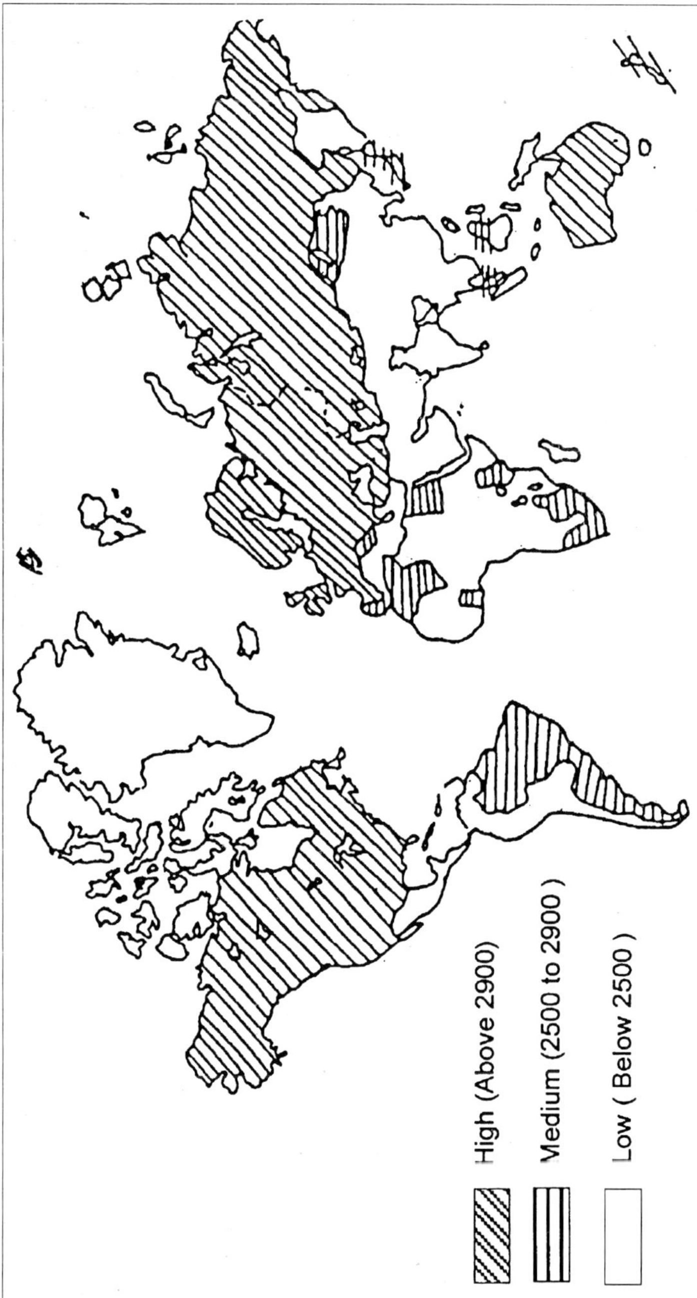

and New Zealand have a high calorie intake food. The pressure to produce food caused by a growing population or by crises such as droughts or floods can result in long-term damage to environment.

We can conclude this chapter with the observations of John Bongaarts, in March 1994 issue of *Scientific American,* as under:

> Feeding a growing world population a diet that improves over time in quality and quantity is technologically feasible. But the economic and environmental costs incurred through bolstering food production may well prove too great for many poor countries. The course of events will depend crucially on their governments' ability to design and enforce effective policies that address the challenges posed by mounting human numbers, rising poverty and environmental degradation. Whatever the outcome, the task ahead will be made more difficult if population growth rates cannot be reduced.

3

The Ecosystems

The whole earth and its parts, viz., land surface, water bodies, atmosphere as well as living organisms are working in an integrated system, which not only directs but also determines the pattern of life and is also an indicator of environmental relationship with living organisms as well. Each and every part of the earth's surface is having its own ecosystem but at the same time it is also a part of a larger system, which may cover the whole of the continent, parts of various continents or even whole of the earth. The single giant ecosystem is the 'biosphere'. The term 'ecosystem' was coined by A.G. Tansley in 1935, who defined it as "the system resulting from the integration of all the living and non-living factors of the environment". He further stated that "the whole system includes not only the organism complex but also the whole complex of physical factors forming what we call the environment of the biome–the habitat factors in the widest sense. It is the systems so formed which are basic units of nature on the face of the earth".

Although the concept of ecosystem is much older than the term itself, many terms parallel to it have been used by bio-scientists, such as *biocoenosis* (Mobius, 1877), *microcosm* (Forbes, 1887), *holocoen* (Friederichs, 1930), *biosystem* (Thienemann, 1939), *geobiocoenosis* (Sukachev, 1944), *ecosphere* (Cole, 1958), etc. However, the term 'ecosystem' is now accepted and most preferred, where 'eco' implies the environment, and 'system' means interdependent, interacting complex.

According to Monkhouse and Small (1970), ecosystem is "an organic community of plants and animals viewed within its physical environment or habitat". The habitat or physical environment controls the whole world of organic community, viz., plants and animals. With the change in physical environment, the type of plants and animals too have changed. Similar views have been expressed by Haggett (1975): "Ecosystems are ecological systems in which plants and animals are linked to their environment through a series of feedback loops."

Strahler's have defined ecosystem as "the total assemblage of components entering into the interactions of a group of organism". He further elaborated that "to the geographer, ecosystems are the part of the physical composition of the life layer".

Ecosystem has also been defined as a unit that includes all the organisms (biological factors) in a given area interacting with the environment (physical factors) so that a flow of energy leads to a clearly defined trophic (nutrient requiring) structure, biotic diversity, and material cycles (i.e., exchange of materials between living and non-living sectors).

In fact, our earth has a giant ecosystem in the form of the biosphere, where biotic and abiotic components are constantly acting and reacting upon each other, bringing forth structural and functional changes in it. The biosphere is a vast ecosystem and difficult to study as a whole. Therefore, for the convenience of study, it can be divided into two parts:

1. *Terrestrial* as forest, grassland, desert, mountains, etc.
2. *Aquatic* (water-open): (a) *freshwater*, which may be *lotic* (running-water like spring, stream, rivers) or *lentic* (standing water like lake, pond, swamp, pools, etc.); and (b) *marine*, such as deep sea or shallow sea, delta, etc.

Components of the Ecosystem

The two major components of ecosystem are:

— the biotic components, comprising all living organisms, and
— the abiotic components, including the physical (non-living) environment.

Biotic Components

In an ecosystem, organisms are usually divided into two categories on the basis of their nutritional (trophic) relationship. These are: (a) autotrophic components, and (b) heterotrophic components.

(a) *Autotrophs* are those organisms, which can produce their own food. These are green plants (with chlorophyl) and certain bacteria, which obtain their energy from the sun and through photosynthesis produce food. Since these organisms produce food for all the other organisms, they are known as producers.

(b) *Heterotrophs* are those organisms, which depend directly or indirectly upon the autotrophs for their food, thus known as consumers. The consumers are of two types:

(i) *Macroconsumers* also known as herbivores, carnivores or omnivores. Herbivores are the plant eaters, while carnivores are animal eaters. On the other hand, omnivores eat all kinds of food. They all are phagotrophs which include chiefly animals that ingest other organic and particulate organic matter. These are also known as primary consumers.

(ii) *Microconsumers* are also known as decomposers or osmotrophs. They are decomposers because of their role in decomposition of dead organic matter. They secrete digestive enzymes to break down food into simpler substances and then absorb the digested food.

Functionally, the biotic components can be divided into three types, viz., producers, consumers and decomposers. Producers produce their own food like plants, which are primary producers, while man and animals obtain food from plants. Similarly, consumers are also primary, secondary or tertiary. Man, cow, goat, etc., are primary consumers, while meat eaters are secondary consumers. Tertiary consumers are those animals, which eat meat such as snakes eat frogs, peacocks eat snakes, etc. Among decomposers those bacteria, fungi, etc., have been included, which are responsible for decomposition of a product and release inorganic nutrients in environment.

Abiotic Components

The physical environment with its several interacting variables constitutes the abiotic component of ecosystem. It consists of (i) the lithosphere, i.e., the solid mineral matter of the earth; (ii) the water in the oceans, rivers, lakes, etc., or in other words, the hydrosphere; (iii) the gaseous mixture in the air (the atmosphere); and (iv) the radiant solar energy.

Figure 3.1 below is a generalized depiction of the structural elements of an ecosystem and their functional linkages:

Figure 3.1

Ecosystem Model Showing its Structure and Function

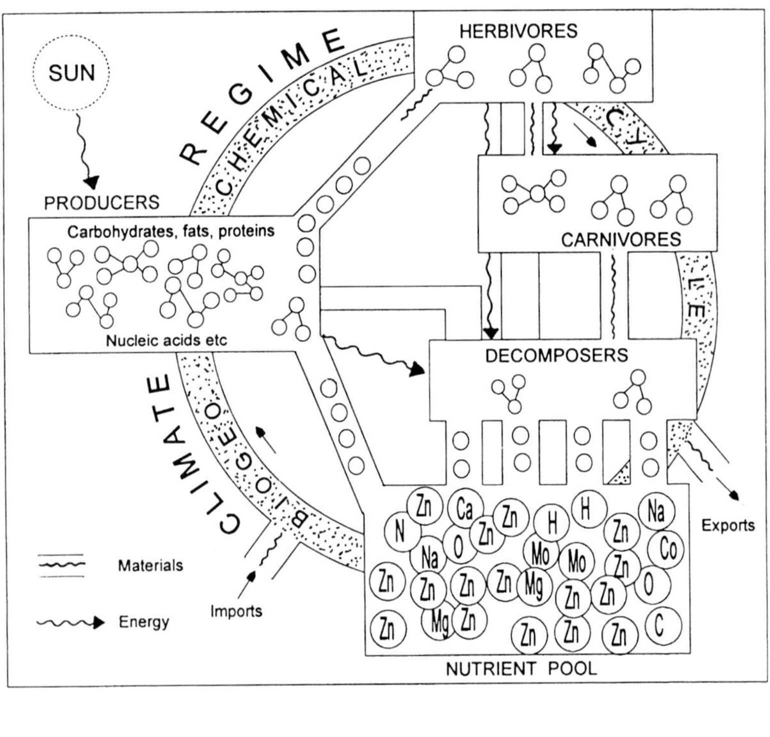

Ecosystem Functioning

The functional pattern of an ecosystem is a very important and basic aspect of study, because all its components are dynamic in one way or the other and are responsible for the creation of an unique state of man-environment relationship as well as a habitat, different from other regions. Ecosystem functioning can be studied under three heads, viz., energy flow, productivity and biogeochemical cycling.

Energy Flow in an Ecosystem

Energy is defined as the ability to do work and is the essence of life. Without energy transfers, there could be no life and no ecological systems. The energy used for all the life processes is derived from solar radiant energy. The behaviour of energy is described by the laws of thermodynamics: (i) energy may be transformed from one type into another but is never created or destroyed, and (ii) no process involving an energy transformation will spontaneously occur unless there is a degradation of the energy from a concentrated form into a dispersed form, etc.

The radiant energy produced in the sun travels through space in the form of waves. But, only a small fraction of solar radiation reaches the earth to provide energy for the biotic components of the ecosystem. Figure 3.2 indicates the fate of radiant energy reaching the earth's atmosphere. It becomes clear from the figure that most of the radiation is lost in space by processes of reflection, absorption as well as through scattering. Its energy is greatly altered as it passes through cloud cover, water and vegetation. The daily input of sunlight to autotrophic layer of an ecosystem varies mostly between 100 and 800 to 300-400 gcal per cm^2 (= 3,000 to 4,000 kcal per m^2) in the temperate zone. The total radiation flux within different strata of the ecosystem varies from season to season as well as with nature of the earth's surface, thus controlling the distribution and response of organisms accordingly.

The energy reaching the earth's surface is transformed and/or absorbed by plants and other organisms. It is used by the green

Figure 3.2
Radiant Energy Reaching Earth's Atmosphere

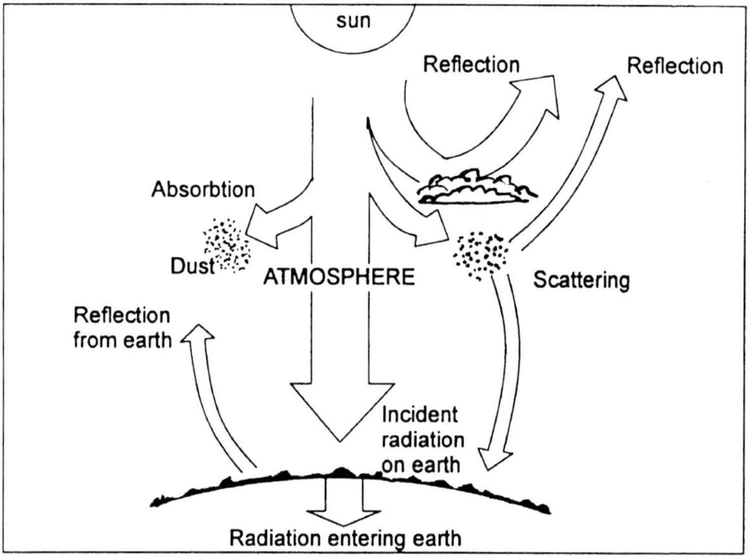

plants during photosynthesis by converting the light energy to chemical energy and making it available to other organisms as food. Such energy transfers along the food chain were studied for the first time by Lindeman in 1942. He stated that all the functions of an ecosystem could be explained in terms of energy by the knowledge of two attributes of each trophic level—the level of energy storage and the efficiency of energy transfer. Odum (1957), Golley (1960), Slobodkim (1959, 1960, 1962), Teal (1962) and Kozlovsky (1968) have made further detailed investigations. The process of energy flow in an ecosystem has been depicted by Odum in a simplified diagram as shown in Figure 3.3, where the 'boxes' represent the trophic levels and the 'pipes' depict the energy flow in and out of each level. It becomes clear from this simplified model that the energy flow is greatly reduced at each successive trophic level from producers to herbivores and then to carnivores.

Figure 3.3

Energy Flow in a Food Chain

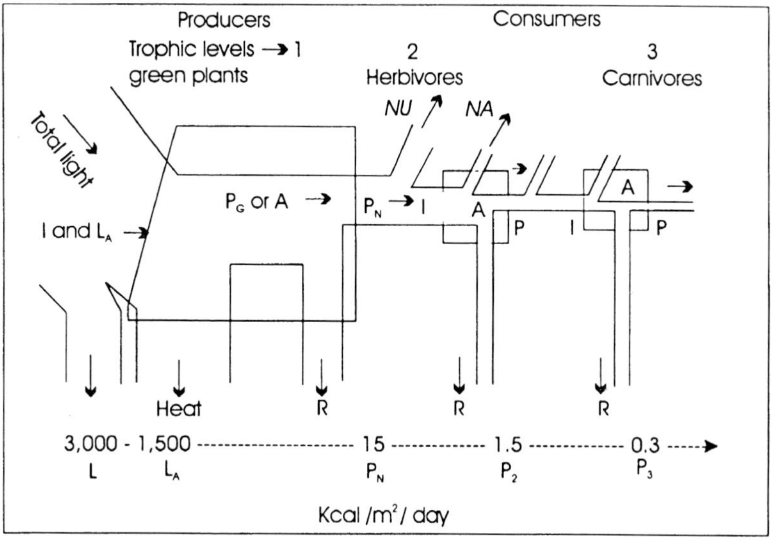

(After E.P. Odum)

(I-total energy input; LA-light absorbed by plant cover; PG-grass primary production; A-total assimilation; PN-net primary production; P-secondary (consumer) production; NU-energy not used (stored or exported); NA-energy not assimilated by consumers (egested); R-respiration; bottom line in the diagram shows the order of the magnitude of energy losses expected at major transfer points, starting with a solar input of 3,000 Kcal per metre per day.)

Productivity of Ecosystem

The productivity of an ecosystem refers to the rate of production, i.e., the amount of organic matter accumulated in any unit of time. It is of primary, secondary and net productivity.

(i) *Primary productivity* is defined as "the rate at which radiant energy is stored by photosynthetic and chemosynthetic activity of producer organisms (chiefly green plants) in the form of organic substances which can be used as food materials". Primary productivity is of two types:

(a) *Gross primary productivity* is the total rate of photosynthesis including organic matter used up in respiration during a particular period.

(b) *Net primary productivity* is the rate of storage of organic matter in plant tissues in excess of respiratory utilization by plants during the measurement period.

(ii) *Secondary productivity* is the rate of energy storage at consumer level. It actually remains mobile from one organism to another and does not live *in situ* like primary productivity.

(iii) *Net productivity* refers to the rate of storage of organic matter not used by the consumers. Thus, it is the rate of increase of biomass of the primary producers which has been left out by the consumers.

Food Chains in Ecosystems

The transfer of food energy from the producers, through a series of organisms (herbivores to carnivores to decomposers) with repeated eating and being eaten, is known as a *food chain*. Producers utilize the radiant energy of sun, which is transformed to chemical form, ATP, during photosynthesis. Thus, green plants occupy, in any food chain, the first trophic (nutritional) level—the producers level, and are called the *primary producers*. The energy, as stored in food matter manufactured by green plants, is then utilized by the plant eaters—the herbivores, which constitute the second trophic level—the primary consumers level, and are called the *primary consumers* (*herbivores*). Herbivores, in turn, are eaten by the carnivores, which constitute the third trophic level—the secondary consumers level, and are called the *secondary consumers* (*carnivores*). These, in turn, may be eaten still by other carnivores at tertiary consumers level, i.e., by the *tertiary consumers* (*carnivores/omnivores*). Some organisms are omnivores eating the producers as well as the carnivores at their lower level in the food chain. Such organisms thus may occupy more than one trophic level in the chain. This classification of all the living organisms of any ecosystem in one of their functions and not of species. Species that are taxonomically different from each other may occupy the same trophic level as they all have the similar function in the food chain. In any food chain, energy flows from primary producers to primary consumers (herbivores), from primary consumers to secondary consumers (carnivores), and from secondary consumers to tertiary consumers (carnivores/omnivores) and so on. This simple chain of eating and being eaten away is known as food chain. A food chain in grassland ecosystem starts with grasses and forbs and goes through grasshoppers, the frogs, the snake, the hawk in an orderly sequential arrangement based on the food habits, whereas in a pond the order would start with phytoplanktons, going through water fleas, smaller fish, bigger fish, birds, larger animal and so on.

In nature, we generally distinguish two general types of food chains:

Grazing Food Chain

Grazing food chain starts from the living green plants, goes to grazing herbivores (that feed on living plant materials with their predators), and on to carnivores (animal eaters). Ecosystems with such type of food chain are directly dependent on an influx of solar radiation. This food chain thus depends on autotrophic energy capture and the movement of this captured energy to herbivores. Most of the ecosystems in nature follow this type of food chain. From energy standpoint, these chains are very important. The phytoplanktons-zooplanktons-fish sequence or the grasses-rabbit-fox sequence are the examples of grazing food chain.

Detritus Food Chain

Detritus food chain goes from dead organic matter into micro-organisms and then to organisms feeding on detritus (detritivores) and their predators. Ecosystems with such type of food chain are thus less dependent on direct solar energy. These depend chiefly on the influx of organic matter produced in another system. For example, such food chain operates in the decomposing accumulated litter in a temperate forest. A good example of a detritus food chain is based on mangrove leaves described by Heald (1969) and Odum (1970). In the brackish zone of southern Florida, leaves of the red mangrove—*Rhizophore mangle*—fall into the warm, shallow waters. The fallen leaf fragments (acted on by such saprotrophs as fungi, bacteria, protozoa, etc., and colonised mainly by phytoplanktonic and benthicalgae) are eaten and re-eaten (coprophagy) by a key group of small animals. These animals include crabs, copepods, insect larvae, grass shrimps, mysids, nematodes, amphipods, bivalve molluscs, etc. All these are detritus consumers. These animals are in turn eaten by some minnows and small game fish etc., i.e., the small carnivores, which in turn serve as the main food for larger game fish in particular. The mangroves considered generally as of less economic value make a substantial contribution to the food chain that support the fisheries—an important economy in that region. Similarly, detritus from seagrasses, saltmarsh grasses and seaweed support fisheries in many estuarine areas.

But, under natural situations, a system must always be self-sufficient. In fact, the detritus food chain is simply a sub-component of another ecosystem. And, the above said two types of food chains in nature are indeed linked together belonging to the same ecosystem.

Food Webs: Interlocking Pattern of Organisms

However, food chains in natural conditions never operate as isolated sequences, but are interconnected with each other forming some sort of interlocking pattern, which is referred to as *food web*. Under natural conditions, the arrangement of food chains hardly occurs and these remain indeed interconnected with each other through different types of organisms at different trophic levels. For example, in grazing food chain of a grassland, in the absence of rabbit, grass may also be eaten by mouse. The mouse in turn may be eaten directly by hawk or by snake first, which is then eaten by hawk. Thus, in nature, there are found alternatives, which all together constitute some sort of interlocking pattern, known as the food web.

In such a food web in a grassland system, as shown in Figure 3.4, there may be seen as many as five linear food chains, which in sequences are:

(1) Grass→Grasshopper→Hawk
(2) Grass→Grasshopper→Lizard→Hawk
(3) Grass→Rabbit→Hawk (or vulture or fox or even man, if present)
(4) Grass→Mouse→Hawk
(5) Grass→Mouse→Snake→Hawk

Figure 3.4
Food Web in a Grassland Ecosystem

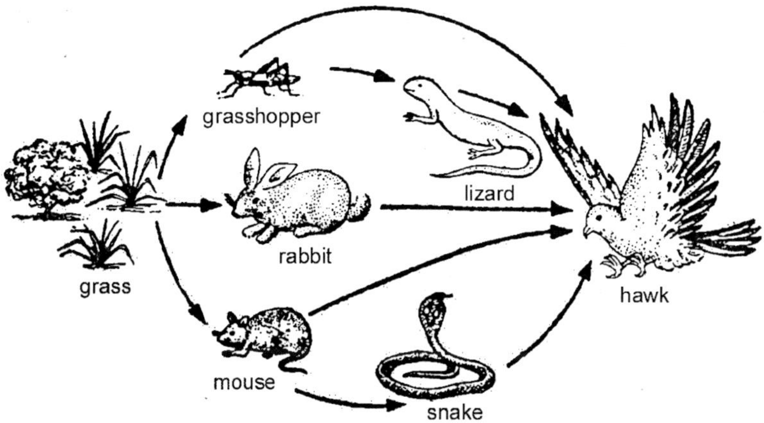

Besides those shown in Figure 3.4 above, there may also be present some other consumers such as vulture, fox and man, in grasslands, and if so, the food web may be even more complex. However, all these five chains are interlinked with each other at different points, forming a food web. A similar food web in a pond, with different interlinked chains, is shown in Figure 3.5. The food webs are very important in maintaining the stability of an ecosystem in nature. For example, decrease in the population of rabbit would naturally cause an increase in the population of alternative herbivore—the mouse. This may decrease the population of the consumer (carnivore) that prefers to eat rabbit. Thus, alternatives (substitutes) serve for maintenance of stability of the ecosystem. Moreover, a balanced ecosystem is essential for the survival of all living organisms of the system. For instance, had primary consumers (herbivores) not been in nature, the producers would have perished due to overcrowding and competition. Similarly, the survival of primary consumers is linked with the secondary consumers (carnivores) and so on. Thus, each species in an ecosystem is indeed kept under some sort of a natural check so that the system may remain balanced.

Figure 3.5
Food Web in a Pond

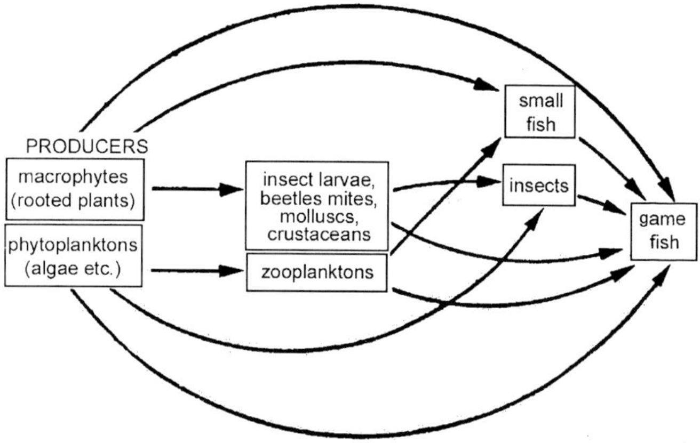

The complexity of any food web depends upon the diversity of organisms in the system. It would accordingly depend upon two main points:

(i) *Length of the food chain:* Diversity in the organisms based upon their food habits would determine the length of food chain. More diverse the organisms in food habits, more longer would be food chain.

(ii) *Alternatives at different points of consumers in the chain:* More the alternatives, more would be the interlocking pattern.

In deep oceans, seas, etc., where we find a variety of organisms, the food webs are much complex.

Biogeochemical Cycles

The chemical elements, including all the essential elements of protoplasm, tend to circulate in the biosphere in circular paths from environment to organism and back to the environment. These move in a more or less circular path, thus known as *biogeochemical cycles.* The growth of life process requires about 40 elements. Hydrogen, carbon and oxygen are the basic elements, while nitrogen, phosphorus, potassium, calcium, sulphur, magnesium and iron are the other important elements. All the elements continue to cycle at the ecosystem level, they are also an integral part of the larger and/or global cycle. The cycling of various elements can be grouped into two categories, viz., (i) gaseous cycles of elements like hydrogen, carbon, oxygen, nitrogen, sulphur; and (ii) sedimentary cycles of those elements which are present in the soil and organisms. The process of biogeochemical cycles can be understood through following examples:

Hydrological Cycle

The hydrological cycle or water cycle is the most important one among biogeochemical cycles. It involves interchange of water between earth's surface and the atmosphere through rainfall and evapotranspiration. The water from water bodies like oceans, lakes, rivers, etc., gets evaporated by solar energy. These water vapours, after cooling and condensation form clouds, which result in rainfall, snowfall, etc. A large part of the rainfall occurs over oceans, and a sizeable part of the water vapours goes back to the oceans via rivers and streams. Some part of it infiltrates into the become soil or underground water. A small quantity of water is also absorbed by the plants and consumed by other animals. The same is released during respiration and transpiration of plants. Thus, there is a continuous cycling of water as shown in Figure 3.6.

Carbon Cycle

Like the hydrological cycle, carbon cycle is also very important for man. The small amount (0.03%) of carbon dioxide in the atmosphere is the only source of all carbon that passes through the organisms along the food chains. As shown in Figure 3.7, carbon moves from the atmospheric pool to green plants (producers), then to animals (consumers) and finally to bacteria and other micro-organisms (decomposers) that return into the atmosphere, through decomposition of dead organic matter. The carbon dioxide has the unique property of absorbing infra-red radiation and its small quantity helps in keeping the earth warm. A part of this cycle also operates in the ocean.

Figure 3.6
Hydrological Cycle

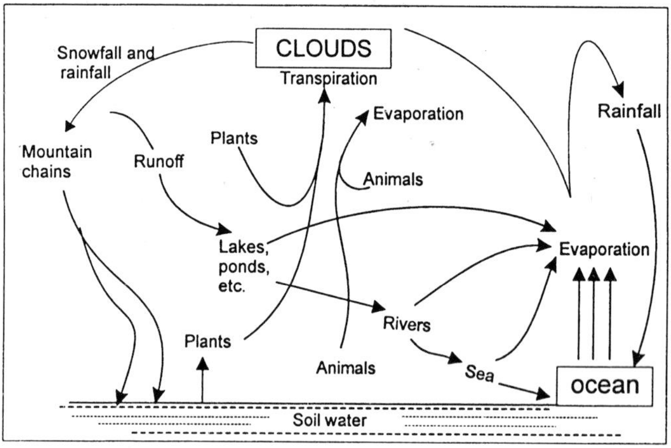

Oxygen Cycle

The oxygen constitutes 21 per cent of the atmosphere. It also occurs in a bound state as oxides and carbonates in rocks and in water. The plants release oxygen in photolysis of water during photosynthesis. Again, gaseous oxygen is used in respiration of all the organisms and in the oxidation of the organic matter. Another phase of the oxygen is the ozone layer of the outer stratosphere which serves an important function of protecting the life from the ionizing ultra violet waves. The pattern of oxygen cycle has been depicted in Figure 3.8.

Nitrogen Cycle

Nitrogen is an essential element of all forms of life and in atmosphere, its percentage is 79. But, it is never taken directly from the atmosphere. The chief sources of nitrogen for plants are nitrates in the soil. During the cycle, the reduced and oxidized forms are involved at one or other stage. The chief symbiotic nitrogen fixers are bacteria belonging to the genus *Rhizobium*

Figure 3.7
A Simplified Carbon Cycle

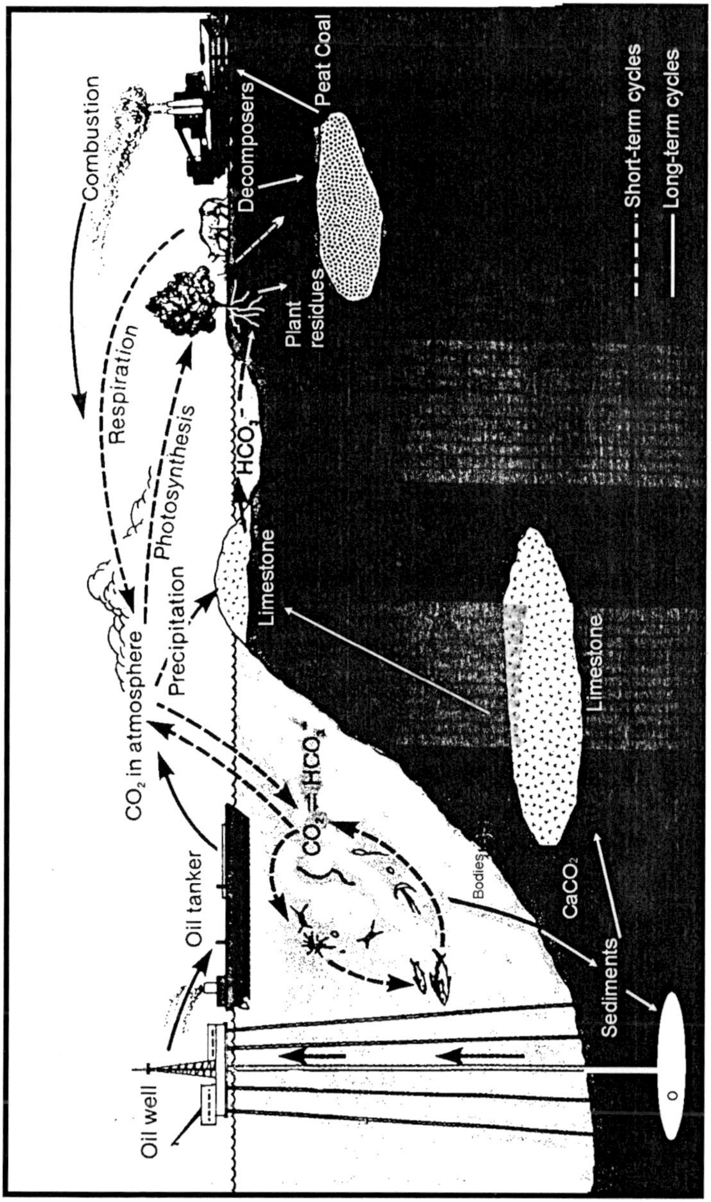

Figure 3.8
Oxygen Cycle

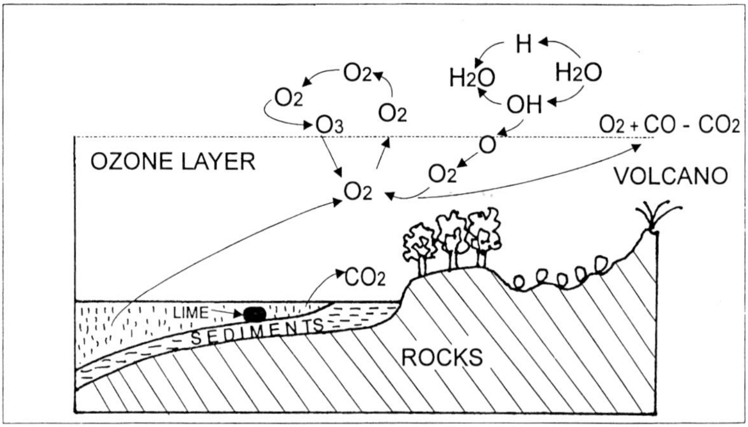

found in the root nodules of legumes, while asymbiotic nitrogen fixers are some blue-green algae. Plants in turn are eaten by animals. The dead organic matter formed due to death of plants and animals is decomposed by bacteria, fungi, etc., which releases nitrogen either in free state to atmosphere or as ammonia gas. Ammonia gas may also reach the soil as nitrates through the activity of nitrifying microbes. The whole pattern of the nitrogen cycle becomes clear from Figure 3.9.

Phosphorus Cycle

This is a sedimentary cycle and a simpler one, in comparison to nitrogen cycle. As shown in Figure 3.10, phosphorus, an important and necessary constituent of protoplasm, tends to 'circulate', the organic compounds being broken down eventually to phosphates which are again available to plants. The great reservoir of phosphorus are rocks or other deposits which have been formed in past geological ages. These erode and release phosphates to ecosystems. A major portion of phosphates goes into the sea in the form of sedimentation. Sea birds also have a role in returning phosphorus to the cycle from sea to land. The general pattern of phosphorus cycle is more or less similar to that of other minerals.

Figure 3.9
Nitrogen Cycle

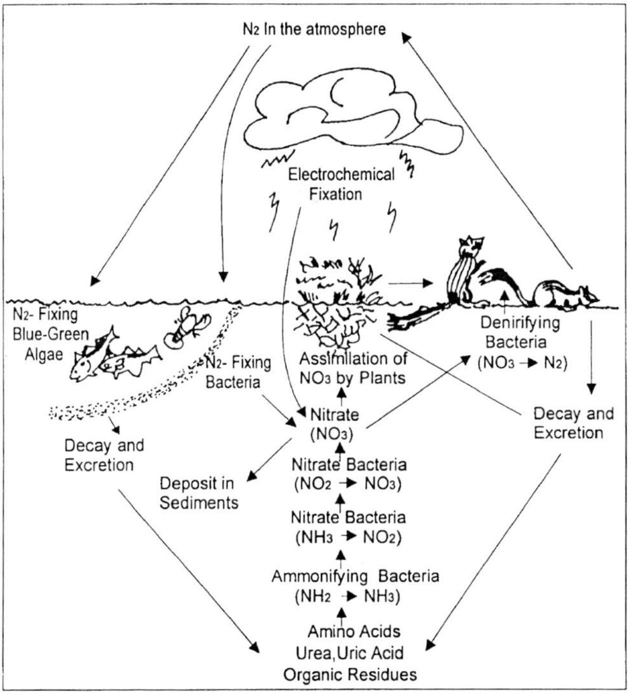

Figure 3.10
Phosphorus Cycle

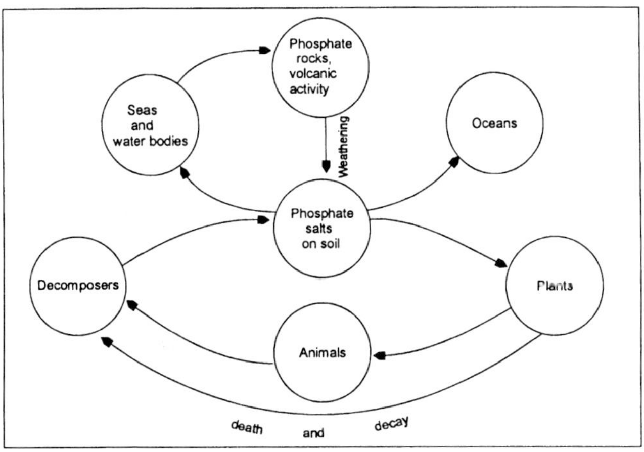

Figure 3.11
Sulphur Cycle

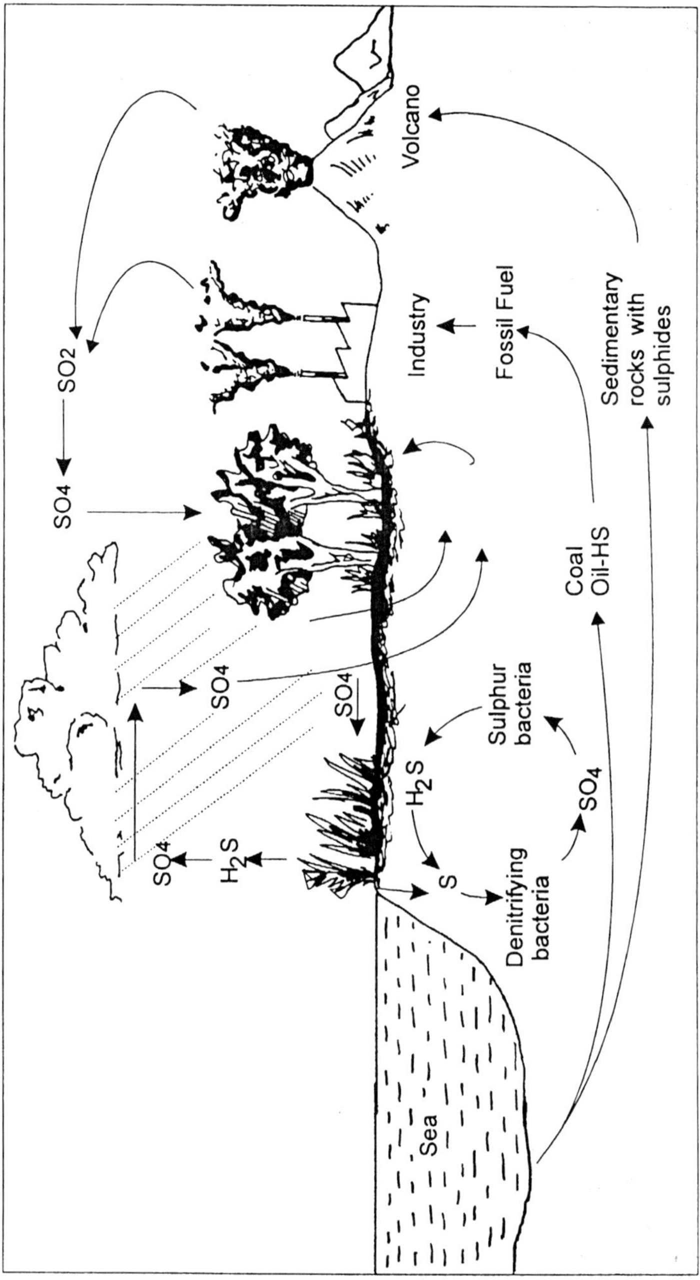

Sulphur Cycle

The sulphur cycle, as shown in Figure 3.11, links air, water and soil, where microbes play an important role. The reserve pool of sulphur is the soil. It is made available to the plants in the soil by the activity of sulphur bacteria. Some quantities are added to the atmosphere by the burning of the fossil fuels. Later, sulphur dioxide and hydrogen sulphide return to the soil as sulfates or sulphuric acid, with the rain. In tissues of organisms, sulphur is in the form of proteins. The decomposition of proteins releases sulphur. The sulphur cycle is a good example of the interaction and complex biological and chemical regulation between different mineral cycles.

Apart from above mentioned cycling of elements, other elements too follow an almost similar pattern of cycling. The cycles of these elements are usually restricted to the same ecosystem but some of them are widespread and a part of the global system.

Major Ecosystems

In the world, there are several ecosystems working at macro or micro level. As pointed out earlier, the biosphere is the biggest ecosystem, which combines all the ecosystems of the world. But, with the difference in physiography, climate, natural vegetation, soil and water bodies, separate ecosystems have been developed. The biosphere can be divided into following major ecosystems (see also Figure 3.12):

Natural Ecosystems

(i) Terrestrial ecosystems
  (a) Forest
  (b) Grassland
  (c) Desert

(ii) Aquatic ecosystems
  (a) Freshwater
  (b) Marine

Man-Engineered or Artificial Ecosystems

Peter Haggett, in his book *Geography: A Modern Synthesis* (1972), has described the major ecosystems/environmental regions as follows:

Figure 3.12
Basic Types of Ecosystems

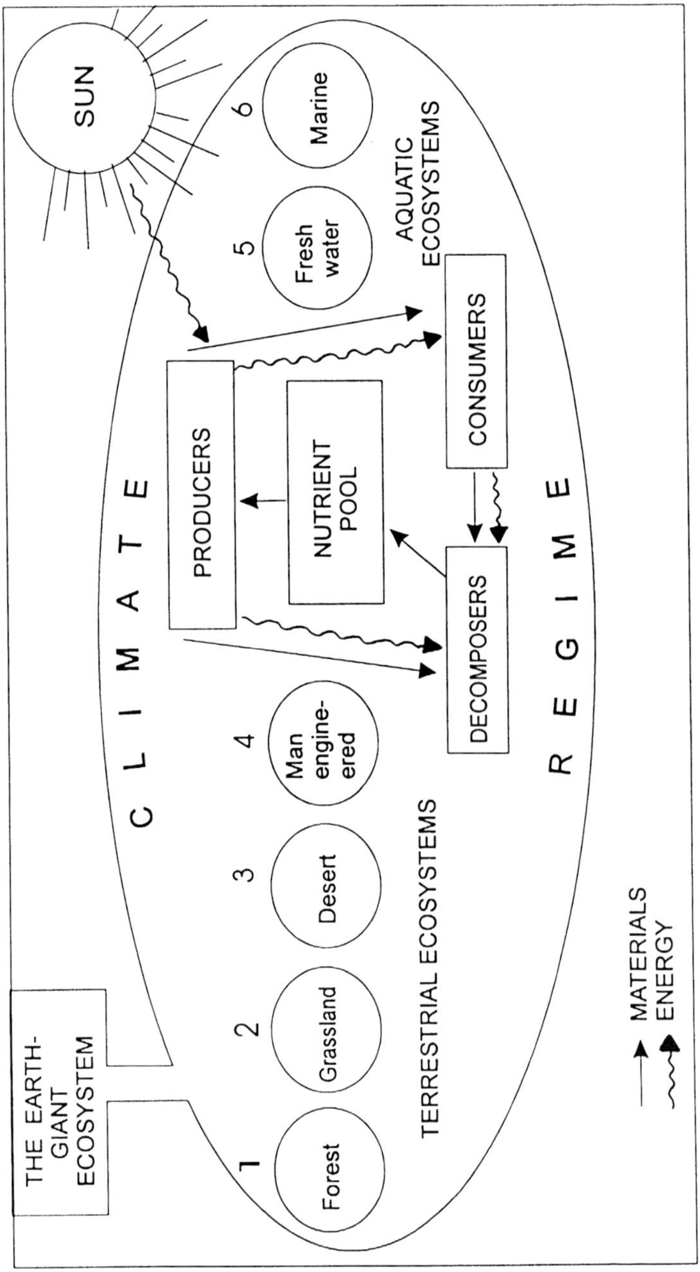

(a) Forested
  (i) Equatorial
  (ii) Mid-latitude (peripheral)
  (iii) Boreal
(b) Intermediate
  (i) Savannah
  (ii) Mediterranean
  (iii) Mid-latitude grassland
(c) Barren
  (i) Arid and semi-arid
  (ii) Tundra
  (iii) Polar

The above classification of ecosystems is more geographical, but from the approach of 'habitat' there are several micro ecosystems working in a geographical region. The regions represent the biomes, which has been defined by Odum thus: "Regional climates interact with regional biotic and substrate to produce large, easily recognizable community units, called biomes." These are primarily the biotic zones also referred to as major life zones.

The major ecosystems are described as under:

Freshwater Ecosystem

Freshwater habitats can be divided into two categories:
(i) Standing water or lentic (calm)—lake, pond, swamp or bog.
(ii) Running water or lotic (washed)—river, spring, stream.

Although freshwater habitats occupy a small portion of the earth's surface, they are of great importance to man because they provide drinking water as well as water for domestic and industrial needs. Freshwater ecology, in Odum's words, emphasizes the organisms in environment relationship in the freshwater habitat in the context of the ecosystem principle.

A pond is a good example of freshwater ecosystem, which exhibits a self-sufficient, self-regulating system. A pond is a place where living organisms not only live but interact with abiotic and biotic components, thus forming an ecosystem, which is different from other systems. Similarly, lakes, swampy regions and delta regions of rivers have their own ecosystems in which producers, consumers and decomposers interact and are responsible for the unique ecosystem of each.

Marine (Ocean) Ecosystem

The marine ecosystem is different from freshwater ecosystem mainly because of its salty water and also because (i) the sea covers 70 per cent of earth's area, (ii) the sea is deep, (iii) the sea is continuous, and (iv) the sea water is in continuous circulation. According to Odum (1971), "marine ecology emphasizes the totality or pattern of relationship between organisms and the sea environment". In a marine ecosystem, the ecology of shallow and deep waters as well as estuarine part are different from each other. Each ocean also represents a very large and stable ecosystem.

Grassland Ecosystem

Grasslands occupy about 19 per cent of the earth's area, which include tropical and temperate grasslands. In this, the savannah ecosystem is very important. The abiotic components are the nutrients present in the soil and aerial environment. The elements like carbon dioxide, water, nitrates, phosphates, sulfates, etc., are present in the air and soil of the area. The producers are mainly grasses and small trees and shrubs. The primary consumers include cows, buffaloes, sheep, goats, deer, rabbits, and other animals, while secondary consumers are animals like foxes, jackals, snakes, frogs, lizards, birds, etc. The microbes are active in the decaying and dead organic matter of different forms. They bring the minerals back to the soil, thus making them available to producers. Pastoralism and livestock ranching are the main occupations in these regions.

Forest Ecosystem

About 30 per cent of the land area of the earth is under forest cover, but due to man's intervention this area is gradually becoming smaller. But still forest ecosystem is very important. The coniferous forests stretch as broad belts across North America and Eurasia. On the other hand, temperate deciduous forests occupy areas in eastern North America, parts of Europe, Japan and also in Australia. Among forests the tropical evergreen forests are found in the tropical regions.

In the forest ecosystem, the abiotic components are the organic substances present in the soil and atmosphere and also minerals present in dead organic debris. The producers are trees of different species. The primary consumers are animals of various types, while secondary consumers include carnivores like lions, tigers, snakes, birds, lizards, foxes, etc. The forest ecosystems are of great concern from the environmental point of view. The rate of exploitation of forest by man is growing day by day, thus causing a great concern to all nations of the world because of its impact over global climate and on several animal species.

Desert Ecosystem

Deserts generally occur in regions having less than 25 cms of rainfall and are unevenly distributed. Scarcity of rainfall may be due to: (i) high sub-tropical pressure, as in the Sahara and Australian deserts, (ii) geographical position in rain shadows, or (iii) high altitude as in Tibetan, Gobi, Bolivia deserts. There are three life forms of plants that are adapted to deserts: (i) the annuals, which avoid drought by growing only when there is adequate moisture; (ii) the succulents, such as the cacti, which store water; and (iii) the desert shrubs, which have numerous branches and a special root system which help them to adapt to desertic conditions. The most common animals, apart from camels and goats, are reptiles and insects, who are able to live under xeric conditions. Due to poor vegetation, dead organic matter is less and some fungi and bacteria act as decomposers. Apart from hot desert, there are also widespread cold deserts encircling the north and south poles, where permanent ice caps have developed an entirely different type of ecosystem, sustainable to cold climatic conditions.

Cropland Ecosystem

Apart from the above-mentioned natural ecosystems, there are also man-engineered ecosystems in which man is very much involved in their operation. One such is the cropland ecosystem, in which man has developed croplands after considering the soil, climatic and other environmental conditions. These are ecosystems of dominant crop species like wheat, maize, jowar, paddy, sugarcane, cotton, tea, coffee, etc.

The abiotic components of this ecosystem include climatic conditions and mineral contents of the soil. In case of any deficiency, man used chemical fertilizers and/or water for irrigation, etc. The various types of foodgrains, pulses and commercial crops are grown in these croplands, which provide food and fodder not only to man and animals, respectively, but in the fields several types of animals like birds, rats, rabbits, and other smaller reptiles insects, etc., also survive. The decomposition of dead organic matter of plants and animals make the minerals available again.

There is a need that every ecosystem should be studied in detail. Apart from above mentioned macro or global ecosystems, there are also several meso and micro regions existing in each region. For example, India has the following major ecosystems:

1. Himalayan mountain ecosystem
2. Plain ecosystem
3. Desert ecosystem
4. Central India plateau ecosystem
5. Peninsular (Deccan plateau) ecosystem
6. Coastal plain ecosystem
7. Island ecosystem

These ecosystems have been identified on the basis of physiography, which also controls climate, natural vegetation, soil and also man's adoption to nature. Each major region can be divided into sub-ecosystem regions; for example, Rajasthan has the following ecosystems:

(i) Arid ecosystem
(ii) Irrigated arid ecosystem
(iii) Sub-arid ecosystem
(iv) Aravalli hills ecosystem
(v) Eastern plains ecosystem
(vi) Hadoti plateau ecosystem

Further identification of micro-ecosystems will help not only in understanding the ecosystem but also in regional development and planning. The goal of sustainable development can only be achieved, when our developmental policies are based on the micro-ecosystem of each region.

4

Biodiversity and Its Conservation

Biodiversity or biological diversity refers to the variety of life on earth. The term encompasses three categories: genetic diversity, species diversity and ecosystem diversity. Genetic diversity describes the variation of genes within a species; species diversity describes the variety of species within region; and ecosystem diversity refers to the number and distribution of ecosystems. The increasing interest in biodiversity is a result of concerns regarding species extinction, depletion of genetic diversity, and disruptions to the atmosphere, water supplies, fisheries and forests.

The environment is a complex of ecosystems made up of a variety of species, themselves represented by a number of strains, each with its own genetic identity. This diversity is a condition for the long-term sustainability of the environment and the maintenance of its integrity is, therefore, recognized as being indispensable to sustain human life. The taxonomic knowledge of species is incomplete and, therefore, it is essential to guard against the extinction of the largest possible number of species and strains, among which are some that may in the future provide us with food and medicine or be used in the biological control of pests and pathogens.

Biological diversity encompasses all species of plants, animals, and micro-organisms and the ecosystem and ecological processes of which they are part. As stated above, biodiversity is usually described at three levels: genetic, species and ecosystem. *Genetic diversity* is the sum total of genetic information, contained in the genes of individual plants, animals, and micro-organisms that inhabit the earth. *Species diversity* refers to the variety of the living organisms on earth. *Ecosystem diversity* refers to the variety of habitat's biotic communities and ecological processes in the biosphere as well as the enormous diversity within ecosystems in terms of habitat difference and the variety of ecological processes.

Biodiversity provides the basis for life on earth. The fundamental social, ethical, cultural and economic values of these resources have been recognized in religion, art and literature from the earliest days of recorded history. Wild species and the genetic variations within them make substantial contribution to the development of agriculture, medicine and industry. Perhaps, even more important, many species have been fundamental to stabilization of climate, protection of watersheds, protection of soil, and the protection of nurseries and breeding grounds. It is difficult to determine the total economic value of the full range of goods and services which biodiversity provides.

Biological resources have made substantial contribution to human welfare, specially in the rural areas of developing countries. For example, fuelwood and dung provide over 90 per cent of the energy needs in many areas in Nepal, and in many other countries. Human beings have used about 7,000 kinds of plants for food, but only 20 species supply 90 per cent of the world's food, and just three—wheat, maize and rice—supply more than half. Although the major food crops in use today were domesticated thousands of years ago, the potential for other species to play prominent role in world agriculture is great. Numerous locally important, though yet much less known, species of wild and domesticated plants could be cultivated and used much more widely.

Genetic diversity of a crop is the total genetic variation of the species available for further crop improvement. With an ever-increasing growth in human population, more food has to be grown to satisfy its needs. The key to better yielding varieties is provided by plant breeding to increase their food value, resistance to fungal, bacterial and viral diseases and insects, nematodes and other pests. This inbuilt genetic resistance and adaptation may eliminate the need for environmentally undesirable pesticides.

More than four lakh varieties of germplasms of important crops have been collected in international gene banks. Some countries including India have specific crop gene banks. There are numerous facilities in the world that conserve collection of vegetatively propagated crops like fruit trees, tuberous crops, palms, nuts coffee, cocoa, grasses and shrubs. World collection also includes varieties of wheat, rice, maize, barley, potatoes, sweet potatoes, sorghum, millet, lentils, legumes, etc.

Estimation of World Species (Biodiversity at Global Level)

How many species exist in the world is a big question before the scientists and they have given their estimates, but it still requires a long way to go to unfold the entire biodiversity pattern of the world. So far, about 1.6×10^6 species have been described and of those fewer than 10^5 are familiar, interesting, or pretty enough to have been studied in detail. More are being discovered all the time. In 1988, two primates and one deer were discovered, another primate (a tamarin) was found in 1990, and since 1908, 11 species of cetaceans (whales and porpoises) have been added to the global inventory, amounting to 13 per cent of all known members of that order. Between 1978 and 1987, the newly identified animal species were 5 birds, 26 mammals, 231 fish, and 7,000 insects. Clearly, the species that have been found represent only a proportion of the total number, and estimating that number must necessarily involve an extrapolation from what is known to what is unknown. Many scientists have attempted the task, producing estimates of up to 100×10^6 species, but a conservative and probably more realistic estimate puts the total at 5.10×10^6. Robin Pellew, director of the UK branch of the World Wide Fund for Nature, has taken a median estimate of around 8×10^6 broken down as in Table 4.1.

Table 4.1

Number of Species Described and the Likely Total Number

(in '000)

Group	*Described*	*Estimate*
Viruses	5	500
Bacteria	5	400
Fungi	7	1,000
Protozoa	40	200
Algae	40	200
Nematodes	15	500
Molluscs	70	150
Crustaceans	40	100
Arachnids	75	600
Insects	950	4,000
Vertebrates	45	50
Higher plants	250	300
Total	1,605	8,000

The true total is likely to be higher, because the list omits a number of invertebrate groups, such as the annelids (worms), sponges (porifera), and cnidarians (hydras and jellyfish). It also omits such plant groups as the ferns, mosses, and bryophytes. Further uncertainties arise from taxonomic disagreement between 'lumpers' and 'splitters' that can alter significantly the number of species recognized in certain groups.

Only 13 per cent species are supposed to be known of the world's existing microbial resources covering algae, bacteria, fungi lichens viruses and protozoa. Diversity of micro-organisms is preserved through culture collections, to be used beneficially in mining for metals, getting rid of methane from coal mines, cleaning up oil spill, creating perfumes, monitoring air pollution, controlling insect pests, destroying patricides in the soil, etc.

Many plants and invertebrate species, particularly associated with tropical forests, are still not identified and remain unknown. Most developing countries are concerned about how to safeguard their interests so that these resources are not lost to the technologically and financially more powerful developed countries. And, to do this, the genetically rich developing countries including India must develop technological capabilities to safeguard the migration of vast germplasm resources through international agreements or financial attractions.

Like other natural resources, the above distribution of living species in the world is not uniform. Species richness increases from the poles to the equator. Freshwater insects, for example, are three to six times more abundant in tropical areas than in temperate zones. Tropical regions have also the highest richness of mammal species, per unit area, and vascular plant species diversity is much richer at lower latitudes.

Biodiversity in India

India has a rich heritage of species and genetic strains of flora and fauna. Overall, 8 per cent of world species are found in India. It is estimated that India is tenth among the plant-rich countries of the world. India has diversity in its ecosystem consisting of forests, wetlands, grassland, deserts, marine areas, coral reefs, etc., and each system supports thousands of species. The total number of living species identified in India so far is 2,00,000 (many more not yet discovered). The pattern of biodiversity in India is given below in Table 4.2:

Table 4.2
Biodiversity of India

Species	*Number*
Total plants	45,000
Mammals	340
Reptiles	420
Amphibians	2,000
Fishes	1,693
Insects	67,000
Molluscs	4,000
Birds	1,200
Invertebrates	6,800

Source: Negi, S.S. (1991), *Environmental Degradation and Crisis in India*, Indus Pub., New Delhi, pp. 68-69.

But India's rich biological diversity is rapidly eroding. More than half its forests are gone, two-thirds of its wetlands drained out or polluted, almost all of its dry scrub and grassland habitats destroyed. Habitat destruction, hunting and overexploitation, pollution and poisoning and introduction of exotics have caused a decline in many species. Many species have gone extinct, and of what remains, over 10 per cent of flowering plants, 21 per cent mammals and 5 per cent of birds are believed to be under threat.

In the Earth Summit in 1992, India was the first country to sign the Convention on Biological Diversity (CBD). Not only this, several efforts have also been made to conserve the rich heritage of biodiversity in the country; for example, 358 wildlife sanctuaries and 63 national parks have been developed. There is also need to implement the laws pertaining to the protection of forests and wildlife. But, what is needed more is the people's participation. Two measures, which might greatly help, are:

1. Local communities must be given much more secure and meaningful rights over public lands and waters in their own localities, following the lead to joint forest management (JFM) programmes.
2. Local communities should be given substantial incentives to continue conserving biodiversity resources on private and public lands in their own localities by linking financial inputs.

Biogeographical Regions of India

As Indian sub-continent is characterized by a variety of climate types, flora of the country is also correspondingly of different types in different parts. For the study of flora, the country has been divided into following nine biogeographical regions: (1) Western Himalayas, (2) Eastern Himalayas, (3) West Indian Deserts, (4) Gangetic Plain, (5) Assam, (6) Central India, (7) Malabar, (8) Deccan, and (9) Andamans.

Figure 4.1
Biogeographical Regions of India

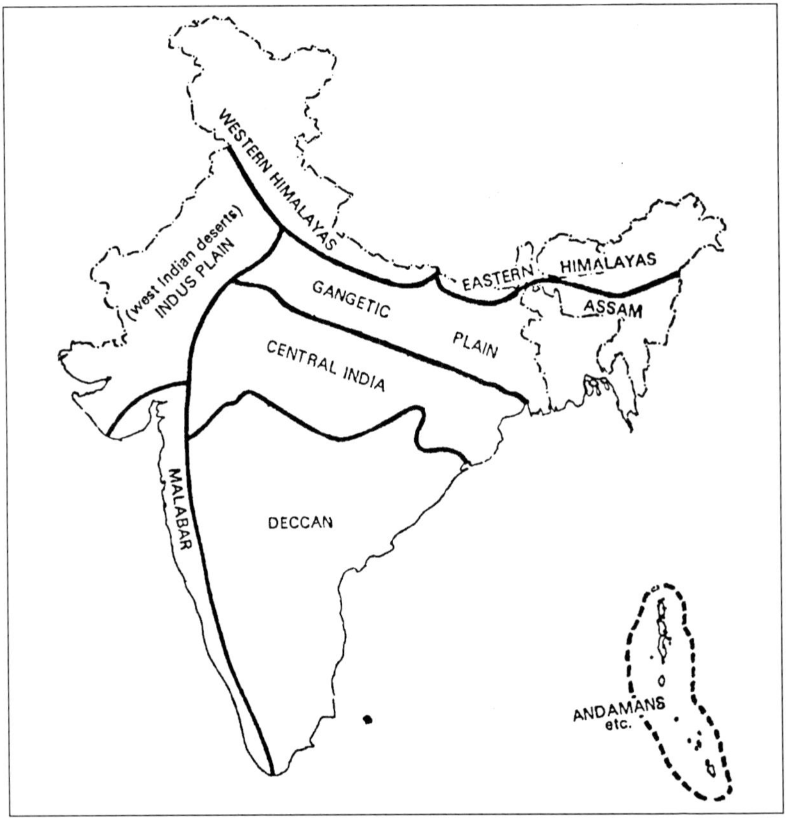

Western Himalayas

It extends from central region of Kumaon to northwest region of Kashmir. Altitudinally, there are three zones of vegetation corresponding to three climatic belts.

(i) Submontane or Lower Zone (Tropical and Subtropical)

This zone lies from about 300 to 1,500 metres above sea level in Siwalik and adjacent areas. The forest is dominated by timber trees of *Shorea robusta*. In riverain regions, trees of *Dalbergia sissoo* are most noticeable, while in more moist soils, *Cedrela toona, Ficus glomerata* and *Eugenia jambolama* are found in plenty.

(ii) Temperate or Montane Zone

This zone extends from 1,500 to 3,000 metres above sea level. At about 3,000 metres, *Pinus longifolia* is generally replaced by *Pinus excelsa.* From 1,500 to 10,000 metres, *Cedrus deodara* is quite abundant forming pure forest stands. At these altitudes, *Quercus incana* is also grown as separate patches. At higher altitudes, *Aesculus indica* (horse chestnut), *Quercus semecarpifolia, Quercus dilatata,* along with the conifers such as *Abies pindrow, Picea morinda, Cupressus torulosa, Taxus baccata*, etc., are most common components of vegetation.

(iii) Alpine Zone

It is the limit of tree growth at about 3,600 metres, known as timber or tree line, where the plant height is considerably reduced. Plants are mostly dwarfed and cushion-shaped shrubs and grasses. At about 4,500 metres and above—snow line—plant growth is almost nil. On lower levels of this zone, some rhododendrons, *Betula utilis* and small junipers are present. Above this zone, there are present many types of herbs, with short period of vegatative growth and flowering.

Eastern Himalayas

It consists of regions of Sikkim and extends in the east up to NEFA. In its vegetational zones, it is similar to the western Himalayas. On the whole, the eastern Himalayan region has more tropical elements, greater variety of oaks and rhododendrons and less of conifers than the western Himalayas. This region is also divided into three zones, viz., submontane, temperate and alpine.

(i) Submontane Zone

Due to warm and humid weather, it is typically tropical with dense forests of *Shorea robusta*. It extends from the plain foot of the hill up to 1,800 metres altitude. In riverain areas, there are forests of *Dalbergia sissoo* and *Acacia catechu*. Mixed forests of deciduous trees like *Sterospermum, Cedrela toona, Bauhinia, Anthocephalus cadamba and Lagerstroemia parviflora* are predominant.

(ii) Temperate Zone

It ranges between 1,800 and 3,600 metres altitude above sea level. The lower region has several species of oaks, such as *Quercus lemellosa, Quercus lineata, Michelia, Cedrela* and *Eugenia.* The upper region, which is cooler, has such conifers as *Juniperus, Cryptomeria, Picea, Abies* and *Tsuga.*

(iii) Alpine Zone

It is situated above 3,600 metres, where vegetation is devoid of trees. Shrubby growth of *Juniperus* and *Rhododendron* is found in grassy areas.

West Indian Deserts (Indus Plain)

This region consists of parts of Rajasthan, Kutch, Delhi and Gujarat. The climate is characterized by very hot and dry summer and cold winter. Rainfall is less than 70 cm and plants are mostly xerophytic, such as *Acacia nelotica, Prosopis spicifera, Prosopis juliflora, Salvadora oleoides, Salvadora persica, Tecomella, Capparis aphylla, Tamarix dioica* and *Zizyphus nummularia.*

Gangetic Plain

Comprising Uttar Pradesh (UP), Bihar and Bengal, this is the most fertile region. The chief climatic factors, viz., temperature and rainfall together, are responsible for distinct type of vegetation. Rainfall is less than 70 cm in western UP, whereas it is more than 150 cm in Bengal. Vegetation is chiefly of tropical moist and dry deciduous forest type. In northwestern UP, near foothills of the Himalayas, *Dalbergia sissoo* and *Acacia nelotic* are most common. In southwestern UP, there are desert areas, where characteristic species are *Capparis aphylla, Saccharum munja, Acacia nelotica*, etc. In eastern UP, *Butea monosperma* (dhak), *Madhuca indica* (mahua), *Terminalia arjuna* (arjun), *buchanania lanzan* (chiraunji), *Diospyros melanoxylon* (tendu), *Cordia myxa* (lisora), *Sterculia urens,*

Boswellia serrata (salai), *Acacia catechu* (khair), *Azadirachta indica* (neem), *Mangifera indica* (mango), *Ficus bengalensis* (bargad), *Ficus religiosa* (pipal) are most dominant trees.

Assam

This region receives the heaviest rainfall, with Cherrapunji (Meghalaya) as much as more than 1,000 cm. Both the temperature and wetness are very high, which are responsible for dense tropical evergreen forests. Some of the important trees are *Diperocarpus macrocarpus, Mesua ferrea, Michelia champaca, Shorea robusta, Artocarpus chaplasha, Alstonia scholaris, Sterculia alata, Lagerstroemia flos-regina, Ficus elastica*, etc.

Central India

It comprises Madhya Pradesh, parts of Orissa and Gujarat. Depending upon the amount of rainfall, forests have developed into thorny, mixed deciduous and sal types. The forest vegetation is chiefly constituted by *Tectona grandis, Diospyros melanoxylon, Butea monosperma, Terminalia tomentosa* and *Dalbergia latifolia.* The thorny vegetation consists of *Carissa spinarum, Zizyphus rotundifolia, Accacia leucophloea, Acatechu, Butea frondosa*, etc.

Malabar

This region comprises the western coast of India extending from Gujarat in the north to the Cape Camorin in the south. Rainfall is heavy. The vegetation is of four types: tropical moist evergreen forests, mixed deciduous forests, subtropical or temperate evergreen forests and the mangrove forests. The tropical wet evergreen forests are very luxuriant and multi-storied, with such tall trees as *Dipterocarpus indicus, Sterculia alata, Cedrela toona, Tectona grandis* and *Dalbergia latifolia.* Bamboos, like *Dendrocalamus strictus* and *Bambusa arundinacea*, are also present.

In the Nilgiri hills, there are temperate evergreen forests of such trees as *Eurya japonica, Michelia nilagirica* and *Gordonia obtusa*, also known as the *sholas.*

Deccan

This region is drier with rainfall of only 100 cm. It includes Andhra Pradesh, Tamilnadu and Karnataka. It has central hilly plateau with forests of *Boswellia serrata, Tectona grandis* and *Hardwickia pinnata,* and the low eastern dry Coromandal coast, with tropical dry evergreen forests of *Santalum album* (chandan), *Cedrela toona* and plants like *Capparis, Phyllantuhus, Euphorbia,* etc.

Andamans

It has a wide range of spreading coastal vegetation like mangroves, beech forests and in the interior evergreen forests of tall trees. There are some pockets of dry areas also. Important species of the island are *Rhizophora, Mimusops, Calophyllum, Dipterocarpus, Lagerstroemia* and *Terminalia.* Most of the area is now cleared for paddy and sugarcane cultivations.

Endangered and Endemic Species of India

Several plant and animal species in the country are endangered and endemic. Some of them are vulnerable and rare, while others are interminate and threatened.

Among important endangered animals are included tiger, elephant, rhino, Indian wild ass, Harigul or Kashmir stag, the golden langur, the pygmy hog and a host of others.

There are also endangered bird species like the Siberian crane, the great Indian bustard, the florican, etc. Many plant species are now increasingly threatened due to changes in their habitat induced by human activity. There are thousands of small herbs, which are greatly threatened by habitat loss. Many plants are threatened due to overharvesting and excessive use of chemicals.

Threats to Biodiversity

Due to unsustainable resource use and developmental activities, biodiversity is at threat in the entire world as well as in each ecological region. Man himself is responsible for the loss of biodiversity. The main causes of the loss of biodiversity are:

— habitat loss,

- changing agricultural and forest practices,
- invasion by introduced species,
- overexploitation for commercial agriculture,
- environmental pollution,
- poaching of wildlife,
- global climatic change,
- loss of traditional knowledge,
- international trade, and
- growing demand, etc.

The primary threat to biodiversity is due to habitat loss because of the growth of human population, industrialization and changes in land use pattern. The loss of habitats, due to rapid human population growth and economic development, is the major contributor to the rapid global destruction of biodiversity.

Extinction of Species or Loss of Biodiversity

Today, the extinction of several species or loss of biodiversity is a much debated issue among the environmentalists at the international level. Species are disappearing rapidly and there is growing consensus within the international community that a system should be put in place to slow or halt the process of extinction. All the species are the integral part of ecosystem and extinction of some species diminishes the well-being of the remaining species, including human beings. The concern about biological diversity is the shrinking genetic pool. It is estimated that tropical forests contain at least 50 per cent and perhaps 90 per cent of the world's species. According to an estimate, 20 to 75 species are becoming extinct each day because of deforestation in the tropics.

Species do not persist indefinitely. Indeed, it was the realization that fossils are the remains or traces of organisms no longer to be found alive that led to the development of our present understanding of evolutionary processes. Estimating the number of species existing at present as a proportion of all the species that have ever lived is difficult, but the plants and animals alive today probably constitute around 2 to 4 per cent of all the species that have lived in the last 600 million years.

Extinctions have not been spread evenly. There is a general background rate at which species go extinct, but there have also been at least five mass extinctions in which 65 to 85 per cent (and at the end of the Permian period, around 225 million years ago, 95 per cent or more) of all species disappeared. Background extinctions have little or no effect on biodiversity, because their rate is matched or exceeded by that of speciation, in which one species divides into two and thus increases the number of species. Nor do mass extinction produces more than a temporary reduction in the number of species, because historically they have been followed by the rapid adaptive radiation of surviving species into the vacated niches. The extinction of the dinosaurs, for example, was followed by rapid speciation among mammals. Today, the number of land-dwelling species alive is about twice the average of the last 450 million years.

Throughout the geological history of the earth, species of plants and animals had been subjected to various evolutionary processes. Some species became extinct during the different geological periods. The last major extinction of some species occurred at the close of the Cretaceous period, some 65 millions years ago, when birds and mammals were particularly affected. The total disappearance of all dinosaurs occurred during that great extinction. It is generally agreed that they were triggered by natural environment phenomena during geological evolution of the earth. In recent history, biological resources have been lost at an accelerated rate, mainly due to anthropogenic causes. Tropical deforestation between 1990 and 2020 may eliminate between 5 and 15 per cent of the world's species. The World Conservation Monitoring Centre has recognized that some 22,000 species of plant and animals are actually threatened with extinction.

Amongst the causes identified for the loss of biological diversity are: (i) habitat loss, fragmentation and modification: as forests are cleared, wetland drained, valleys flooded and roads built, so habitats are transformed and have led to loss of certain species; (ii) overexploitation of resources, both land and sea, is responsible for the extinction of some large terrestrial animals, as well as of many marine species; (iii) pesticides and pollution have affected several species of birds and other organisms; and (iv) the impact of introduced exotic species as the threaten natural flora and fauna by predation, competition or altering natural habitat.

Besides, the introduction of new high yielding wheat and rice varieties, since the mid-1960s, has caused a loss of gene pool in many centres of crop diversity as Turkey, Iraq, Iran, Afghanistan, Pakistan and India.

The intense pressures on biological diversity are a direct reflection of the increasing human numbers. These pressures are expected to increase until population stabilizes, as projected by the United Nations, by about the period 2050-2070, at about 10 billion. Such stabilization would be achieved only if present efforts to curtail growth of human population are pursued vigorously.

Evolution of the Biodiversity Regime

The Stockholm Conference was not the first occasion at which issues related to biodiversity were placed on the international agenda. A variety of legal instruments already existed. Some of these were regional, such as the Convention on Nature Protection Wildlife Preservation in the Western Hemisphere (Washington, 1940) and the African Convention on the Conservation of Nature and Natural Resources (Algiers, 1968). Other measures dealt with specific species, such as birds and marine and polar region species. Prior to Stockholm, the only major international legal instrument for conserving biodiversity was the 1971 Convention on Wetlands and Wildlife Habitats. The 61 parties to this convention pledged to make an inventory of designated wetlands, to promote their conservation, and also to establish nature reserves in the important wetlands.

But, no comprehensive international treaty addressed the problem of biological diversity. Although Stockholm did not produce such a document, it is was the first time when the issue was addressed in such a holistic manner. The issue of biodiversity was debated, and the conference document included provisions aimed at protecting biodiversity.

The area of genetic resources and biotechnology was already controversial in 1972, at the time of the Stockholm Conference. Developing countries were concerned about their lack of access to the biotechnology that was developed from the use of their resources, and they tried to use linkage politics to gain access to this technology. They pressed their demand for the transfer of technology on non-commercial terms. This demand was rejected by the developed countries, and the final statement of the conference diluted the language that addressed this linkage between economics and the environment.

Both the declaration of the United Nations Conference on the Human Environment and the Action Plan for the Human Environment included language that addresses biodiversity. Principles 2, 4, and 6 of the declaration included provision for safeguarding flora and fauna and preserving ecosystems. The action plan addressed the importance of protecting forests, which among other thing, are important habitats for wildlife; it recommended that wildlife be monitored to assess the impact of pollutants and that the economic value of wildlife be assessed. Governments were asked to take steps to protect ecosystems that have international significance. Recommendations 39 through 45 dealt generally with the issue of preserving genetic resources.

In the period between the Stockholm and Rio conferences, the body of legislation concerning biodiversity continued to grow. Relevant major international legislations included the Convention on the Protection of the World Culture and Natural Heritage (1972), the Convention on International Trade in Endangered Species of Wild Fauna and Flora (1973), and the Convention on Conservation of Migratory Species of Wild Animals (1979). Other conventions on biodiversity include May 1992 at Nairobi, June 1992 at UNCED; while in December 1993 Convention on Biological Diversity entered into force. The highlights of the convention were:

(i) National identification and monitoring of biological diversity.
(ii) The development of national strategies and programmes for conserving biological diversity.

(iii) National *in situ* and *ex situ* conservation measures.
(iv) Environmental assessment procedures to take into account the effects of projects on biological diversity.
(v) National reports from parties on measures taken to implement the convention and the effectiveness of the measures.

In the aftermath of Stockholm, developing countries continued their push for greater access to the biotechnology that resulted from their biological wealth. A non-binding International Undertaking on Plant Genetic Resources (Resolution 8/33) was passed by the FAO in 1983. It stated that access to genetic resources should not be restricted, and it declared that all seed resources were the common heritage of humanity; therefore, both primitive stocks and those developed by proprietary means should be free to all. Some developed world producers were opposed to this declaration, and many industrialized countries were not parties to it because it was incompatible with their patent rights. Third World members, however, accepted its provisions.

A 1991 Costa Rican deal is considered one possible model for future bilateral arrangements. The parties to the deal were the National Biodiversity Institute, a non-profit research centre, and Merck & Co., the world's largest pharmaceutical company. Merck agreed to pay the institute US$1.1 million, as well as royalties from any product developed, in return for plant, insect and microbe samples from all over Costa Rica. Costa Rica is estimated to have about 5 per cent of any royalties go directly into conservation. Although this agreement provides for compensation, some critics say it gives away Costa Rican resources for too little money. Nevertheless, many developing countries are studying this arrangement with interest.

The years between Stockholm and Rio saw incremental progress with regard to the items on the Third World's biodiversity agenda. Developing states wanted to make their own arrangements concerning resources access, and as the Merck deal illustrates, the slow process of norm change had begun. But, the progress of these states in the campaign for transfer of technology and financial assistance is more difficult to assess. Although developing countries continued to push for change in these areas, developed countries maintained their determined resistance. These conflicting perspectives were reflected in the preparatory negotiations for the Rio Conference.

The issue of biodiversity should be seen as a common problem; as such, action by a country has implications for other countries too. The biodiversity of every country should be protected with mutual cooperation and exchange of biotechnology.

In fact, this is a common property resource (CPR) concern as a decrease in biodiversity has consequences for all species. But, this CPR has some distributional characteristics that make it different from other environmental issues. The bulk of the world's biological diversity is found in tropical forests, which are located in the Third World. The loss of biological diversity has tremendous implications for agriculture. The range of food resources has declined over time. One estimate says that more than 3,000 plant species have been used for food throughout human history, however, there certainly has been a significant reduction in variety. Now, most of the world's food comes from 20 species. The issue of patents is at the core nowadays, because several developing countries have a fear that the use of traditional plant species will be restricted by scientifically advanced countries. After Uruguay Round of GATT, much debate has taken place and still continues to standardize intellectual property rights. The controversy over patent right of 'Neem' tree, which has been used by Indians for centuries, is one example.

To conclude, one can quote from a stanza in *Isho-Upanishad* which says: "The Universe along with its creatures belongs to the land. No creature is superior to any other. Human beings should not be above nature. Let no one species encroach over the rights and privileges of the other species."

Conservation of Biodiversity

Several measures have been taken at the international as well as the national level for the conservation of biodiversity. In India, legislative measures that have been taken for conservation of diversity are:

(i) The Environmental Protection Act, 1986;
(ii) The Fisheries Act, 1897;
(iii) The Forest (Conservation) Act, 1980;
(iv) The Wildlife (Protection) Act, 1972;
(v) The Amendment Act, 1991;
(vi) The Wildlife (Protection) Amendment Act, 2002; and
(vii) The Biodiversity Act, 2002.

These Acts have been discussed in detail in Chapter 6.

In Situ Conservation

In situ conservation, as defined by the UNEP is, "the conservation of ecosystem and natural habitats and the maintenance and recovery of viable populations of species in their natural surroundings". This is an effective conservation strategy since it ensures the maintenance of ecosystems and species in their natural conditions.

India has taken several measures to conserve in situ wild biodiversity by developing a network of protected areas throughout the country. India has 89 national parks and 500 wildlife sanctuaries sprawled in an area of 1,56,000 sq. km. These protected areas have helped in conserving habitats and their biodiversity.

Ex Situ Conservation

It is a method of conserving species outside natural habitats. This could be in zoological parks and botanical gardens or through forestry or research institutes. There is also another form of conserving a plant by preserving its germ plasm in a gene bank so that it can be used if needed in future. The Madras Crocodile Bank was the first crocodile-breeding centre in Asia. A lot of efforts are under way to collect and preserve the genetic material of crop, animal, bird and fish species by Government of India.

5

Environmental Pollution

Pollution is the result of human activities, mainly those associated with industries and automobiles. The word 'pollution' is derived from the Latin word *'polluere'*, which means "to soil or defile". Any alteration to air, water, soil or food that threatens the health, survival capability or activities of humans or other living organisms, is called pollution. Pollution is the effect of undesirable changes in our surroundings that have harmful effects on plants, animals and human beings. Environmental pollution is a man-made problem, mainly of affluent countries, now a serious problem of developing countries as well.

The common forms of pollution are air, water, soil, noise, thermal and radioactive pollution, which can be divided into (i) non-degradable, (ii) degradable, and (iii) slowly degradable or persistent pollutants. The main pollutants are deposited matter, carbon monoxide, sulphur dioxide, sulphuric acid droplets, hydrogen sulphide, fluoride and other halogens; metals like lead, iron, zinc, bromine, iodine; agricultural pollutants like pesticides, insecticides, herbicides, fungicides and fertilizers; and complex organic pollutants, photochemical pollutants, pollutants from automobiles, radioactive minerals, unwanted noise, municipal waste, etc.

Air Pollution

Air, which is a mixture of gases, moisture and some inert material, controls life on earth. It is a reservoir of oxygen needed by man and other animals and of carbon dioxide essential for plants. Any contamination in air may disturb the whole atmospheric system, which is an insulating blanket round the earth. Without air there would be no clouds, no winds, no rain, no snow and no fire. In other words, there would be no life on earth. The atmosphere, which shields the earth from ultraviolet radiation, becomes progressively tenuous with increasing distance from the earth. About 75 per cent of earth's atmosphere lies within 16 kilometres from the surface, and 99 per cent of it lies below an altitude of 30 kilometres.

Table 5.1

Composition of Clear, Dry Air at Sea Level

Components	*Per cent by Volume*
Nitrogen	78.084
Oxygen	20.9476
Argon	0.934
Carbon dioxide	0.0314
Neon	0.001818
Helium	0.000524
Methane	0.0002
Krypton	0.000114
Sulphur dioxide	0 to 0.0001
Hydrogen	0.00005
Nitrous oxide	0.00005
Xenon	0.0000087
Ozone	Summer 0.000007
	Winter 0.000002
Nitrogen dioxide	0 to 0.000002
Iodine	0 to 0.000001
Ammonia	0 to trace
Carbon monoxide	0.1 ppm-0.2 ppm

Source: H.J. Sanders (ed.), *Chemistry and the Atmosphere*, The American Chemical Society.

The structure of the atmosphere is controlled by various gases present in the air. The clear, dry air at sea level contains 78 per cent nitrogen, 21 per cent oxygen, 1 per cent argon, 0.03 per cent carbon dioxide and other gases as shown in Table 5.1.

Sources of Air Pollution

Air pollution is the result of the combined effects of several pollutants. These pollutants are associated with each other and also react with other elements. Therefore, it is difficult to categorize them, but for proper understanding, they can be divided into the several categories on the basis of their origin, nature, size, impact, etc.

Particulate matter can be divided into two types, viz., natural and man-made. The natural form of particulate matter is the result of volcanic dust and gases, mineral dust and sea-salt crystals. Another class of natural particulate matter is smoke from forest fires and grass fires. Living plants release pollens and spores into the air, which are called organic compounds. From forest trees certain hydrocarbons called terpenes are also released into the atmosphere.

Man-made particulate matter comes from many sources, but the major source is the combustion of hydrocarbon fuels like petroleum products, coal, peat and wood. Combustion of solid wastes is another source. Other kinds of matter introduced into the atmosphere are industrial chemicals, fly ash, refining fossil fuels, mining and smelting ores, as well as pollutants discharged through quarrying, farming activities, etc. Use of various types of solvents and also radioactive elements are other causes of air pollution created by man.

Another classification is (i) primary, and (ii) secondary pollutants. The primary pollutants are those gaseous and other solid micro particles inducted into the atmosphere. These pollutants are emitted and as such are not found in the air. The most important gaseous pollutants are carbon monoxide, oxides of sulphur, hydrogen sulphide, hydrocarbons, oxides of nitrogen, ozone and other oxidants. Secondary pollutants are the result of chemical reactions. Evidences and experiments indicate that exhaust gases of automobiles contribute more in the formation of secondary pollutants. For example, oxides of nitrogen produced in the combustion of petroleum and other fuels emitted into the atmosphere, yield ozone in the presence of sunlight. It is to be noted that ozone is not emitted as such into the atmosphere but formed only from primary pollutants.

According to chemical composition, air pollutants can be divided into organic pollutants and inorganic pollutants. Others have divided them into solid, liquid and gaseous pollutants. The gaseous pollutants are carbon monoxide, sulphur dioxide, hydrogen sulphide and organic sulphide, hydrogen fluoride, hydrogen chloride, oxides of nitrogen, aldehydes and organic acids, etc. Particulate pollutants consist of both solid and liquid particles. They vary in size from 0.01 micron to 20 microns. Dust, fume, mist, spray and smoke are included in this category.

According to source type, pollutants can be classified as being produced from:

(i) combustion,
(ii) transportation emissions,
(iii) industrial processes,
(iv) use of solvents, and
(v) radioactivity.

Combustion processes yield particulates such as fly ash and smoke and oxides of sulphur and nitrogen. The amount of sulphur dioxide emitted depends upon the contents in the fuel. High temperature processes, such as thermal fixation of atmospheric nitrogen, yield larger quantities of oxides of nitrogen. Carbon monoxide is also emitted from combustion. The other contaminants that are produced by combustion include acids and aldehydes.

The simplest form of combustion is the use of fuels in domestic use. In India, as well as in many developing countries, wood, coal, cowdung and kerosene oil are commonly used. All these materials yield carbon dioxide, carbon monoxide, sulphur dioxide, etc.

Automobiles may be considered as the main source of air pollution, specially in urban areas. Automobile exhausts release smoke and to a certain extent lead particles also. Smoke contains the gaseous pollutants carbon monoxide, hydrocarbons and oxides of nitrogen. The pollutants emitted by petrol- and diesel-driven vehicles are as shown below in Table 5.2:

Table 5.2

Pollutants Emitted by Petrol- and Diesel-Driven Vehicles

Emissions	*Petrol Engine*	*Diesel Engine*
Carbon monoxide	3	-
Sulphur dioxide	40 ppm	400 ppm
Nitrogen oxides	1100 ppm	300 ppm
Unburnt hydrocarbons	150 ppm	20 ppm
Particulate matter	0.1 g/m^3	0.01 g/m^3

The rapid rate of industrialization has resulted in more and more air pollution. Various industrial processes release almost all types of pollutants into the air. Some industries like cement, iron and steel, fertilizer, petrochemical, etc., are of great concern because of the difficulty in controlling the emission of pollutants from them. Acid rain has become a great threat to the environment. The use of solvents is increasing with the growing use of paints, spray, polish, etc. Due to presence of hydrocarbons in these materials, air pollution is caused, which is dangerous for health. Similarly, spray of pesticides in agriculture is also responsible for air pollution even in rural areas.

Nuclear material, when released into the air, is hazardous for all living organisms. Nuclear weapon testings, nuclear reactors, chemical processing plants, research institutes and hospitals contribute many radionuclides to the atmosphere.

It becomes clear from the above analysis that the problem of air pollution is increasing with the growth and expansion of industries and automobiles. It is high time that all of us should know the harmful effects of air pollution and also evolve technology to control it.

Table 5.3 indicates at a glance the main sources of air pollution and their impact.

Table 5.3
Main Pollutants of Air and their Impact on Health

Pollutant	*Sources*	*Health Hazards*
Carbon monoxide	Automobiles: due to incomplete combustion/burning of carbon in the fuel of internal combustion engines.	Displaces oxygen in blood, reduces amount of oxygen to blood tissues. Dulls mental performance, causes accident proneness, extra burden on anaemic, heart and lung patients.
Particulates (soot, smoke, fly ash, etc.)	Stationary fuel combustion in industrial processes.	Occurrence of photochemical smog which can cause widespread deaths in a few days.
Oxides of sulphur	Mainly industrial processes involving burning of coal and oil as fuel.	Temporary or permanent injury to the respiratory system, irritate the upper respiratory tract and lung tissue.
Hydrocarbons	Automobiles, fuel combustion in electric power plants, industrial processes, combustion in solid waste disposal and agricultural burning.	Gaseous hydrocarbons in atmosphere are not toxic but help in forming photochemical smog.
Oxides of nitrogen	Burning of fuel at very high temperatures as in transport vehicles, power plants and industrial boilers.	Nitrogen oxides combine with hydrocarbons in the presence of ultraviolet rays of the sun to form secondary pollutants called photochemical oxidants.
Others	Photochemical oxidants.	Photochemical oxidants feroxy-acetyl nitrogen, aldehydes and acrolein) cause eye irritation and flu, when they combine with particulates to form smog.

Effects of Air Pollution

Air pollution has now become a widespread problem and every individual in one way or the other is facing. At local and regional levels its manifestations are in the form of alterations in (i) visibility, (ii) intensity of sunshine, (iii) precipitation amount, and (iv) acid rain. Its global effects are: (i) change in natural climate by rise of temperature, melting of snow, (ii) increase in carbon dioxide, (iii) increase in particulates, (iv) holes in ozone layer, etc. Several aspects of air pollution, such as effects on the ozone layer, greenhouse effect, smog and acid rain have already been discussed. The effects of air pollution can be grouped under the following heads:

(i) on human health,
(ii) on animals and plants,
(iii) on atmosphere, and
(iv) other effects.

On Human Health

Some environmental poisons can cause acute illness and even death. Others may be harmful, although the disease may take years or even decades to appear. Air pollution mainly affects the respiratory system. Bronchitis, emphysema, asthma and lung cancer are some of the chronic diseases caused due to exposure to polluted air. It is feared that lung cancer is caused mainly due to polluted air because carcinogens are found in the polluted air. Its mortality rate is higher in urban areas. Figure 5.1 shows the various effects of air pollution on the human body. Sulphur dioxide is the most serious

Figure 5.1
Effects of Air Pollution on the Human Body

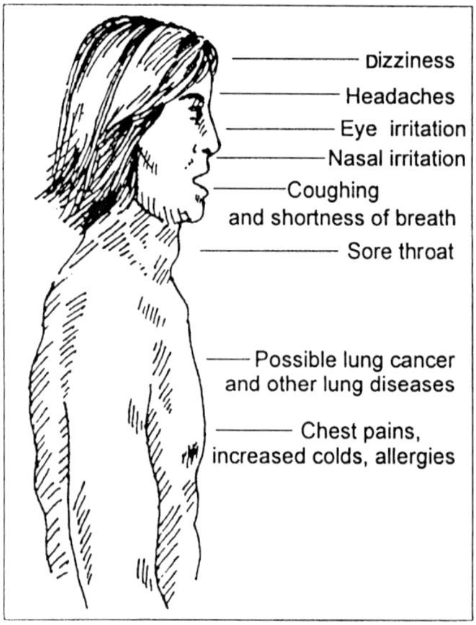

and widespread air pollutant. Its lower concentration is a cause of spasms in the smooth muscle of bronchioles and its higher concentration induces increased mucus production. Sulphur dioxide is also considered to cause cough, shortness of breath, spasm of the larynx and acute irritation to the membranes of the eyes. It also acts as an allergenic agent. When it reacts with some compounds, sulfuric acid is formed which may damage lungs.

Carbon monoxide often affects the oxygen-carrying capacity of blood. Nitric oxide is reported to be a pulmonary irritant and its excess concentration may cause pulmonary hemorrhage. Hydrogen sulphide is also toxic. Lead emitted from automobile exhausts is a cumulative poison and is dangerous particularly to children and may cause brain damage.

The particulate pollutants such as asbestos, silica, carbon, beryllium, lead, etc., are capable of exerting a noxious (fibrotic) local action in the interstitial areas of the lungs. Radioactive elements are also harmful to man and other living organisms. As described earlier, smog has a killer effect, which is the result of air pollution. The death toll by smog varies from few persons to thousands. In December 1952, about 4,000 persons died in London due to smog. Similar cases have been reported in London itself in 1956, 1957 and 1962 in which the death toll was between 700 and 1,000 persons. In other countries also smog deaths have been reported. In fact, the growing air pollution has now become a health hazard for man.

On Animals and Plants

The impact of air pollution on animals is more or less similar to that of effects on man. Chronic poisoning results from the ingestion of forage contaminated with atmospheric pollutants. Among the metallic contaminants, arsenic, lead and molybdenum are important. Fluoride is another pollutant, which causes fluorosis among animals. A number of livestock have been poisoned by fluorides and arsenic in North America. Bone lesions in animals due to excessive fluorides have also been reported.

Air pollution has caused widespread damage to trees, fruits, vegetables, flowers and in general, vegetation as a whole. The total annual cost of plant damage caused by air pollution in USA alone has been estimated to be in the range of 1 to 2 billion dollars. The most dramatic early instances of plant damage were seen in the total destruction of vegetation by sulphur dioxide in the areas surrounding smelters. When the absorption of sulphur dioxide exceeds a particular level, the cells become inactive and are killed, resulting in tissue collapse and drying of leaves. Cotton, wheat, barley and apple are more sensitive to this pollutant.

Fluorides are responsible for various types of injuries to plants. The leaves of apple, apricot, fig, peach, prune are more susceptible to air borne fluorides. Fluorides seem to interfere with the photosynthesis and respiration of plants. Smog also causes injury to plants. Similar impact of ozone can be seen in the lesions to plants. Chlorine, ammonia, hydrogen sulphide, etc., are also harmful to vegetation.

On Atmosphere

Some of the effects of air pollution on atmospheric conditions have already been discussed such as effect on ozone layer, greenhouse effect, etc. There is an increase in the carbon dioxide concentration in the air due to increased combustion of fossil fuels. Carbon dioxide absorbs heat strongly and the radiative cooling effect of the earth is thus decreased. The rising of temperatures and ozone holes are some of the problems, which have attracted the attention of the scientists of the world. These problems are not related to any region or a country but are the global problems and their impact on world climate may be hazardous to the whole world. The local weather conditions are highly susceptible to air pollution. Its impact on temperature, humidity, rainfall and clouds is apparent. The 'smog dom' on large urban centres is the result of air pollution. Due to air pollution visibility also reduces.

Other Effects

Air pollution can also cause damage to property and materials. The smoke, grit, dust and oxides of sulphur have harmful effects on structures. In 1972, when an oil refinery at Mathura was opened, its impact on Taj Mahal became a major issue. Sulphur dioxide is the most damaging gaseous pollutant. Aluminium alloys, copper and copper alloys, iron and steel are corroded when exposed to contaminated air. Hydrogen sulphide reacts with lead paints to form lead sulphide thereby producing a brown to black discolouration. The damage caused by air pollution to structures is not serious but from an aesthetic point of view it is not desirable.

Measures for Containing Air Pollution

Worldwide efforts are going on to contain air pollution. Scientists and technologists have developed certain measures but still progress in this field is not satisfactory. For the control of air pollution, there is need to deal with this problem from two angles: (i) to check the present prevalent air pollution in such a way that their harmful effects can be minimized, and (ii) to develop such methods and technology so that air pollution can be controlled in future. Some of the measures to contain air pollution are as follows:

1. The forest cover should be protected by restricting deforestation and through adoption of afforestation programmes. Trees are the best regulators of air pollution. It is an accepted fact that 33 per cent of the land area should remain under forest/tree cover. It will help in containing air pollution and also help in maintaining the ecological balance.
2. There must be a 'green belt' around every township and village. Similarly, industrial areas should be surrounded by green belts (see Table 5.4).
3. The main source of air pollution is the automobiles, therefore, their engines should be redesigned in such a way that their emissions cause minimum pollution. Several steps have been taken and some technology has also been developed, but still it is in a very preliminary stage. Apart from technological changes, some steps on individual level should be taken by vehicle owners, such as:
   (i) regular service of the vehicle,
   (ii) change or replacement of old engines,

(iii) use of filters and after burner,
(iv) the engine should be well-tuned, and
(v) mixing of anti-tibs in diesel and petrol, etc.

Table 5.4
Width of Green Belt for Various Industries

Industry	*Examples*	*Area of Works (ha)*	*Width of Green Belt*
Heavy industry	Oil refineries, chemical works, metallurgical and seaport industries, nuclear reactors	> 500	< 2 km
Heavy industry	Machine manufacture, ship-building, big harbour industries, power stations	200-500	> 1 km
Medium-heavy industry with much air pollution	Manufacture of straw boards, artificial fibres, and ceramic products, cement works	100-200	500 m or more
Medium-heavy industry with little air pollution	Manufacture of cars, foods, and textiles		200 m or more
Light industry with some air pollution	Tanneries, textiles and food industries	50-100	50-100 m
Light industry with some air pollution	Manufacture of electronic apparatus and domestic machines		
Service industry	Printing works, bakeries, laboratories	10-50	> 100m
Workshops, handicrafts, etc.	Fashion studios, photo printing shops, potteries	1-10	> 50 m

Adapted from *Manual on Urban Air Quality*, WHO Regional Publications, European Series No. 1, Copenhagen, 1976.

4. The use of steam engine by the railways should be stopped or minimized. As far as possible, electrically operated rail engines should be used, which are pollution-free.
5. In countries like India traditional use of fuelwood, coal, etc., should be checked and newly devised smoke-free furnaces be used.
6. The industrial areas should be located at a certain distance from residential areas. The selection of the site should be made with consideration of air direction.

7. Steps should be taken for immediate check on forest fires. For this proper arrangement and sound infrastructure are necessary.
8. In industries, arrangements for pollution control should be made. Only after full arrangement of effluent treatment, permission for production should be given.
9. With the help of chemical reactions harmful effects of pollution can be minimized. Measures for such methods should be taken and the methodology and material should be made available to the concerned persons.
10. Air pollution may also be contained by some other methods like filtering, settling, dissolving, absorption, etc. For these methods cheap devices should be developed.

Actual prevention of air pollution is not so simple as explained above. However, much of the pollution could be minimized or controlled without undue cost by careful planning. For this, the following steps will be helpful:

Control of Gaseous Pollutants

The equipments, which can be used to control gaseous pollutants, are classified as combustion, absorption and adsorption equipments. Combustion is applicable to pollutant gases which are oxidizable. In petrochemical, fertilizer, paint and varnish industries combustion control equipments are useful. Absorption is a diffusional process in which the transfer of gas molecules into a liquid phase takes place. Such equipments include spray chambers, packed towers and sieve plate contractors. Absorption is the means of controlling air pollution which occurs due to some gases and vapours and inflammable compounds and cannot be treated by other means.

Control of Emission from Motor Vehicles

The emission control techniques include tune-ups, catalytic reactors and engine modifications. A high air-fuel ratio will reduce the concentrations of both carbon monoxide and hydrocarbons. The modified engines have an efficient system of burning of the fuel. At present, there is no system of reduction in sulphur dioxide although, researches in this direction are in progress throughout the world.

Control of Aerosol Emissions

Aerosol emissions can be controlled by arresters and scrubbers. Arresters include inertial separators, filters and precipitators. The electrostatic precipitator is considered to be the most effective device for preventing the emission of dust from fuel gases and is the standard equipment for large power stations.

Control by Fuel Selection and Utilization

Coal and oil are the primary fuels in which smoke, grit and sulphur dioxide are the major pollutants. Coal pollutes more because it releases more smoke and carbon in the air. Instead of coal, oil can be used. But, in oil, the amount of sulphur dioxide emission is higher. Therefore, fuel selection should be made properly and the harmful impact be restricted by inducing other chemicals. In order to control smoke, the coal is pulverized before being used. When oil is used for fuel, it is essential that the ratio of air should be maintained constant in order to prevent smoke emissions.

Control of Air Pollution by Site Selection and Zoning

Selection of an industrial site is the most important factor through which impact of air pollution can be minimized. The industrial site should be selected considering: (i) residential areas, (ii) nature of industries, and (iii) climatic conditions, specially the direction of winds. The site of each and every industry should have an approval from the department of environment. It should be approved in taking into consideration the long-term perspective rather than immediate effects. Within the city the location of industrial zone is a critical aspect and town planners should have a check over its location as well as unorganized growth.

Water Pollution

Water pollution simply means contamination of water due to any external material, or in other words, introduction of something to natural water, which makes it unsuitable for human consumption. WHO has defined water pollution as "any foreign material either from natural or other sources that may contaminate the water supply and makes it harmful to life, cause of their toxicity, leads to reduction of normal oxygen level of water, causes aesthetically unpalatable effects and spread of epidemic diseases". Owen (1971) has defined it as "any unreasonable contamination of water which lessens its value to man". In general, water pollution implies the adverse change in composition or condition of the water that makes it less suitable for the purposes for which it would be suitable in its natural state. The changes include, physical changes, chemical changes and biological changes. According to Gilpil (1978), the deterioration in chemical, physical and biological properties of water, brought about mainly by human activities, is the water pollution. Whatever additions are done to the water either by natural processes or by human activities, they change its natural qualities. The problem of water pollution was first recognized by Hippocrates (450 BC), who suggested filtration and boiling as remedial measures. With the fast industrial development and modern civilization, the demand for water is also increasing day by day. At the same time, population explosion, urbanization, improper sewage disposal, unsafe industrial wastes, radioactive wastes, oil leakages, etc., have polluted our water resources so much so that about 70 per cent rivers and streams, not only in India but in all the countries, contain polluted water.

Sources of Water Pollution

Water pollution is caused by several sources, which are not independent in nature but interact with one another. Generally, one or two factors become prominent and may be considered the primary sources of water pollution. The various sources of water pollution can be broadly classified as natural and human.

Natural Sources

Natural elements, which create water pollution, are gases, soil, minerals, humus material, and wastes created by animals and other living organisms present in the water. During rains, one can see the

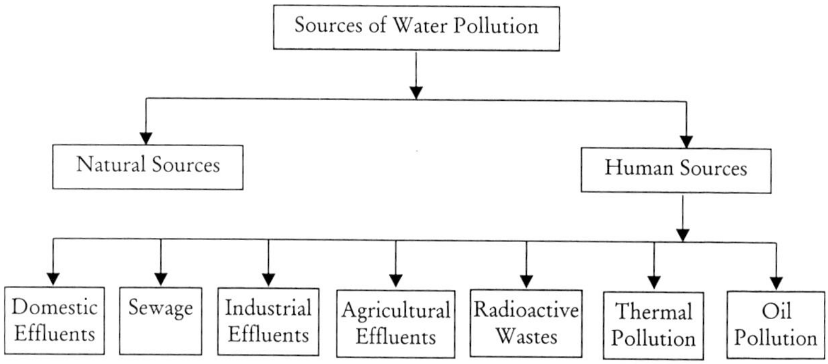

direct impact of soil on the water of rivers, tanks and other water bodies. The brown and dirty water is the result of mud mixed in the water, which becomes clear after some time. Similarly, several types of natural suspended and colloidal impurities are also found in the water. These elements may be organic or inorganic and may even be harmful. The minerals like sodium, potassium, calcium, magnesium, iron, etc., are also present in the water, and if their quantity is more than the permissible limit, these are may also prove dangerous. Besides some poisonous minerals, such as nickel, beryllium, cobalt, lead, mercury, cadmium, etc., are also responsible for water pollution. Sometimes, water-borne vegetation too becomes a cause of pollution.

Human Sources

There is no doubt that water pollution is the result of human activities. The rapid growth of population, urbanization, industrialization and increasing use of chemicals have resulted in water pollution and this problem is increasing day by day in spite of several measures taken in this direction. This is not only a problem of developed countries also developing countries. Besides, both urban and rural people are badly affected by it. A misconcept developed right from the dawn of human civilization is that water bodies can be used as dumping grounds for all types of wastes and this is responsible for water pollution throughout the world. This is not only hazardous to human health and other organisms but also disturbs the delicate ecosystem. Table 5.5 indicates sources or types of contaminants responsible for water pollution and their impact:

Table 5.5

Water Pollution Contaminants and their Impact

Source or Type of Contaminant	*Impact*
1. Degradable Wastes	
Domestic and municipal sewage and other oxygen demanding industrial wastes - they are acted upon by the bacteria and oxygen dissolved in water and reduced to inorganic form, as also in quantity.	Depletion of dissolved oxygen in water - harmful for fish and other aquatic life.
2. Plant Nutrients	
Phosphatic and nitrogenous compounds dissolved in water from industrial wastes, or due to washing away of fertilizers due to heavy rains from fields.	Stimulate growth of algae/plankton and other plants resulting in clogging of waterways and rendering the water unfit for human use.
3. Infectious Agents	
Polluted, stagnant water breeding grounds for parasites, bacteria, viruses of all kinds.	Cause water-borne diseases and outbreak of epidemics such as ameobiosis, dysentery, cholera, typhoid, etc.
4. Synthetic Organic Compounds	
Such as pesticides, agricultural chemicals, detergents, industrial wastes, DDT, etc.	Instance of cadmium, lead and mercury poisoning in human beings. Cause neurological impairment and even death.
5. Inorganic Minerals and Other Chemicals	
Asbestos and acids, etc.	Asbestos produces lung cancer. Acids cause allergies, ulcers, skin diseases. Also have catastrophic impact on fish and aquatic life.
6. Radioactive Elements	
Wastes from nuclear power plants and nuclear fuel reprocessing plants are packaged and buried under water/oceans.	Potentially hazardous in the event of leakages and induce radiation-related illness.
7. Sediments	
Soil and mineral particles washed into streams or water.	Reduce amount of sunlight available for marine plants, cause clogging of filter plants.
8. Thermal Pollution	
Water used for cooling in electric, thermal, nuclear power plants, when recirculated in water bodies.	Can raise lake water temperature by 70-100°c aggravate diminution of dissolved oxygen, kills marine fish and plant life.

For detailed analysis, the human sources of water pollution can be classified into the following categories:

(i) domestic effluents and sewage,
(ii) industrial effluents,
(iii) agricultural effluents,
(iv) radioactive wastes,
(v) thermal pollution, and
(vi) oil pollution.

(i) Domestic Effluents and Sewage

Man, for his various domestic purposes, such as drinking, preparation of food, bathing, cleaning, cooling etc., uses on an average 135 litres of water per day. About 70 to 80 per cent of this is discharged and drained out, which through municipal drains poured into, in many cases, a river, tank or lake. This water is known as domestic waste water and when other waste materials such as paper, plastic, detergents, cloth, etc., are mixed in it, it turns into municipal waste or sewage. The domestic waste water and sewage is the main source of the water pollution. This is the inevitable and unfortunate fallout of urbanization. As it decays, this organic waste depletes the oxygen from water and upsets the natural balance of the aquatic ecosystem.

Municipal sewage is considered to be the main pollutant of water. Most of the sewage receives no treatment before discharge, specially in developing countries like India. In Delhi alone, 120 crore litres of water is consumed per day, out of which 96 crore litres is drained into the Yamuna river through 17 big drains. All the 47 towns located on the bank of river Ganga drain their sewage into it. With the growth of population the quantity of waste water is also increasing in addition to the production of large quantities of sewage. Sewage contains decomposable organic matter and exert an oxygen demand on the receiving waters. The common organic materials found in a sewage are soaps, synthetic detergents, fatty acids, and proteinaceous matters such as amines, amino acids, amides and amino sugars. In addition to the above components, it also contains numerous micro-organisms. Untreated waste water is often the carrier of viruses and bacteria and, along with household sanitation practices, has been linked to high infant mortality rates in developing countries. Even in the developed world, where most sewage is treated, recent measurements of faecal coliforms indicate increasing pollution. Sewage supports the growth of other forms of life that consume oxygen, which is measured in terms of biochemical oxygen demand (BOD). It is the lack of oxygen that kills fish and other aquatic life.

In recent years, there has been considerable growth in the use of detergents, which causes severe water pollution. Many modern detergents contain phosphates, which are an essential component of agricultural fertilizers. When phosphate detergents are discharged into waterways, they supply a needed nutrient and promote rapid growth of algae. This enrichment process is known as 'eutrophication'. In many areas of the world, aquatic weeds have multiplied explosively. They have interfered with fishing, navigation, irrigation and even production of hydroelectricity. In developing countries, human population and settlements are growing much faster than waste water treatment facilities can be provided. Thus, much of the untreated waste water and sewage is discharged into rivers and other water bodies, making the water unsuitable for drinking and is a main cause of water pollution.

(ii) Industrial Effluents

Industrial activities generate a wide variety of waste products, which are generally discharged into water courses. Major contributors are the pulp and paper, chemicals, petrochemicals and refining, metal working, food processing, textile, distillery, etc. The wastes, broadly categorized as heavy metals or synthetic organic compounds, reach bodies of water either through direct discharge or by leaching from waste dumps. In developed countries of the world, many industrial discharges are strictly controlled. Yet, water pollution continues from accumulations of wastes discharged over the past 100 years. But, in developing countries, industrial discharges being largely uncontrolled, thus, are a main cause of water pollution.

All the Indian rivers have been polluted by industrial effluents. The holy river Ganga has become a highly polluted river due to various types of industrial discharges. Along the Ganga, several chemical, textile, tanning, pulp and paper, petrochemical, rubber, fertilizer and other heavy industries are located and all of them discharge their waste water and other effluents, directly or indirectly, into the river, resulting in the pollution to such an extent that even the Ganga Action Plan, to control water pollution, has failed. From Delhi industrial area alone, more than 8 lakh tonnes of industrial waste is discharged into the river Yamuna.

The Damodar river of Bihar is another highly polluted river due to industrial wastes discharged from Bokaro, Rourkela, Indian Iron and Steel Company (CISCO), Bengal Paper Mills, Sindhri Fertilizer Factory, etc. A study reveals that from Durgapur plant alone 1,800 cu/m washed coal is discharged into the river. Similarly, from CISCO 15,000 cu/m and from Bengal Paper Mills 12,000 cu/m industrial waste is discharged into the river per day. Likewise, about 10 to 15 tonnes of sulphuric acid from Sindri and 5 to 10 tonnes toxic chemicals are discharged into the river water. The story of the Hooghly river of West Bengal is more or less same. Its water has been polluted to such an extent that even fish fertilization becomes difficult. The paper mills located along the river discharge about 11.4 tonnes liquid wastes into the river. Same is the story of other rivers in India excluding rivers of the north-east region. Chambal, Narbada, Kaveri, Godavari, Mahanadi and other small rivers have been polluted and this has not yet been stopped, rather more and more pollutants have been discharged, resulting in greater water pollution.

The nature and effects of the pollutants from the effluents of paper and pulp, textile, food processing, chemicals, metal, petroleum are as follows:

Paper and pulp industries: Effluents from paper and pulp industries include wood chips, bits of bark, cellulose fibres and dissolved lignin, in addition to a mixture of chemicals. All these produce a sludge, which blankets fish spawning grounds and destroys certain types of aquatic life. The effluents contain chlorine, sulphur dioxide, methyl mercaptan, etc., which are considered to be highly poisonous to fish.

Textile industries: Effluents from textile industries are alkaline in nature and have a higher demand for oxygen.

Food processing industries: These industries include dairies, breweries, distilleries, meat-packing, etc., where the waste products constitutes fats, proteins and organic wastes. These industries discharge wastes containing nitrogen, sugar, proteins, etc. All these wastes have a higher BOD and are responsible for water pollution.

Chemical industries: These industries include acid manufacturing industries, alkali manufacturing, fertilizer, pesticides and several other industries. The effluents from these industries contain acids, which have corrosive effects. The effluents from fertilizer industries contain phosphorus, fluorine, silica, and large amounts of suspended solids.

Metal industries: These industries usually discharge effluents containing copper, lead, chromium, cadmium, zinc, etc., which are toxic to human as well as aquatic life. These wastes also contain acids, oils, greases and cleansing agents.

Petroleum industries: These industries include oil refineries and petrochemical plants. The effluents discharged include hydrocarbons, phenolic compounds and other organic and inorganic sulphur compounds.

Aprat from the above, other industries, which pollute water, are tanneries, soaps and detergent industries, glass, electroplating, bleaching, atomic plants, explosive factories, etc. Besides, mining operations can result in metals leaching into the acidic effluents, thus adding to the metal load in rivers, lakes and groundwater. Discharge of mercury from gold mining activities has polluted some streams in Brazil and Ecuador and created serious health problems. With reference to water pollution through mercury, mention of Minimata Gulf incident must be made. In 1950, near the Japanese coast, in Minimata Gulf, fishermen suffered from blindness, weakness, mental illness, paralysis, etc. It was found that effluents discharged from a plastic factory contained mercury which entered the fish and by eating those fish, all the fishermen suffered from effects of mercury poisoning. The problem of water pollution through industrial effluents has become a major environmental problem and sufficient measures should be taken to contain it.

(iii) Agricultural Effluents

Agricultural water pollution is caused by fertilizers, insecticides and pesticides, farm animal wastes and sediments. In recent years, use of chemical fertilizers has increased manifold. The Green Revolution of India is a reflection of the increased use of fertilizers. The chemicals used in fertilizers enter the ground water by leaching and the surface water by run-off. The nitrates, when mixed with water, may cause methemoglobinemia in infants. Incidences of nitrate poisoning are also there in livestock. The plant nutrients, nitrogen and phosphorus are reported to stimulate the growth of algae and other aquatic plants.

The use of various types of pesticides and insecticides in agriculture is also one of the important causes of water pollution. Their presence in water is highly toxic to man and animals, because all these have a high persistence capacity, i.e., their residues remain for long periods.

The farm animal wastes often pose serious problems of odour and water pollution. These wastes also contain pathogenic organisms which get transmitted to humans. Sediments of soil and mineral particles, washed out from fields, also cause water pollution. They fill stream channels and reservoirs and reduce the sunlight available to aquatic plants.

(iv) Radioactive Wastes

Radioactive elements, such as uranium and radium, possess highly unstable atomic nuclei. This disintegration results in radiation emission, which may be highly injurious. During nuclear tests, radioactive dust may encircle the globe at altitudes of 3,000 metres or more, which often comes down to the earth as rain. Eventually, some of the radioactive material, such as Strontium 90 (which can cause bone cancer), percolates down through the soil into groundwater reservoirs or is carried out into streams and rivers. In both cases, public water supplies may be contaminated. The construction of more nuclear reactors and the increasing use of radioactive materials in medical research represent other potential contamination sources.

(v) Thermal Pollution

Most of the thermal and electric power plants also discharge considerable quantities (about 66%) of hot effluent water into nearby streams or rivers. This has resulted in thermal pollution of our water courses. Thermal pollution is undesirable for several reasons. Warm water does not have the same oxygen-holding capacity as cold water. Therefore, fishes like black bass, trout and walleyes, etc., which require a minimal oxygen concentration of about 4 ppm, would either have to emigrate from the polluted area or die in large numbers. When the temperature of the receiving water is raised, the dissolved oxygen level decreases and the demand for oxygen increases, hence anaerobic conditions will set in resulting in the release of foul gases. Thermal pollution is considered hazardous for the whole aquatic ecosystem. Several industries have installed cooling towers, where the heated water is cooled. But even so, thermal pollution has become a serious problem for water bodies located near thermal plants.

(vi) Oil Pollution

The spread of oil in the sea has become a common feature nowadays. Oil is transported across oceans through tankers and either due to some accident or leakage oil spills onto the water and causes the degradation of aquatic and marine environment. Between 1968 and 1983, there were more than 500 tanker accidents that involved oil spills. Altogether, more than one million tonnes of oil was released. A dramatic incident was that of the tanker Torrey Canyon, when it struck off the southern tip of the British Isles in March 1967. The Torrey Canyon was the largest oil spill up to that time. The pollution caused widespread destruction of many forms of marine life despite strenuous efforts to clean up the spill. Similarly, on March 16, 1978, the oil tanker Amoco Cadiz, lost its steering off the coast of Brittanny in France and the total spilling of oil was 1.6 million barrels. Such accidents have become very common due to technical problems or heavy marine traffic. During the 1991 Gulf War, there was heavy bombing on oil tanks, which resulted in the spilling of oil. The impact of this oil spill on the marine ecosystem in this area has not yet been remedied. Offshore drilling operations also contribute their share of oil to the sea. The total quantity of oil that finds its way into sea each year is very large. It has been estimated that about one million tonnes of oil spills into the ocean each year from tankers and oil drilling operations.

Effects of Water Pollution

Since use of water is universal to all living organisms, the impact of its pollution is also widespread. The effects of water pollution become severe because water is the controlling factor in the 'food chain'. The harmful effects of water pollution can be divided into three groups, viz., (i) effects on man, (ii) effects on aquatic life, and (iii) other effects.

On Man

On a worldwide scale, the water pollution is probably responsible for more human illness than any other environmental factor. The diseases so transmitted are chiefly caused by micro-organisms and parasites. Sewage and polluted water are responsible for several water-borne diseases. Some of the diseases caused by polluted water are cholera, typhoid, infantile diarrhoea, dysentery, infectious hepatitis, polio, giardiasis, amoebic dysentery, jaundice, zondic, etc. Cholerais, an illness caused by ingestion of the bacterium Vibriocholeral, results rapidly in massive fluid depletion and death in a very large percentage of patients. It is transmitted by drinking water contaminated with the faces of infected individuals. In developing countries, deaths by cholera are still common. Guineaworm is another disease caused by polluted drinking water. In India alone, about 18 lakh people suffer from this disease. Schistosomiasis is a group of diseases caused by infection through worms in water. There are certain chemicals present in polluted water, which may cause diseases like nepurities, wrist drop, foot drop, etc. In spite of full measures taken for the supply of purified drinking water in USA, there are incidents of diseases caused by water contamination in one way or other. The developing countries of Africa, Asia and Latin America, where arrangements of water treatment are limited or negligible, a large section of the population is susceptible to water-borne diseases.

On Aquatic

The effect of water pollution is more on aquatic life, because their existence depends on water and when there is any disturbance in their ecosystem, the impact is maximum on them. In polluted water, due to abundant growth of algae, the oxygen content becomes lesser, causing the death of fishes and other organisms. It is estimated that during the last 20 years, there is a decrease of about 40 per cent in aquatic life. Algae are responsible for imparting a peculiar taste and odour to many of the water supplies and also a cause of gastroenteritis. A report by Wheler indicates that algal poisons usually act on the central nervous system and skin and are also reported to be capable of producing cirrhosis of the liver.

There are many cases on record of the destruction of marine life by polluted waters. Mass killing of fish was among the earliest and most dramatic result of indiscriminate pollution of water. Another type of fish killer is pollution from municipal sewage. Industrial, thermal and radioactive pollutions are also threats to marine life. Because of water pollution a large number of ducks also die every year. For example, 1,40,000 ducks died of botulism in California during 1970. Occasional deaths of animals have also been reported by drinking of polluted water. If water pollution is more severe, the process of photosynthesis is also obstructed, which affects the growth of aquatic vegetation. All the chemicals that are drained into the water have harmful effects on every organism that survives there.

Other Effects

Due to water pollution, the physical and physiological nature of water has also changed. The colour of water changes due to pollutants, mainly due to organic dyes. The colour in itself is not harmful, however, aesthetic considerations make coloured water unsuitable for any purpose. The turbidity caused by the presence of colloidal or suspended matter is the characteristic trait of sewage and industrial effluents. Generally, the more the turbidity, the stronger is the sewage or effluent and the effects are worse. Foam is the product of water mixed with soaps and detergents. It consists of a suspension of air bubbles in water medium. Industrial effluents containing chemical substances as iron, chlorine, phenols, etc., affect the taste of the water. The decomposition of organic matter and algae, fungi and filamentous bacteria also imparts peculiar tastes. Similarly, the odour of water also changes due to the presence of pollutants. Even small amount of sulphides cause bad odour in water. The pollutants also reduce the transparency of water. Oil spills have their effect over evaporation. The industrial effluents which contain several types of chemicals are also responsible for the loss of soil fertility. In fact, the effects of water pollution are multidimensional in nature. Apart from above-mentioned direct effects, there are several indirect effects also. In general, water pollution has now become a threat to the ecosystem and an important cause of environmental degradation.

Measures for Containing Water Pollution

As described earlier, water pollution now has become a worldwide problem. Not only developing countries but developed countries are also facing this problem. However, developed countries have initiated several methods not only to contain water pollution but also for the purification of polluted water. But, most of these techniques are expensive and even those countries are facing difficulties in checking water pollution. Apart from technological methods, there are other measures, which are useful in minimizing water pollution. Some of them are as follows:

(i) All domestic and municipal effluents should be drained in water bodies only after proper treatment.
(ii) As far as possible domestic waste water should be used for irrigation; it is also very useful for horticulture.
(iii) Similarly, if sewage can be mixed with soil, it will act as a fertilizer.
(iv) The drinking water source and its nearby area should be kept clean.
(v) There must be strict regulations for industrial effluents, that they must not discharge highly toxic water into water bodies. Every industry should develop its own effluent treatment plant.
(vi) Use of pesticides in agriculture should be limited and only standard quality pesticides should be allowed to be used.
(vii) There is also need to conserve several water purifying organism.
(viii) In the Indian context, there should be a complete ban on the disposal of dead bodies in rivers. The banks of water bodies are often used as public latrines, which should be strictly checked.
(ix) Algae and other water-borne vegetation should be cleaned regularly.
(x) Chemicals such as potassium permanganate should be spread regularly in order to protect water from micro-organisms.
(xi) Under present practices, pure, clean, drinking water is used to flush toilets and irrigate lawns. There are two possibilities to check this loss—first, waste water from bathrooms and sinks be recycled and used for irrigation and flushing of toilets, and second, separate water supply system be provided for drinking water and water for other uses.
(xii) The most important aspect would be to educate people not to pollute water. Such awareness will help in solving this problem to a great extent.

Noise Pollution

Sound is a normal feature of our life and a medium through which communication is possible. It may be pleasant, like the sound of running water of a stream or the sweet sound of birds in the forest or the pleasant sound produced by musical instruments. On the other hand, it may be the noisy and harsh sound of lightning and thunder or noise produced by machines, automobiles, railways, aeroplanes or even the blaring sound of loudspeakers or some musical instruments. But all sounds are not noise. Noise is any sound that is not wanted. It is one of the more common forms of atmospheric pollution. Sound is caused by the vibration of molecules, while noise radiates from vibrating surfaces. More and more noise is the creation of modern civilization and has now become a major environmental pollutant, specially in urban areas. It was only in 1972, when in the UN Environment Conference at Stockholm, noise pollution was first accepted as a problem, which needs proper attention.

The perception of noise as a problem is different for different people. Noise at certain levels might be an aggravation or nuisance for some, while at higher levels, it might become a more widespread or general aggravation. At still higher levels, noise might fall within 'discomfort range' and at even higher levels, it may lead to physical and psychological damage.

Measurement of Sound/Noise and Its Intensity

The most popular measure of noise level is the 'decibel', which is measured by an instrument known as decibel metre. A sound between 0 and 1 decibel is the weakest that an average human can hear. For testing purposes, 0 decibel is considered to be the threshold of hearing. A whisper is about 20 decibels and an average speaking voice is about 60 decibels. The loudest sound that a person can stand without discomfort is about 80 decibels. Automobile horns may reach 90 decibels and a jet airplane may have an intensity of about 140 decibels. The intensity of various sounds is shown in Table 5.6 whereas levels of common noise have been depicted in Figure 5.2.

Table 5.6
Intensity of Various Sounds

Sound Source	*Intensity (in decibels)*	*Response Criteria*
	0-10	just audible
Broadcasting studio	20	-
Soft whisper (15 feet)	30	very quiet
Library, bedroom slow radio	30-50	quiet
Light auto traffic, air conditioning unit	50-70	intrusive
Freeway traffic, freight tram	70-80	annoying
Motorcycle, heavy traffic	80-100	very annoying; hearing damage
Rail noise	110-130	intolerable
Lighting-thunder	120	intolerable
Carrier deck jet operation	140-150	painfully loud

Figure 5.2
Levels of Common Noise

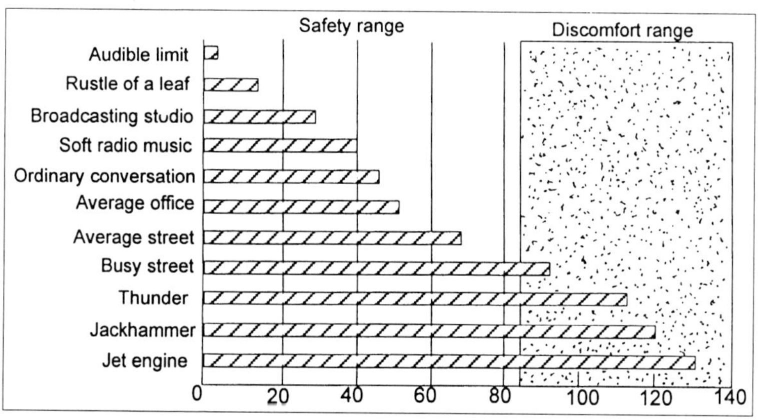

(After T. Berland)

In most of the countries, maximum limit fixed for noise is 75 to 85 decibels. According to scientists, noise above 90 decibels for a long time may result in deafness. In most of the cities in India, the noise level is 75 to 90 decibels but it is more in industrial areas, near airports, railway stations, highways, etc. But, since noise pollution is increasing enormously day by day, planning for its control should be done without any delay or hesitation. Actually, loudness alone is not the sole cause of noise problem, although this the most apparent characteristic of noise that creates environmental problems. Pitch of the noise also influences the degree of annoyance—the higher the pitch, the greater the annoyance. Similarly, duration of the noise also determines how annoying or irritating noise will be. The degree of noise in an enclosed space or indoor is different from the level of outdoor noise.

Sources of Noise Pollution

The sources of noise can be divided into two categories, viz., natural and artificial. Natural sources are associated with natural phenomena like lightning, thunder, volcanic eruption, earthquakes, sound of the ocean waves, etc. These reasons are local or regional and generally their impact is very limited and not very harmful. On the contrary, noise produced by artificial sources is much harmful.

The sources of noise pollution in an industrial society are manifold. In cities and other highly developed countries, these are mainly associated with transportation, automobiles, motorcycles, rail engines, buses, fire brigades, police cars, ambulances, aero planes, industries, high pitched musical instruments, etc. During religious or domestic functions as well as in political meetings during elections, noise pollution often increases due to use of loudspeakers.

The main source of noise, however, comes from transport. The number of road vehicles, particularly diesel engine vehicles, has increased the level of noise enormously. This problem is more in metropolitan cities where a number of vehicles ply simultaneously and their noise is unbearable. The horns and sirens used by these vehicles, specially the pressure horns, are very noisy. The value of horns and sirens, except in emergencies, is questionable. The whistle of rail engines is very harmful to the ears. Busy traffic streets, highways, bus stands and railway stations have also problems of noise pollution. Larger and faster jet aircrafts have been built over the years and have become one of the most troublesome sources of noise pollution. For example, O'Hare International Airport, in Chicago, the busiest airport in the world, has more than a thousand operational jet flights on an average day. This means a flight in or out every 40 seconds. The residents within 20 kilometres radius from the airport face great problem not only in their conversations, television viewing, sleep and relaxation but it has also affected their health adversely. The air traffic has increased to such an extent that nobody likes a new airfield in the neighbourhood.

Noise associated with manufacturing, building construction, mining, road building, etc., comes second in intensity after transportation noises. But, their impact is felt more by factory and other workers. It is reported that noise inside factories can become a health hazard causing deafness. Industrial noise, particularly from mechanical saws and pneumatic drills, is unbearable and a nuisance to the ears. The impact of noise in a factory varies with age groups. For workers below 30 years of age, the 95 decibels noise is not harmful, but for 40 to 50 years age group this limit is 84 decibels and for 50 to 60 years the bearable limit is 80 decibels. In mining, noise produced by blasting and digging is also a source of uncomfortable noise.

Nowadays, music has also become noisy and the electronic media and instruments have further developed its intensity. In a closed space, high volume music is harmful and is also responsible for noise pollution. Similarly, during social and religious functions, marriages and other gatherings, including political meetings, the use of high volume loudspeakers has become a common feature and an irritating cause of noise pollution. The popular 'pop music' may be entertaining but its ultimate impact is not healthy on man. Besides, use of crackers at Deepawali in India, has become a major sources of both noise and air pollution.

Effects of Noise Pollution

The most notable effect of noise pollution is on hearing. Violent noise can cause temporary or permanent impairment of hearing, thus a cause of deafness. Continual noise can lead to gradual decline in auditory acuity and eventual deafness. Acute damage occurs to the ear drum when exposed to very loud sudden noises.

Noise causes several undesirable effects also. Damage to hearing and loss of sleep are only two of the obvious results. Noises produce irritability and a feeling of fatigue and may reduce a worker's efficiency. There is evidence that noise is one of the major causes of stress and anxiety. It also has an impact on blood pressure and is a cause of other cardiovascular diseases. The rate of heart beat may also be affected by noise. A recent report indicates that blood is also thickened by excessive noises. Eosinophilia, hyperglycemia, hypokalaemia and hypoglycemia are also caused by a change in blood and other body fluids due to noise. Noise also causes headaches and irritability. The effects of noise on the foetus are not fully known. Medical scientists have noted that an unborn child will move and kick when there is a loud noise. Some of studies indicate that children born in areas of high noise have some defects in comparison to the children born in peaceful areas.

Control of Noise Pollution

Since noise pollution is created by man, it can be controlled by adopting certain measures. Some of the measures are as follows:

(i) Noise producing industries should be located away from residential areas.

(ii) Inside industries proper arrangements to minimize noise should be made by constructing sound-proof walls and also to provide such instruments to workers, which can protect their ears from noise.

(iii) Old machines often create more noise, therefore, all such machines should be well maintained, and replaced, if necessary.

(iv) The automobile horn should be designed in such a way that the noise it produces may not be harmful.

(v) Use of horn should be minimum and pressure horn should be banned as has been done in many countries.
(vi) The noise created by musical instruments, and other indoor equipments, can be checked by individuals in their own interest.
(vii) The noise created by railways can be checked by construction of ballastless rail tracks.
(viii) Special arrangements should be made to check noise near air bases. Control of aircraft noise requires several changes, which should be done.
(ix) Dense tree plantations around or nearby areas of noise can also reduce its intensity.
(x) Every government has enacted certain laws to control noise pollution. The basic need is the proper implementation of these laws and regular monitoring. In countries like India, the problem of noise pollution is still in its primary stage, therefore, measures to control this problem are necessary.

Soil and Land Pollution

Solid Waste Disposal

Although one-fourth of the earth surface is land, half of this surface is not useful to man due to permanent snow cover, deserts, mountains, etc., and only about 448 lakh sq kms of land can be used by human being for multifarious activities. Any misuse or wastage of land may create problems not only for the present generation but for the future ones as well. The problem of land and soil pollution is growing day by day with the rapid growth of population, urbanization, industrialization, agricultural and other developmental activities. Land pollution is the result not only of man's misuse of land but more due to solid waste disposal. The disposal of solid wastes, more a problem of developed nations till now, has also become a grave problem of all the countries of the world. Solid wastes are dumped in the ocean or open grounds; mining wastes are produced at the rate of millions of tonnes a day; slag heaps and mill tilings accumulate near processing operations; and industrial refuse contaminates streams and lakes. In USA alone, solid waste produced annually includes 30 million tonnes of paper and paper products, 4 million tonnes of plastics, 30 billion bottles, 60 billion cans, 100 million tyres, 8 million junked and abandoned automobiles and millions of major appliances of innumerable makes, sizes and kinds. No one knows the total amount of the world's wastes, but it is certain that the problem of solid waste disposal now has become a threat to our environment, specially in our cities.

Land pollution can be defined as the "changes in physical, chemical and biological conditions of the soil through man's intervention or misuse of land and resulted into degradation in quality and productivity of the soil". The problem of land pollution differs from that of water or air pollution in the respect that the pollutants remain in place for relatively longer periods. Rapid urbanization with the consequent increase in buildings has resulted in the reduction of lands for the wastes to be disposed of. Dumping of industrial and municipal wastes causes leaching by toxic materials, which seep into the soil and affect the groundwater. Agricultural practices introduce pesticides, fertilizers and manures to the land resulting in both biological and chemical contamination. Thus, land and soil pollution is increasing day by day by hazardous materials and micro-organisms enter the food chain or water and are consequently ingested by man. Therefore, there is an urgent need not only to control soil pollution but also for its proper management.

Sources of Land Pollution

The soil and land pollution is the result of several sources, which can be categorized under following heads:

(i) domestic and municipal wastes,
(ii) industrial and mining wastes,
(iii) agricultural wastes,
(iv) radioactive materials, and
(v) biological agents.

Domestic and Municipal Wastes

One of the main causes of land and soil pollution is the growing quantity of domestic and municipal wastes. Household garbage includes food scraps, old newspapers, a variety of plastic items, bottles, discarded papers, wood, lawn trimmings, glass, canes, old appliances, tyres, worn-out furniture, broken toys and a host of other items. The total quantity of solid wastes is large and increasing. In United States, municipal solid wastes averaged 1.2 kg per person per day in 1920. The quantity rose to 2.3 kg in 1970 and 3.6 kg in 1980 and now it is more than 4.5 kg. Urban wastes comprise both commercial and domestic wastes including dried sludge of sewage. In general, all the urban solid wastes are referred to as 'refuse'.

It has been estimated that in 45 major cities of India, the quantity of average per day municipal wastes is about 50,000 tonnes. The National Environmental Engineering Institute (NEERI), Nagpur, has given details of the municipal wastes in Indian towns as shown below in Table 5.7:

Table 5.7

Nature of Solid Wastes in Indian Towns

(in percentage)

Material Composition	*Towns According to Population Size*			
	up to 2 lakh	*2 to 5 lakh*	*5 to 20 lakh*	*above 20 lakh*
Paper	3.09	4.74	3.80	7.07
Plastic	0.57	0.59	0.81	0.86
Metals	0.51	0.39	0.64	1.03
Glass	0.29	0.34	0.44	0.76
Ash and dust	46.60	39.97	41.81	31.74
Mixed material	33.41	39.76	40.05	41.74
Carbon	12.36	12.51	11.95	15.92
Nitrogen	0.60	0.61	0.50	0.51
Phosphorus, phosphate	0.70	0.71	0.67	0.59
Potassium	0.70	0.73	0.72	0.67

It becomes clear from the above table that in our cities 90 per cent wastes include ash, dust, mixed material and carbon, while in developed countries, paper, plastic, glass, metal, etc., dominate.

The dumping of domestic and municipal wastes is a serious problem in cities because of its impact on environment and public health. Solid wastes may or may not cause diseases but are definitely hazardous to human health. Diseases such as dysentery, diarrhoea, plague, malaria and numerous others are the result of the indiscriminate dumping of wastes.

Industrial and Mining Wastes

The disposal of industrial solid wastes is the major source of soil pollution by toxic chemicals. The industrial wastes are mainly discharged from coal and mineral mining industries, metal processing industries and engineering industries. They contain toxic metals such as lead, copper and chemicals having acids and are responsible for soil pollution. It has been reported that about 50 per cent of raw materials ultimately turn into waste products in industry and about 15 per cent of it is toxic. The chemicals discharged from the industries often enter the surface or ground water or poison the soil or crops. The production of consumer goods also involved environmental problems including land and soil pollution. Table 5.8 below lists some of the effects of the production of consumer goods:

Table 5.8

Production of Consumer Goods and its Effects on Land/Soil

Process	*Activity*	*Effects*
Extraction	Mining and oil drilling	Surface land disruption, acid mine drainage, mine failings, sludge ponds, oil spills.
	Agriculture	Disruption of natural habitats, soil erosion, fertilizer run-off, poisonous pesticides.
	Forestry	Habitat disruption, soil erosion, pesticides.
Processing	Manufacturing	Soil and underground water pollution, loss of soil productivity, air and water pollution.
Energy	Energy conversion and transmission	Depletion of resources, thermal and radioactive pollution, disruption of land for transmission rights of way. Litter, land-use disruption, release of hazardous wastes, dust, etc.

The expansion of mining activities in many countries of the world has now become a main cause of land pollution due to loss of soil and destruction of land. Mining has become a threat to the environment because it leads to the huge quantity of wastes generally not useful to man and its reprocess is not economical. Mining operations produce about 1.35 billion tonnes of debris each year.

Agricultural Wastes

Agricultural practices also pollute the soil. According to an estimate, agricultural activities produce more than 1.8 billion tonnes of wastes each year. About three-fourths of this is manure. Much of this manure is piled in dumps, where it pollutes streams and waterways. Yet, at the same time, farmers across the continent are suffering from worn-out and depleted soils. Other agricultural wastes include branches and slash left over from logging apart from animal wastes. In addition to fertilizers and pesticides, soil conditioners and fumigants are used in agriculture. Organic compounds containing lead, mercury and arsenic, when applied to a land, accumulate on the soil permanently and introduce these toxic metals into plant products.

Radioactive Materials

The radioactive wastes produced by nuclear testing laboratories and industries reach the soil and accumulate there. Wastes from nuclear reactors contain ruthenium-106, rhodium-106, iodine-131, barium-140, lanthanum-140, cerium-144, etc. All the radionuclides deposited on the soil emit gamma radiations, and are harmful to soil as well as for plant growth.

Biological Agents

The excreta of humans, animals and birds is also a source of soil pollution by biological agents. Digested sewage sludge, which is used as a manure, also causes soil pollution. In the developing countries, intestinal parasites constitute the most serious soil pollution problems. Faulty sanitation, waste water and wrong methods of agriculture also induce soil pollution. There are three groups of pathogenic organisms that pollute the soil, viz., (i) pathogenic organisms excreted by man, (ii) pathogenic organisms excreted by animals, and (iii) pathogenic organisms found in contaminated soil.

Effects of Land/Soil Pollution

The following are the harmful effects of the land and soil pollution:

(i) Land and soil pollution is responsible for loss of fertility and productivity of soil.

(ii) The decomposition of the various types of waste material causes harmful gases and bad smell, which not only pollute environment but is also harmful if mixed with chemicals.

(iii) The municipal and domestic waste is often discharged in water bodies, thus responsible for water pollution.

(iv) The dumping of waste in oceans is a common practice and a main cause of imbalance of the marine ecosystem.

(v) Particles in the sewage may clog the micro holes of the soil and also destroy the micro-organisms necessary for the soil.

(vi) Industrial and chemical wastes are also responsible for the pollution of underground water.

(vii) Those bacteria, which are transmitted from soil to man infect man causing dysentery, cholera, tuberculosis, typhoid, paratyphoid fever, etc.

In fact, land and soil pollution is one of the main causes of air and water pollution, therefore, its control and proper management is necessary not only in developed countries but also in developing countries.

Control of Land and Soil Pollution: Methods of the Disposal of Wastes

Land and soil pollution can be controlled by adopting measures for the disposal of solid wastes, which unfortunately involves large finances and technology. Prior to disposal, the wastes have to be collected from the places by trucks to the disposal area. It is estimated that about 80 per cent of the total cost of solid waste management is spent for collection only. The methods used for the disposal of wastes are open dumps, ocean dumping and sanitary landfills.

Dumping is a popular and an inexpensive means of solid waste disposal. *Open dump* is the least acceptable method but prevalent in most of the developing countries, including India, and a cause of soil as well as general environmental pollution. In this method, waste is collected and hauled to a site where it is dumped on the ground. Organic matter rots or is consumed by insects, rats or hogs. In some communities, the pile is set afire in the evening to reduce the total volume and the odour. All this creates serious ecological problems. The dump itself is a potential source of disease. Rain erodes the dump, and the polluted water flows into nearby rivers and ground water reserves.

Sanitary landfill is commonly used for final disposal of solid wastes. This is cheaper than other disposal methods and has the advantage of avoiding acute pollution problems associated with discharging wastes into waterways or polluting air from incineration. But, the main disadvantage over open dumps is in the aspect of public health. Leaching by surface water or ground water may contaminate streams and other water supplies. The availability of land for the dumping of the growing volume of wastes is also a problem.

Ocean dumping of wastes is practised by many coastal cities. It was considered to be the favourite disposal method under the prevalent notion that the ocean is an inexhaustible sink. We are now learning that the ocean does not have an infinite capacity for covering, holding, absorbing or decomposing materials, nor the capacity for anywhere near the load of pollution that would result if the rate of ocean disposal continues, as in the past. There were seven major categories of waste, viz., harbour dredgings, industrial wastes, municipal sewage sludge, refuse and garbage, construction and demolition debris, military explosives and chemicals and miscellaneous wastes like agricultural land run-off, pesticides, fertilizers, sewage and garbage from vessels, oil spills, etc. Now, the environmentalists have warned that ocean dumping is neither a safe nor a desirable method for the disposal of wastes. In 1970, the Council on Environmental Quality recommended a series of drastic actions to control ocean dumping because it upsets the ecological balance of regions of the sea.

Incineration is a method through which the volume of wastes can be reduced by 60 per cent, which, in turn, lessens the public health problems. This method is adaptable over a wide range of capacities from small domestic incinerators to large centralized municipal plants. It can handle a mixture of garbage and rubbish, and the physical nature of the residue, called *clinker*, aids in the disposal of the wastes, although it aggravates the problem of air pollution.

Chemical processing of solid wastes is also applied but it is costly and technically not feasible for poor countries. But, due to prospect of energy production and recovery of certain usable materials, the salvage of some wastes by chemical methods is now considered economically feasible. The reclamation of non-ferrous scrap metals has long been an established industry.

Composting municipal refuse to convert it into a fertilizer and soil conditioner is appealing not only because it appears to be a good way to recycle the resources in solid wastes, but also because of the beneficial nature of the compost. This may be considered as a useful method for the disposal of municipal refuse, specially in developing countries.

New methods of waste disposal that are under trial in various parts of the world are:

— The transformation of the organic content into sugar or proteins.
— The heating of organic refuse under anaerobic conditions to convert it into useful gases such as methane, which is usable as fuel, or into a liquid product.
— The compression of refuse into building blocks that can be sheathed with more durable materials. One such plant is in operation in Japan.
— The compression of refuse into briquettes that can be used as fill. A mixture of fly ash, dried sewage sludge, incinerator residue and river and lake dredgings is under study.
— The use of degradable plastic bags instead to trash cans in the collection and transport of municipal refuse.
— The transport of refuse as a liquid slurry in pipelines is now under study.

Apart from refuse and recycling of wastes, there are methods through which wastes can be utilized properly.

Energy from Refuse

In many metropolitan areas of developed countries the garbage is burnt in a well-engineered furnace. The heat from the fire is used to boil water and produce steam. Then, the steam is used in industries. But, there are problems in this type of burning as wet garbage and food scraps are difficult to burn and burying PVC products produces hydrogen chloride gas, which reacts with water to produce a strongly corrosive liquid—hydrochloric acid. In spite of these difficulties, incineration may become profitable in the future because of the following reasons:

1. Increasingly large quantities of dry paper and cardboard have appeared in refuse, thereby increasing the fuel content of the trash.
2. The price of fuel has skyrocketed and therefore the value of steam has also gone up, thus it will be more economical day by day.
3. The rising cost of land has made it harder to find adequate sites for landfills, thus demanding alternative solutions and burying of refuse is the most suitable alternative.

Recycling of Waste Material

Most refuse contains a wealth of raw materials that can be easily reused or recycled. A large quantity of metals can be obtained from waste dumps, as also paper, glass, tyres, manure, etc. Table 5.9 indicates the possibilities of recycling the various waste materials.

It becomes clear from the table that if the recycling process is adopted properly, not only the problem of waste disposal can be minimized but it will also save financial resources. An estimate indicates that about 21 per cent of the paper in the United States was recycled, compared with about 50 per cent in Japan. If the rate of recycling was increased to 50 per cent in the United States, approximately 100 million trees would be saved annually, and the energy saved would be enough to supply 7,50,000 homes with electricity. If people would separate their household trash into piles of aluminium, steel, paper, plastic and food scraps, then perhaps all these materials could be recycled.

Table 5.9

Various Recycling Routes for Some Common Wastes

Waste	*Recycling Possibilities*
Paper	Use the backs of business letters for scrap paper or personal stationery, lend magazines and newspapers to friends
	Repulp to reclaim fibre
	Compost
	Incinerate heat
Glass	Purchase drinks in deposit bottles and return them, use other bottles as storage bins in the home
	Crush and remelt for glass manufacture
	Crush and use as aggregate for building material or antiskid additive for road surface
Tyre	Recap usable casings
	Use of swings, crash guards, boat bumpers, etc.
	Shred and use of manufacture of new tyres
	Grind and use as additive in road construction
Manure	Compost or spread directly on fields
	Ferment to yield methane; use residue as compost
	Convert to oil by chemical treatment
	Treat chemically and re-use as animal feed
Food scraps	Save for meals of leftovers
	Sterilize and use as hog food
	Compost
	Use as culture for yeast for food production
Slaughter house and butcher shop-wastes	Sterilize and use as animal feed
	Render compost

New Approach

The above-mentioned methods have proved quite useful for waste management. But, nowadays, there is more emphasis on people's participation in waste management. There is a growing adoption of the polluter-pays principle, i.e., NIMBY and NIABY, which is as follows:

The Polluter-Pays Principle: NIMBY and NIABY: The public are becoming better informed on environmental issues, and may object to real or imagined pollution and waste hazard or nuisance. Special-interest groups or the public can adopt a "not-in-my-backyard" (NIMBY) attitude. NIMBY is often invoked when authorities are proposing to site a hazardous or 'nuisance' waste or pollution treatment plant. Some proposals are opposed by environmental activists and NGOs whenever they are to be sited (for example, deep underground storage of high-level nuclear waste)—a "not-in-anybody's-backyard" (NIABY) response.

Apart from the polluter-pays principle, over last few decades, pollution and waste management have been aided by:

— a trend towards more proactive planning and management;
— increased release of information on pollution and waste risks, as a result of government, NGO, media and international agency activity;
— improved legislation;
— development of better policing;
— spread of better environmental quality standards more widely applied;
— better methods and equipment for monitoring and assessment, etc.

Radioactive Pollution

Nature and Sources

Radioactive substances are among the most toxic materials known to the mankind. The magnitude of their injurious effects is in a range that might be said figuratively to represent a 'quantum jump'. H.P. Jammet, Chief of Atomic Hygiene and Radio Pathology, French Atomic Energy Commission, France, defines radioactive pollution of the environment as "the increase in natural background radiation, emerging from the activities of man involving the use of naturally occurring or artificially produced radioactive materials. The atmosphere screens out much of the sun's radiation, including most of that which would be lethal to life".

Naturally occurring, radioactive elements are present in the rocks, water and air, and in all living organisms. The composite of all forms of natural radiation that we are exposed to, is called background radiation. For millions of years, background radiation remained at a relatively constant level. Recently, however, the radiation that we are normally exposed to has increased and can be expected to increase further. Man-made radiation includes that from x-ray machines, radioactive fallout, nuclear reactors, research laboratories, industrial and medical uses of radioactive materials and radioactive wastes from the production of radioactive materials.

Environmental radiation may be divided into two types: (i) natural, and (ii) man-made.

Naturally occurring radiations are: (a) cosmic radiations from the outer space reaching the earth's surface, and (ii) terrestrial radiation from natural radio-isotopes present in the earth's crust. Cosmic ray bombardment of the atmosphere continuously produces a few radioactive materials of short half-life. The half-life of a radionuclide refers to its period of radioactivity and has a bearing on the length of time that a radioactive substance might remain active as an environmental pollutant.

Man-made radiations originate from the activities of man involving the use of radioactive materials. They are used for the production of nuclear weapons, nuclear fuel and electric power. One of the most harmful uses of radioactive material is in the nuclear weapons, specially in atom bombs. The world has already seen the nature of destruction as well as impact of radioactivity on man and environment during the Second World War when atom bombs were dropped over Hiroshima and Nagasaki–the two Japanese towns. During the last fifty years, there have been a number of nuclear weapon testings either in sea or underground, resulting in the increase in the level of radiation of the environment. A study revealed that the radioactive materials, which cause such explosions, are fission products as Strontium-90, Caesium-137, Iodine-131 and unused explosives. These elements either settle down in the soil or water or remain suspended in the atmosphere, thus becoming a major cause of radioactive pollution.

Nuclear fuels used in operation of reactors also contribute to pollution. The heat liberated during fission and activation process is converted into electricity. During this process, two types of wastes are formed: (i) the fission products remaining in both the primary and secondary fuels, and (ii) extraneous activation products in the coolant. The disposal of radioactive or nuclear wastes is a great problem and a cause of environmental pollution. It includes remaining metal products at the site of mines, fission products and activation products. These are of three categories, viz., low level, intermediate level and high level. Among these, high level products remain in the environment for several hundred years. Similarly, leakage in nuclear reactors often became the cause not only of environmental pollution but also of the death of hundreds of people as happened in case of leakage at Chernobyl atomic reactor in erstwhile USSR on 26 April 1986.

Effects of Radioactive Pollution

Different forms of radiation have different effects. Visible light and infrared heat rays and certain kinds of radiation are generally beneficial. Some of the other forms of radiation, for example, x-rays, are more energetic and are, therefore, biologically injurious because of their destructive action on cells and tissues. Because these highly energetic forms of radiation tend to split substances, including living matter, into ions, they are called ionizing radiation. The other forms include electromagnetic radiation and particulate radiation. Ultraviolet radiation is highly injurious to the tissues of some organisms. It is well recognized that sun-burn is caused largely by the ultraviolet content of the sun's radiation and that excessive exposure can cause serious injury to both the superficial and deep layers of the skin.

The environmental hazards from fission reactors include: (i) the possibility of a serious accident that releases a large amount of radioactivity, (ii) the hazard of even the usual small radioactive emissions with normal operations, and (iii) the pollution caused by radioactive wastes. The fate of a radioactive contaminant is also dependent on ecological conditions. Radioactive pollution causes deposition of the contaminants on ground and surface waters. The water consumed by plants thus acts as a medium for radioactivity. This contamination is passed on to vegetation and animals through the nourishment from soil and water.

Man is considered to be the ultimate sufferer through reactions and interactions. Radioactive particles present in air have a direct impact on man's respiratory system, while indirect contamination occurs by consumption through the food chain. The ill-effects of radioactive pollution are numerous. Radiation can cause cancers, abnormal births, skin diseases and mutations in man. Chronic exposure to radiations leads to leukemia in an individual and even affects an unborn child in the womb. The radiations from medical x-rays, colour TV, luminous dials of clocks and watches, x-ray fluoroscopes are also contributing to the risks. As described earlier, any leakage of radioactivity from reactors is not only a health hazard but is also a cause of death and other disorders to thousands of people. Similarly, nuclear testing in sea waters not only creates disorder in the oceanic ecosystem but also becomes a cause of the destruction of marine life.

Control of Radioactive Pollution

In spite of certain harmful effects of radioactivity, nuclear power and other uses of radioactive elements have become an integral part of modern development. Many of the environmentally conscious countries in the world depend on nuclear power significantly for their electricity generation. At present, 17 per cent of the world's electricity is generated through nuclear sources. Nuclear source is considered clean, compact and concentrated. It is clean because its impact on the environment is minimal compared to other energy-generating sources. To make it environmentally safer still, there is a need for monitoring and prevention measures.

Monitoring of radiation is very necessary for the control of radiation. For this, sampling as well as its proper analysis is necessary. The samples of air, water and soil have to be collected regularly and their analysis—both manual and instrumental—be done, not only to know the actual level of radioactive pollution but also for its control.

Prevention and control measures are to be adopted to control radioactive pollutants. All measures should so aim that the level of radioactive pollution should not exceed the maximum permissible limit. The industrial wastes having radioactive elements only should be discharged after proper treatment. The high activity wastes should not be discharged. Now, a few techniques have been developed through which these wastes can be used if treated properly. The disposal of the wastes into sea is also not a safe method but if nothing is possible, these wastes should be sealed in concrete-filled steel drums and discharged into depths of 1,000 fathoms or more.

The emission of radioactive pollutants should be controlled. In uranium mines, wet drilling should be employed. Closed-cycle systems with gaseous coolants of very high purity may be used in the case of nuclear reactors to prevent extraneous activation products. There is a need to control radiation hazard for workers and officials working in reactors or other places having danger of radioactivity. There is also a need for regular monitoring and clean-up of surface, careful washing is necessary, apart from this proper kit to protect from radiation effects and health care of workers is also necessary. What is more, personnel at power stations must be trained in radiation protection and radiation hazard control measures. The UN and other agencies of the world are in favour of total ban on nuclear weapons but very little progress has been made in this field. Let us hope that the time will soon come when our world will be free from the danger of atom bombs and other nuclear weapons.

Disaster Management

In the world, most common and disastrous hazards are volcanism, earthquakes, landslide, floods, droughts, and famines, thunder storms, tornadoes and tropical cyclones.

Volcanism

The eruption of volcanoes is one of the most dreadful natural phenomena. The molten rocks, boiling lava and hot gases penetrate out of that part of the surface, which is comparatively weak. When this material comes out of these spots, an explosion takes place, with thunderous noise, molten rocks, lava and gaseous clouds rise up towards the sky. All this results in a threat to the environment as well as to life.

Volcanism is not common throughout the world but is limited to the Circum-Pacific belt extending from Andes in South America, through the Cascades and the Aleutians into Japan and then south into the East Indies and New Zealand. There is also an important belt in the Mediterranean, which includes the active volcanoes of Italy.

A volcanic explosion poses a great threat to environment. On an average, a volcano, in an explosion, ejects 150 cubic km of material. This material is of three types: solid material in the form of small and large pieces of rocks, ash particles and also pieces or volcanic bombs which shoot into the sky. The liquid material called *magma* comes out of volcano is known as *lava*. A huge amount of gaseous material also comes out of volcano, which includes steam, carbon dioxide, and sulphur in vapour form. They produce poisonous gases when combined with other gases. Gases like chlorine, fluorine, etc., are also emitted in large quantities.

The eruptions of volcanoes and lava flows are environmental hazards of the severest type, often taking a heavy toll of plants and animal life. Loss occurs from sweeping clouds of incandescent gases and suspended matter that descend the volcano slopes like great avalanches. When Mont Pele burst in 1902 in the West Indies, its burning material ejected out of it moved in the form of a cloud over the city called St. Piere and only two people out of total 30,000 population survived. The explosions of Etna and Vesuvious in Italy destroyed many beautiful cities. In 1943, when Paracutin, 320 km west of Mexico city, exploded, created a mountain 167 metre high. In 1991, volcanic explosions in Japan and Philippines have damaged a lot of property and caused loss of human life and also polluted the environment. Similarly, volcanic activity in the Andaman & Nicobar Islands was responsible for the environmental degradation in this area.

Earthquakes

Earthquakes are tremors, which are produced by the passage of vibratory waves through the rocks of the earth. The devastation caused by earthquakes to the life of man and property, as well as to the ecosystem, is very high. The earthquake belt of the world is also associated with the volcanic belt, but several other regions too have occurrence of earthquakes. Wherever earthquakes occur, apart from loss of life and property, landslides, change in course of rivers, loss of vegetation and animal life, destruction of dams and development of faults and fractures in earth's surface are common and all these events lead to environmental degradation. The list of devastating earthquakes in the world is too long to be enumerated here. In India, the occurrence of earthquakes in areas of Jammu & Kashmir, Himachal Pradesh, Uttar Pradesh, Bihar, West Bengal, Punjab, Delhi, Haryana, northeastern states as well as in Maharashtra, are common. Recently an earthquake has been occured in Pakistan and parts of Kashmir in which heavy loss of property and life was reported, apart from the whole regional ecosystem being disturbed.

Floods, Droughts and Famines

Both floods and droughts are natural hazards and are related with rainfall. If there is heavy rain in the catchment area of a river, flood will occur. On the other hand, if there is less rain or failure of monsoon, drought will occur. In both the situations, their impact on environment creates problems and also affects the regional ecosystem.

Flood is a hydrological phenomenon that occurs in any drainage basin. Its magnitude and frequency varies primarily on the precipitation conditions in the catchment area. Most of the river valleys are subjected to varying degrees of flood incidences, either creating minor damages or devastating havoc at times. Such calamities pose a serious problem to the whole environmental set-up of a region, bringing about some phenomenal changes in the physical environment ushering in accelerated erosional transportional and depositional activities of the river with the consequent effects on soil. The devastating effects of flood can be seen on vegetation, agricultural, industry settlement, sometimes causing loss of human and animal lives and of material also.

The main cause of flood is excessive rainfall but its occurrence is also due to earthquakes, deforestation in the upper catchment areas, failure of dams, excessive snow melting, etc. The beneficial effects of floods have been established beyond doubt in the form of fertilization of soil, but, its devastating effects far exceed the benefits.

In India, the problem of flood and challenge to the environmental setting is of gigantic magnitude, because of (i) typical seasonal rainfall, and (ii) erratic nature of tropical cyclones and rainstorms. The following are the areas, which may be termed as flood-prone areas:

(a) Upper catchment and piedmont zone of the Himalayan river basins.
(b) Ganga river valley—upper, middle and lower deltaic zone.
(c) Brahmaputra valley and its tributaries.
(d) Deltaic region of Mahanadi, Godavari, Cauvery and Krishna rivers.
(e) Narmada and Tapti basins.

The common measures of the flood control are as follows:

(i) Control of erosion in upper catchment areas.
(ii) Construction of dams and reservoirs at suitable sites.
(iii) Prevention of overflow in channels.
(iv) Construction of multiple channels for distribution of the excess river water.
(v) Development of shelters in flood-prone areas.

The flood problem should be taken up with more intensive preventive measures, in order to avoid environmental problems.

Drought is also a natural hazard, which has its impact on the regional ecosystems. The areas, which get less rainfall, i.e., amount of rain is too less to support agricultural production or even grasslands, are usually called drought-prone areas. When droughts become severe, they cause famines, which are devastating for man, animals and also environment. Generally, droughts occur when rainfall is less than 25 to 50 per cent of the average. If it is below 50 per cent of the average, famines occur. In 1899, India faced the severest famine known as *Chappan-ka Akal.* A similar famine also occurred in 1977. In both these famines several lakhs of people lost their lives. In 1992 93, Ethiopia also suffered from the grips of a bad famine, in which more then 30 lakh people died. Famine conditions are common in Rajasthan, Gujarat, Haryana, Madhya Pradesh, Orissa and Andhra Pradesh in India. In Rajasthan, famine has now become a regular phenomenon.

Thunderstorms, Tornadoes and Tropical Cyclones

Due to abrupt changes in atmospheric conditions, thunderstorms, lightning, hailstorms, tornadoes and cyclonic storms occur and are the cause of environmental hazard. A *thunderstorm* is an intense local storm caused by strong conventional activity. Thunder and lighting normally accompany the storm, and rainfall is heavy, sometimes due to cloudburst also. Violent surface wind may occur at the onset of the storm. The speed of the rising air in a thunderstorm is about 112 kilometres per hour. *Lightning* is also one of the environmental hazards that results annually in the death of many persons and livestock and causes forest and building fires. One of the most destructive products of the thunderstorm is the hailstorm. Hail consists of rounded lumps of ice ranging from 0.5 to 5 cm in diameter. Large hailstorms are an environmental hazard as they can be extremely destructive to crops and flimsy buildings.

A *tornado* is a small, intense cyclone in which the air spirals at a tremendous speed. Associated with frontal air mass interactions in mid-latitude, tornadoes are the most violent storms. These storms are most frequent and violent in the United States although occurring in Australia and in other places of mid-latitudes. A tornado moves across the country with a wind speed of upto 400 kilometres per hour in a funnel-like shape. The end of the funnel cloud may alternately sweep the ground, causing complete destruction of anything in its path.

Tropical cyclones are the most powerful and destructive types of cyclonic storms, which are also known as hurricane or typhoon. These storms develop over oceans in latitude 8° to 15° N and S, but not close to the equator. The tropical cyclone is an almost circular storm having low pressure in which winds spiral at high speed accompanied by heavy rainfall. The environmental impact of tropical cyclones lies in the form of destruction of life, infrastructures as well as of forest and animals. In islands and coastal regions, large-scale destruction of cities and their inhabitants has been reported on several occasions. Bangladesh is a country which has suffered a lot by heavy destruction caused by tropical cyclones—the death toll by tropical cyclones in Bangladesh is almost unbelievable. In 1822, the toll was 40,000 while in 1876 and 1897, it was 1 lakh and 1.75 lakh respectively. In 1970, 3 lakh lives were lost and in 1991, the death toll was 5 lakh. These storms are also responsible for change in atmospheric and environmental conditions.

6

Social Issues and the Environment

Sustainable Development: From Unsustainable to Sustainable Development

Man has continually, and at an increasing rate, been changing the forms and modes of his interaction with the environment. Natural processes and factors that depend on the structure and other characters of the earth and social processes and factors that depend on structure and characteristic of our society, have been closely interwoven. On the one hand, population of the earth is growing rapidly and by the year 2005 AD, it might have exceeded the 6 billion mark; while on the other hand, with the technological and scientific revolution, developmental activities have been accelerated to such an extent that in certain areas they have become a threat to the environment. The utilization of natural resources is growing at an alarming rate, causing great concern for their conservation. The degradation of the environment, due to industrial and other wastes discharged into the atmosphere and hydrosphere, has also caused great concern and there is a big question mark—what will happen next? All these environmental problems, associated with development, have raised several questions regarding the type and nature of development and this has given rise to the concept of 'sustainable development'.

Concept of Sustainable Development

The concept of sustainable development has a long historical background. In ancient Indian writings, 'nature' or 'environment' has been considered as the controller of all human activities, including economic development. They have accorded the status of the Almighty God to all the components of environment such as air, water, land, natural vegetation, animals, etc. In spite of the fact that there was no need for their conservation, the concept of their protection has been put forward in all the religions of India. In Greek writings, there is a reference of *Ge* or *Gaia* as the Goddess of the Earth—the mother figure of natural replenishment. In fact, that was a time when population was limited and there was mutual adjustment between man and environment.

It was only after the industrial revolution, followed by transport revolution and urbanization, that degradation of the environment started, which has given rise to the concept sustainable development. The sudden interest in sustainable development is, of course, a response to warnings that the world is facing an environmental and, therefore, social catastrophe in the near future unless mankind radically modifies certain practices and perspectives which have created the present crisis. This crisis is characterized, among other things, by the poisoning of our rivers, seas and underground water resources; the thinning of the ozone layer; global warming; the rapid extinction of species, massive deforestation and soil improvement; rapid population growth; and uncontrolled urbanization, with its attendant social problems.

Roosevelt's chief forester and mentor, Gifford Pinchot (1910) has observed that "conservation advocates the use of foresight, prudence, thrift and intelligence in dealing with public matters, demands the application of common sense to the common problems for common good". Conservation of resources, in other words, is the sustainable utilization of the resources, which can be achieved through environmental regulation, management, adequate surveillance as well as accountability. The environmental degradation and associated problems like desertification, soil erosion, tropical forest depletion, etc., in the Third World, are the consequences of present development policies. Therefore, there is a need for positive mutual adjustment between development and natural environment.

Concern about the environment as a central issue in development began to grow in the 1960s and 1970s.The idea was slowly incorporated into development and environment debates by international organizations. Throughout this process, the idea of sustainability was pushed most strongly and effectively by scientists like Sir Julian Huxley, first Director of UNESCO, particularly ecologists engaged in international scientific collaboration. Scientific conservationists began to engage with the impacts of development on ecosystems, publishing books such as *The Careless Technology* (Farvar and Milton, 1973) and the handbook for development planners, *Ecological Principle for Economic Development* (Dasmann, Milton and Freeman, 1973).

The United Nations Conference on the Human Environment, held at Stockholm in 1972, is usually identified as a watershed in the emergence of sustainable development, although it was only partly, and belatedly, concerned with the environmental and developmental problems of the emerging Third World. The growing influence of concern for the environmental aspects of economic development was by no means accepted unopposed. Developing countries saw discussions of global resource management as an attempt by industrialized countries to take away control of their resources, and feared that the environment was being given too high a priority compared with development; far from suffering the impacts of pollution caused by industrialization, poor countries suffered the 'pollution of poverty'. Faced with this concern, the phrase 'sustainable development' was used explicitly to smooth over the apparent dichotomy between economic growth, based on industrialization, and associated adverse environmental impacts. The phrase captured perfectly the idea (or the belief) that it was possible to have development without adverse environmental side-effects. The essence of this idea, and the power of its political appeal, changed very little in the two decades that elapsed before the Stockholm Conference's successor at Rio de Janeiro in 1992.

Several strategies, policies and concepts have been propounded by ecologists and planners to deal with environment resource management, such as the zero growth strategy of Daly (1977), organic agriculture for self-sustaining societies of Naess (1977), a narrow and overspecialized approach of environmental economics by Norgaard (1985) and well-known concept, viz., use of environment-friendly techniques and products.

The publication of *US Global 2000 Report* (1980) and other publications like *Resourceful Earth* (Simon and Kohn, 1984), *The Global Possible* (Repetto, 1985) and *Our Common Future* (WCED, 1987) have generated a general debate highlighting the consequences of overexploitation of resources and neglect of global common interest.

The most conspicuous result of the Stockholm Conference was probably the creation of the United Nations Environment Programme (UNEP), which played an important role in the preparation of *The World Conservation Strategy*, published in 1980. This identified three objectives for conservation: first, the maintenance of essential ecological processes; second, the preservation of genetic diversity; and third, the sustainable development of species and ecosystems (IUCN, 1980). *Our Common Future*, published seven years later in 1987, had a different emphasis, blending environmental concerns (e.g., the need to achieve a sustainable level of population, and the desirability of conserving the resource base and reorienting technology.

Sustainable development has many definitions. The most widely quoted is still that of the Brundtland Commission in *Our Common Future:* "Development which meets the needs of the present without compromising the ability of future generations to meet their own needs." Sustainable development fulfilled LéLé's (1991) prediction and became the development paradigm of the 1990s. Indeed, it became a vital buzzword in the speeches of politicians, company chairs and NGO activists alike. It has come to carry on its deceptively simple back a cast range of hopes and ideals, from near-revolutionary environmentalism to the blandest hint of green in corporate capitalism. Academically, sustainable development seems to contain the promise of new joined-up research, unlocking the doors separating disciplines, and breaking down the barriers between academic knowledge and action. In politics, it promises to tackle both poverty and environmental degradation without requiring that anybody gets any less well off, or affecting corporate profits or shareholder value. Sustainable development implies win-win-win solution (across environment, society and economy), perfect for the decade of the televised soundbite and the spin doctor.

Despite its simplicity, the phrase 'sustainable development' is capable of carrying a wide range of meanings, sometimes allowing quite different ideas about what should be done to exist side by side without the conflict between them being clear. Both radical environmentalists and conventional development policy pragmatists have seized the phrase and used it to express and explain their ideas about development and environment. In the process, they have created a theoretical maze of great complexity. The superficial conformity of writing and thinking about sustainable development hides very real and fierce battles behind the scenes over the meanings.

Sustainable Development at Rio, 1992

The United Nations Conference on Environment and Development (UNCED) at Rio in 1992 (also known as the Earth Summit) was attended by 128 heads of states and in total by the representatives of some 178 governments. Debate at the conference drew very directly on the mainstream ideas about the environment and development that had evolved during the 1980s. The Rio Declaration and the much larger *Agenda 21* were the fruits of endless negotiation at a series of Preparatory Commission meetings and at Rio itself, between teams of diplomats determined to surrender as little as possible of their national interest. A key feature of these debates was the gap between countries in the industrialized North and the underdeveloped South, which became steadily more glaring in the run up to, and during, the conference. The issues of climatic change and biodiversity that dominated the Rio Conference are vitally important to certain countries (especially those vulnerable to sea-level rise), but they are not the principal environmental problems faced by most countries of the South.

The Rio Declaration ended up as a bland list of 27 principles. It was long-winded, and in places self-contradictory: even after long debate, the US delegation released an 'interpretative statement' that effectively dissociated it from a number of the principles agreed. It dissented from principle 3 that there was a right to development, the Americans arguing that development was not a right but simply a shared goal, and from any interpretation of principle 7 that suggested that there was an international liability to make development sustainable (i.e., for rich countries to pay for it). Choices about development and environment were matters for individual countries to make their minds up about, and not an issue over which they should be subject to international opinion.

Agenda 21 was even more burdened by divergent opinions, becoming a bloated volume of more than 600 pages in 40 separate chapters. Its scope was enormous, covering issues from biodiversity and water quality to the role of women, children and organized labour in delivering sustainable development. It reflected previous mainstream thinking about sustainable development in several ways. First, it made the need for economic growth a central theme, as in the Brundtland Report. In the sustainable development mainstream, everything is predicated on economic growth, both globally and nationally. Second, *Agenda 21* emphasized the familiar straightforward issues of environmental management: all the familiar environmental issues from the *World Conservation Strategy* appear developed but unmistakable. Third, *Agenda 21* was technocentric. The first six key themes make this quite clear: growth will power and technology will direct the evolution of policy towards more efficient use of the environment and hence towards a more sustainable world economy. The 'essential means' to achieve sustainability also reflect this technocentrism, building on information, science and environmentally-sound technology. Fourth, *Agenda 21* presumed a multilateral benefit to be derived from a sustainable development strategy, as did the Brundtland Report. It suggested that change would arise from the mutual interest of industrialized and non-industrialized countries, and from the concern of present generations about the future. It suggested that this shared interest would cause international financial resources and technology to flow, directed and promoted by international agencies and structured and regulated by international legal instruments. Fifth, like its predecessors, *Agenda 21* called for sustainable development through participation. As in *Caring for the Earth,* women, children, young people, indigenous people, trade unionists, businessmen, industrialists, farmers, local authorities and scientists are all summoned to play a role—a rainbow coalition to put flesh on the endless skeleton of the text of *Agenda 21.*

The various programmes of the UNO, specially the UNEP, have emphasized the need for sustainable development, also referred as 'eco-development'.

Eco-Development

Eco-development is a concept of sustainable development in which all developmental activities are performed or designed in such a way that regional ecological balance can be maintained. This was originally advocated by UNEP for environmental planning and was defined as "development at regional and local levels consistent with the potentials of the area involved, with attention given to the adequate and rational use of the natural resources, and to application of technological styles".

Dasmam (1985) represented eco-development as a triangle, one side of which is *basic needs*, the second *self-reliance*, and the base *ecological sustainability*. Each of these variables needs to be considered, since development will not be sustainable unless poor people are involved in meeting their aspirations. In fact, "the environment and development are means, not ends in themselves. The environment and development are for the people, not people for environment and development" (Chamber, 1986). There is a need for 'environment thinking' with 'development thinking' and 'sustainable livelihood thinking'. In Third World countries, the main consideration should be given to 'basic needs' and 'self-reliance' which can be achieved through social planning norms. While designing eco-development for a region, consideration should be given both to short-term and long-term planning. For sustainable eco-development it is necessary to give priority for the livelihoods of the poor; this can be achieved through political changes at the local, national and international levels. The political, economic and social forces should be directed to fulfil the needs of population in such a way that environment remains protected.

Basic Aspects of Sustainability

The question of sustainable development has emerged not only due to overexploitation of resources but also mismanagement of technology. The aspects which require monitoring of sustainability include climatic change, biodiversity, disposal of hazardous and toxic wastes, disposal of pollution-generating industries and food and ecological security.

Swaminathan (1991) has identified nine principles for desired success in promoting ecologically-sound agriculture. These are: (i) land, (ii) water, (iii) energy, (iv) nutrient supply, (v) genetic diversity, (vi) pest management, (vii) post-harvest system, (viii) systems approach, and (ix) location-specific research and development.

The deterioration in the ecological base in various countries in spatio-temporal terms due to irrational management of the resource and environmental systems having damaging repercussions are reflective of unsustainable policy frame and planning strategies followed so far. Their observable signs can be listed as:

(i) extensive deforestation accounting for loss of flora, fauna and some rare species;
(ii) drying up of drinking water resources and fall in the underground water levels;
(iii) intensifying rate and frequency of flood and droughts;
(iv) land degradation due to desertification, wastelands, salinity and waterlogging;
(v) deterioration in quality of air and water;

(vi) pressure of population resulting in unemployment and mass migrations; and
(vii) unplanned urbanization and unprecedented growth of urban slums, etc.

The environmental problems are multidimensional and varied in nature in developed and developing countries. There are global problems, which have had their impact throughout the world. On the other hand, every country has its own development as well as environmental problems. Apart from this, regional and local problems need immediate attention. The problems created by technology transfer from developed countries to Third World countries have become a cause for concern, because in the absence of proper management it has become a cause of environmental degradation. Such alarms are embodied in the unsustainable activities, which may include:

(i) intensive cultivation of land without taking adequate care of soil fertility;
(ii) development of irrigation facilities without proper water management, which leads to waterlogging, alkaline or saline soil;
(iii) improper use of pesticides, fungicides, herbicides, etc., cause soil damage and biological imbalance;
(iv) excessive trapping of underground water accounts for steep fall in underground water level;
(v) replacement of high yielding hybrid varieties lead to spread of diseases capable of wiping out the entire crop as it happened with Irish potato crop in 1985 and Bengal rice famines in 1942;
(vi) excessive use of non-degradable material like plastic creates problems of waste management;
(vii) discharge of industrial and municipal waste in water bodies leads to problems like unmanageable water pollution; and
(viii) automobiles and industries have become a major cause of air pollution.

In fact, development without proper management has become a cause of eco-destruction, for which sustainable development is the only solution.

Towards Sustainability

The aim of ecologically sustainable development is to maximize human well-being or quality of life without jeopardizing the life support system. The measures for sustainable development may be different in developed and developing countries according to their level of technological and economic development. But developing countries like India can focus attention on the following measures:

- ensure clean and hygienic living and working conditions for the people;
- sponsor research on environmental issues pertaining to the region;
- ensure safety against known and proven industrial hazards;
- find economical methods for salvaging hazardous industrial wastes;
- encourage afforestation;
- find out substitutes for proven hazardous materials based on local resources and needs instead of blindly depending on advanced nations to find solutions;
- ensuring environmental education as a part of school and college curriculum;
- encourage use of non-conventional sources of energy, specially solar energy;
- as far as possible production of environment-friendly products be encouraged;
- use of organic fertilizers and other biotechniques should be popularized;
- environment management is a key for sustainable development, it should include monitoring and accountability; and
- need for socialization and also humanization of all environmental issues.

The prime need for sustainable development is the conservation of natural resources. For this, the development policy should follow the following norms:

(i) Make all attempts not to impair the natural regenerative capacity of renewable resources and simultaneously avoid excessive pollution hampering the biospherical capacity of waste assimilation and life support system.
(ii) All technological changes and planning strategy processes, as far as physically possible, must attempt switch from non-renewable to renewable resource uses.
(iii) Formulate a phase out policy of the use of non-renewable resources in general.

Thus, for a worldwide sustainable growth, there is need for efficient and effective management of available resources. In this field, the production of 'environment-friendly products' (EFPs) is a positive step. With the industrialization and technological development, markets are flooded with products of daily consumption. They could however be a source of danger to health and damage to our environment. There is thus need to distinguish the more environmentally harmful consumer products from those which are less harmful, or have a more benign impact on the environment right from the stage of manufacture through packaging, distribution, use, disposal and reusability or recycling.

Throughout the world, now, emphasis has been shifted to the production of EFPs. In India, plans are afoot to market EFPs with combined efforts of Bureau of Indian Standards, Ministry of Environment & Forests and Central Pollution Control Board. Since 1990, a scheme of labelling 'ECOMARK' has also been started. In its first phase, the items included in this scheme are soaps, plastics, paper, cosmetics, colours, lubricating oil, pesticides, drugs and various edible items. The scheme was first notified in the gazette on 20 February 1991. The objectives of the scheme are: (i) to provide an incentive for manufactures and to reduce adverse environmental impact of products, (ii) to reward genuine initiatives by companies to reduce adverse environmental impact of their products, (iii) to assist consumers to become responsible in their daily lives by providing them information to take account of environmental factors in their purchase decisions, (iv) to encourage citizens to purchase products which have less harmful environmental impact, and (v) to improve the quality of the environment and to encourage the sustainable management of resources.

Environmental Ethics in India

India has inherited a culture of tolerance, non-violence, equity and compassion for animate objects. In the olden times they were a part of daily life and synthesized with the religion. Religious teaching, social and political norms, and economic policies treated man as a part of nature, not as a moulder or superior to it. Air, water, land, animals and human beings are the creation of one supreme power—God. Therefore, the fundamental ethic of behaviour was to live in harmony with each other, because it was well realized that each one of them is dependant on one another and destruction or damage to the other is the destruction of self and is complementary to each other.

Since Vedic times the main motto of social life was "to live in harmony with nature". In spite of the fact that in those days environmental problems were not existing because of lesser population and non-existence of pollution but even then all the great teachers of that time have created an environment of co-existence with nature.

The philosophy of peaceful co-existence with nature also got mentioned, in one way or another, in the Indian Constitution. Two provisions relating to environment were incorporated in the form of Articles 48A and 51A(g). Article 48A is a constitutional pointer to the state to protect and improve the environment and Article 51A(g) confers a fundamental duty on the citizens of India to protect and improve the environment and have compassion for living creatures. This clearly shows that the Indian Constitution fell in line with old traditional values. The language used in these constitutional provisions clearly indicates that the principle of equity, co-existence, reverence for nature and non-violence have been given legal recognition. The use of the term 'protect and improve' implies the improvement of the natural environment as well as quality of life. Further, protection of the environment implicitly directs us not to cut trees, keep the water of rivers, lakes, etc., clean and wholesome. This is reminiscent of centuries old

'Chipko movement' of village Kherjarilli in Rajasthan, where Amrita Bai, her four family members and other 359 persons sacrificed their lives to save trees of the village. Thus, we have a culture where trees are regarded more precious and revered than our lives. The government has also declared the villages of Bishnois in Punjab and Rajasthan as 'reserved areas' and cutting of trees and killing of animals have been declared an offence in those territories. If one happens to visit these villages, he can see deers and other innocuous animals roaming there freely and fearlessly.

The phrase "to have compassion for living creatures" used in Article 51A(g) implicitly recognizes the principle that all creatures are made equal and that animal killing should be prohibited as taught by the principle of non-violence, or as the moral code of conduct says that "killing of animals and birds is a sin of highest order". Abiding by this philosophy of olden times, the Indian Parliament has also passed two statutes, viz., The Wild Life (Protection) Act, 1972 and the Cruelty Against Animals Act, 1962. It is also in consonance with another ethical principle that unarmed enemy and mute birds and animals should not be harmed or attacked. This reminds us of an old story of Prince Siddhartha who saved a swan, who was shot at with an arrow by his brother. The same Prince Siddhartha later became Lord Buddha—a great preacher of non-violence (*ahimsa*) and harmonious relationship with nature. The object behind the theory of "to have compassion for living creatures", scientifically speaking, is that animals and birds are the second trophic level of the 'food chain' or foodwebs and help in energy flow. The utility of the animals and their products need no special description here. It should not also be forgotten that wildlife is the guardian and protector of our forests. Decay of wildlife implies decay of forests. Thus, forests and wildlife are interdependent and complementary to each other.

Indian social and moral ethics, relating to environment protection and conservation, have been accepted by Indian judiciary time and again. Some of the judicial pronouncements upholding old Indian traditions concerning environment are quoted below:

> "Water and rivers have dominated the destiny and fortune of man. Plentiful rivers have brought prosperity to those who lived on their banks. If Bhagirath brought salvation, Ganga sustains life... ages have rolled up by it and it has remained eternal" (*F.K. Husian vs. Union of India*, AIR 1990 Ker 321).

> "In order to arouse amongst the people the consciousness of cleanliness of environment, the Government of India and the governments of the states and union territories may consider the desirability of organizing 'keep the city clean week', 'keep the town clean week' and 'keep the village clean week'... at least once a year. During that week, the entire city, town and village should be kept as far as possible clean, tidy and free from pollution of land, water and air" (*M.C. Mehta vs. Union of India*, AIR 1988 SC 1115).

> "Environmental law is based on the realization of mankind of the dire physical necessity to preserve these invaluable and none too easily replenishable gift of Mother Nature to man and his progeny from the reckless wastage and raparious appropriation that common law permits" (*T. Damodhar Rao vs. Municipal Corporation, Hyderabad*, AIR 1987 SC 171).

The essence of their teachings in the form of *Vedas*, *Upanishads*, *Smritis* and *Dharmashastras* was to protect nature and its elements, i.e., air, water, soil, land, vegetation and animals. In Indian culture, a worshipful attitude has been developed towards trees, earth, sky (*aakash*), air (*vayu*), water (*jal*), rivers, sun, mountains, etc. It was regarded a sacred duty of every person to protect them. The Hindu religion enshrined a respect for nature, environmental harmony and conservation. Many verses in the *Rigveda* and *Artharaveda* have been devoted to the praise of *Surya Devta* (Sun), *Vayu Devta* (Lord Air), *Agni Devta* (God of Fire), *Varuna Devta* (God of Water), *Prithvi Mata* (Mother Earth), *Vanya Devi* (Goddess of Forests), etc. Therefore, cutting of trees and polluting air, water and land were regarded as sins. Protection of their purity was considered to be the duty of everyone. *Rigveda, Manusmriti* and *Charak Sanhita* have emphasized on purity of water and its healing and medicinal value. The society, as a whole, has developed a code of conduct (*maryada*) to protect nature and live in co-existence with local and regional environment.

Environmental Legislations in India

Before independence, in India, some laws have been enacted for the protection of the environment. In Indian Penal Code of 1960, Articles 268, 290, 291, 426, 430, 431 and 432 are related to the environment. Similarly, Article 277 was related to water pollution and Article 278 to air pollution. In Motor Vehicle Act, 1938, there was also a provision to control pollution and Indian Forest Act, 1927 also contained similar provisions. After independence, serious efforts have been made in the form of legislations for the conservation and protection of the environment. Originally, the Indian Constitution of 1950 did not have explicit reference to environment protection, so there was no independent and separate provision dealing with the protection or improvement of the environment. But, taking note of Stockholm Conference and growing awareness for environmental pollution and eco-imbalances, the Indian Parliament passed a historic legislation in the form of the 42nd Constitution Amendment Act, 1976. This Act incorporated two significant Articles—Articles 48A and 51A(g)—to protect and improve the environment. Further, it introduced certain changes in the Seventh Schedule of the Constitution. These changes are as follows:

> *Article 48A*: "The State shall endeavour to protect and improve the environment and to safeguard the forests and wildlife of the country."

> *Article 511(g)*: "It shall be a duty of every citizen of India... to protect and improve the natural environment including forests, lakes and wildlife, and to have compassion for living creatures."

The environmental laws, which have been passed by central and state legislatures, are based on the recognition of clean environment as a human right or fundamental right. As it has been recognized that clean environment is the basic need for the survival of humanity and it cannot be ensured without ecological balance, thus, this right belongs to all as survival of mankind depends on clean, healthful or pollution-free environment. Any attempt to defile, damage the natural environment would amount to violation of human right to clean environment. The Stockholm Conference of 1972 also declared that man has the fundamental right to freedom of equality and adequate conditions of life in an environment of a quality that permits a life of dignity and well-being.

To meet these challenges to mankind, various measures have been adopted in India including legal ones. Many laws have been passed by central and state legislatures to contain the air, water, land and radiation pollutions and eco-imbalances. These laws include the Wildlife (Protection) Act, 1972, the Water (Prevention and Control of Pollution) Act, 1974, the Water Prevention and Control of Pollution) Cess Act, 1977, the Forest (Conservation) Act, 1980, the Air (Prevention and Control of Pollution) Act, 1981 and the Environment (Protection) Act, 1986. A brief note on these laws will provide a deep insight into the legislative measures taken in India regarding protection of environment.

Environment (Protection) Act, 1986

The Environment (Protection) Act, 1986 was passed by Indian Parliament in order to fulfil constitutional obligation as provided under Article 48A as well as to show its strong commitment towards Stockholm Declaration of 1972, in which it was suggested that all governments must evolve necessary laws to protect and improve the flora and fauna, non-renewable resources, wildlife and human health.

In fact, concern over the environment has grown the world over since the sixties. The decline in environmental quality has been evidenced by increasing pollution, loss of vegetal cover and biological diversity, excessive concentrations of harmful chemicals in the ambient atmosphere and in food chains, growing risks of environmental accidents and threats to life-support systems. The world community's resolve to protect and enhance the environmental quality found expression in the decision taken at the United Nations Conference on Human Environment held in

Stockholm in June 1972. The Government of India, participating in the conference, strongly voiced the environmental concerns. While several measures have been taken for environmental protection both before and after the conference, the need for a general legislation to further implement the decisions of the conference has become increasingly evident. Besides, existing laws generally focus on specific types of pollution or on specific categories of hazardous substances. Some major areas of environmental hazards are not covered. There also exist uncovered gaps in areas of major environmental hazards. There are inadequate linkages in handling matters of industrial and environmental safety. Control mechanisms to guard against slow, insidious build up of hazardous substances, especially new chemicals, in the environment are weak. Because of a multiplicity of regulatory agencies, there is need for an authority which can assume the lead role in studying, planning and implementing long-term requirements of environmental safety and to give direction to, and coordinate a system of speedy and adequate response to emergency situations threatening the environment.

The Environment (Protection) Act, 1986 is a special law that extends to the whole nation. It was passed in March 1986 and came into force on the 19 November 1986. The Act consists of 26 sections divided into four chapters. Seven schedules dealing with emission standards of air, noise, effluents, etc., have also been appended to it. Various rules, including the Environment (Protection) Rules, 1986, have also been provided with it. They are as follows:

1. Hazardous Wastes (Management and Handling) Rules, 1989
2. Hazardous Micro-Organisms Rules, 1989
3. Manufacture, Storage and Import of Hazardous Chemicals Rules, 1989
4. Chemical Accidents (Emergency Planning, Preparedness and Response), Rules 1996
5. Bio-Medical Water (Management and Handling) Rules, 1998
6. Municipal Solid Wastes (Management and Handling) Rules, 2000

7. Recycled Plastics Manufacture and Usages Rules, 1999
8. Noise Pollution (Regulation and Control) Rules, 2000

According to Section 2(a) of the Act, environment includes: (a) water, air and land, and (b) the interrelationship which exists among and between (i) water, (ii) air, (iii) land, (iv) human beings, (v) living creatures, (vi) plants, (vii) micro-organisms, and (viii) property. Thus, it includes both animate and inanimate objects and their interrelationship.

Section 2(b): 'Environmental pollutant' means "any solid, liquid or gaseous substance present in such concentration as may be, or tend to be, injurious to environment".

Section 2 (c): 'Environmental pollution' means "the presence in the environment of any environmental pollutant".

Section 2 (d): 'Handling', in relation to any substance, means the manufacture, processing, treatment, package, storage, transportation, use, collection, destruction, conversion, offering for sale, transfers or the like of such substance.

Section 3: Power of central government to take measures to protect and improve environment.

Section 4: It authorizes the central government to appoint offices with proper designations.

Section 5: It empowers the central government to issue directions to any person/officer/authority appointed under Section 4 of the Act.

Sections 7 to 17: These are related to prevention, control and abatement of environmental pollution.

The Act also provides power to central government to constitute a Board of Environment Protection. In fact, this Act is a very comprehensive document on environment protection in India. The other legislation on environment have also interconnection with the 1986 Act.

Air (Prevention and Control of Pollution) Act, 1981

This Act was passed by the Indian Parliament in the exercise of its powers conferred under Article 253 of the Constitution. The aims and objects of the Act provide:

"Whereas decisions were taken at the United Nations Conference on Human Environment held at Stockholm in June 1972, in which India participated to take appropriate steps for the preservation of the natural resources of the earth which, among other things, include the preservation of the quality of air and control of air pollution.

And, whereas it is considered necessary to implement the decisions aforesaid in so far as they relate to the preservation of the quality of air and control of air pollution."

The Act aims to achieve the following goals:

(i) to provide for the prevention, control and abatement of air pollution;

(ii) for the establishment of Board with a view to carry out the above-mentioned purpose;

(iii) to confer on and assign to such Board powers and functions relating to prevention, control and abatement of air pollution and other matters connected thereto; and

(iv) to lay down the standards to maintain the quality of air.

This Act is applicable to the whole of India.

The term 'air pollution' means the presence in the atmosphere of any pollutant and 'air pollutant' means any solid, liquid or gaseous substance (including noise) present in the atmosphere in such concentration as may be or tend to be injurious to human beings or other living creatures or plants or property or environment. Thus, air pollutants include smoke, smoot, heat, fly ash, suspended particulate matter (SPM), noise, radioactive substances, etc.

The above definition emphasizes two things: (a) high concentration of solid, liquid or gaseous substances, which (b) is injurious or likely to be injurious to human beings, flora and fauna, property or environment. Some small quantity of gases, SPM or vapour is tolerable or cannot be designated as pollutants, unless and until the concentration of such things reaches such a volume that it becomes injurious. For example, sound at low pitch is acceptable and liked, but sound at a very high pitch (known as noise) is not acceptable and becomes a health hazard. The same is true of other gases, liquids and solid substances. A small quantity of pollutants usually does not affect human health adversely. Such quantity or volume may be described as permissible/tolerable limit as the nature also has its self-purification mechanism. But, if the volume or the quantity of the pollutants is such which is deleterious/injurious to the health of human beings, flora, fauna, etc., it becomes environmental pollution. In Taj Trapezium case, the apex court observed that emission of sulphur dioxide from coke/coal-using industries was causing acid rain (the sulphur dioxide when combined with moisture forms sulphuric acid called acid rain) which had a corroding effect on the gleaming white marble of the Taj Mahal. Therefore, 292 industries were ordered either to close down or to switch to using gas.

Sections 3 to 15 provide for the constitution of a Board, qualifications of its members, terms and conditions of their service, meetings, vacation of seats and temporary association of person with the Board, etc.

The Act envisages two types of Boards—one at the central level and other in the respective states.

Water (Prevention and Control of Pollution) Act, 1974

The main objective of this Act of 1974 is to maintain or restore the wholesomeness of water and to prevent, control and abate water pollution. To achieve this, the Act has provided various provisions, which are very comprehensive. In view of sub-section 2(e) read with sections 17 and 18 of this Act, the fundamental objective of the statute is to provide clean water to citizens.

Section 2 of the Act has defined certain basic terms used in the Act. While defining water pollution it provides that:

> "Pollution means such contamination of water or such alteration of physical, chemical or biological properties of water or such discharge of any sewage or trade effluent or of any other liquid, gaseous or solid substance into water (whether directly or indirectly) as may, or is likely to, create a nuisance or render such water harmful or injurious to public health or safety, or to domestic, commercial, industrial, agricultural or other legitimate

uses, or to the life and health of animals or plants or of aquatic organism" [Section 2(e)].

Thus, water pollution implies:

(a) contamination of water, or
(b) alteration of physical, chemical or biological properties of water, or
(c) discharge of sewage or trade effluent, or
(d) any other solid, liquid or gaseous substance, which may or is likely to create
    (a) nuisance, or
    (b) render such water harmful or injurious to, public health or safety, or to domestic, commercial, industrial, agricultural or other legitimate uses.

Thus, it is a very comprehensive definition and covers all changes in physical, chemical or biological properties of water. The definition also covers the rise in the temperature of water and discharge of radioactive substances in the water.

Further, the Act has used two terms in relation to water pollution: stream and well. The 'stream' here includes (a) river, (b) water courses (whether flowing or for the time being dry), (c) inland water (whether natural of artificial), (d) subterranean water (underground water), and (e) sea or tidal water.

Section 3 provides that a Board shall be appointed and constituted by the central government to perform the functions under the Act.

Noise Pollution (Regulation and Control) Rules, 2000

Noise Pollution (Regulation and Control) Rules, 2000 have been framed by the central government under provisions of the Environment (Protection) Act, 1986 and read with Rule 5 of the Environment (Protection) Rules, 1986. Rule 3 provides for ambient air quality standards in respect of noise for different areas/zones as specified in the schedule annexed to the Rules, which are as under:

Schedule

Ambient Air Quality Standards in Respect of Noise

Area Code	*Category of Area/Zone*	*Limits in dB (A) Leq.*	
		Day-time	*Night-time*
(A)	Industrial Area	75	70
(B)	Commercial Area	65	55
(C)	Residential Area	55	45
(D)	Silence Zone	50	40

Notes: (1) Day-time shall mean from 6.00 a.m. to 10.00 p.m.
(2) Night-time shall mean from 10.00 p.m. to 6.00 a.m.
(3) Silence zone is defined as an area comprising not less than 100 metres around hospitals, educational institutions and courts. The silence zones are zones which are declared as such by the competent authority.
(4) Mixed categories of areas may be declared as one of the four above-mentioned categories by the competent authority.

It is for state government to categorize the areas into industrial, commercial, residential or silence zone and to take measures for abatement of noise including noise emanating from vehicular movements. Clause 4 provides that all development authorities, local bodies and other authorities concerned, while planning developmental activity or carrying out functions relating to town and country planning, shall take into consideration all aspects of noise pollution as a parameter of quality of life to avoid noise menace and to achieve the objective of maintaining the ambient air quality standards in respect of noise.

Rule 4: Responsibility as to enforcement of noise pollution control measures

(1) The noise level in any area/zone shall not exceed the ambient air quality standards in respect of noise as specified in the schedule.
(2) The authority shall be responsible for the enforcement of noise pollution, control measures and the due compliance with the ambient air quality standards in respect of noise.

Rule 5: Restrictions on the use of loudspeakers/public address systems

(1) A loudspeaker or a public address system shall not be used except after obtaining written permission from the authority.

(2) A loudspeaker or a public address system shall not be used at night (between 10.00 p.m. and 6.00 a.m.) except in closed premises for communication within, e.g., auditorium, conference rooms, community halls and banquet halls.

Rule 6: Consequences of any violation in silence zone/area

Whoever, in any place covered under the silence zone/area, commits any of the following offences, shall be liable for penalty under the provisions of the Act:

(i) whoever plays any music or uses any sound amplifiers,

(ii) whoever beats a drum or tom-tom or blows a horn either musical or pressure, or

(iii) whoever exhibits any mimetic, musical or other performances of a nature to attract crowds.

Rule 7: Complaints to be made to the authority

(1) A person may, if the noise level exceeds the ambient noise standards by 10dB (A) or more given in the corresponding columns against any area/zone, make a complaint to the authority.

(2) The authority shall act on the complaint and take action against the violator in accordance with the provision of these rules and any other law in force.

Rule 8: Power to prohibit, etc. continuance of music, sound or noise

(1) If the authority is satisfied from the report of an officer in charge of a police station or other information received by him that it is necessary to do so in order to prevent annoyance, disturbance, discomfort or injury or risk of annoyance, disturbance, discomfort or injury to the public or to any person who dwell or occupy property in the vicinity, he may, by a written order, issue such directions as he may

consider necessary to any person for preventing, prohibiting, controlling or regulating:

(a) the incidence or continuance in or upon any premises of
   (i) any vocal or instrumental music,
   (ii) sounds caused by playing, beating, clashing, blowing or use in any manner whatsoever of any instrument including loudspeaker, public address systems, appliance or apparatus or contrivance which capable of producing or reproducing sound, or

(b) the carrying on in or upon, any premises of any trade, avocation or operation or process resulting in or attended with noise.

(2) The authority empowered under sub-rule (1) may, either on its own motion, or on the application of any person aggrieved by an order made under sub-rule (1), either rescind, modify or alter any such order.

Wildlife (Protection) Act, 1972

In 1972, the Indian Parliament passed a comprehensive national law—The Wildlife (Protection) Act, 1972—with the sole aim of protecting wildlife. It not only prohibits hunting but also created protected areas and controls trade in wildlife products. To achieve these objectives, it has created a separate and independent authority to protect and improve wildlife. The Act has been accepted and adopted by all the states except Jammu & Kashmir.

The first and foremost purpose of this Act is to protect the habitats of wild animals. As a sequel to it, various national parks and game sanctuaries have been established to ensure greater protection to wildlife. Some special provisions also aim to preserve endangered species like Project Tiger, Gir Lion Sanctuary, Himalayan Musk Deer Project, etc. The Act consists of 60 sections and six schedules, divided into seven chapters.

Wildlife, according to the 1972 Act, includes any animals, bees, butterflies, crustacean, fish and moths, and aquatic or land vegetation which forms part of any habitat. This definition is wider in its connotation. The term 'wild animal' has also been defined as any animal found wild in nature and includes any animal specified in Schedule I, II, III, IV or V. Schedule I includes list of mammals (1 to 41-B), amphibians and reptiles (1 to 17-A), birds (1 to 18), crustacea and insects. It has been clarified that 'animal' includes amphibians, birds, mammals, and reptiles and their young, and in the case of birds and reptiles, their eggs.

Hunting of wild animals has been prohibited altogether. But, the Chief Wildlife Warden has been authorized to grant permission to hunt animals under certain circumstances. These are as follows:

1. if he is satisfied that any wild animal specified in Schedule I has become (i) dangerous to human life; or (ii) is disabled; or (iii) diseased as to be beyond recovery; or
2. when the Chief Wildlife Warden, or the authorized officer, is satisfied that any wild animal specified in Schedule II, III, or IV, has become dangerous to human life or to property, or is so disabled or diseased so as to be beyond recovery.

The killing in good faith of any wild animal 'in defence' of oneself or of any other person is not an offence.

The Act has also specified provisions to protect specified plants of sanctuaries, national parks, forests or areas specified by notification. All the specified plants, or part or derivation thereof, have been declared to be the property of the state governments, and if they are a part of a sanctuary or national park, they shall be the property of the central government. Therefore, a person must have a licence from the Chief Wildlife Warden, or other authorized officer, to commence or carry on business or occupation as a dealer in specified plants.

The Act also prohibits to (a) wilfully pick, uproot, damage, destroy, acquire or collect, or (b) possess, sell, offer for sale or transfer by way of gift or otherwise, or transport any specified plant, whether dead or alive or part or derivative. But, this provision is not applicable to the member of a Scheduled Tribe.

Similarly, cultivation, dealing in, possession of specified plants without a licence has also been declared to be a punishable act. Further, no person shall purchase, receive or acquire any specified plant, or part or derivative otherwise than from a licenced dealer.

Laws Relating to Forest Protection

Forest or natural vegetation is an integral element of natural environment. It not only affects but controls the environment and its degradation. As stated earlier, due importance has been given to forests during ancient as well as medieval periods but during British rule overexploitation of forests for commercial purposes had begun. But, soon, its importance has been realized and several laws have been introduced. In Forest Act, 1865, the forest has been considered as a state government property. The Indian Forest Act, 1927 was enacted with the objective to protect the forests. Under this, forests have been classified into four categories, viz., reserved forests, village forests, protected forests and non-government private forests. This Act was a very elaborate one, which deals not only with the use and conservation of forests but also empowers to punish those who are responsible for the unauthorised cutting of forests.

The Forest (Protection) Act, 1980 has been passed in the spirit of the agreement of 1972 Stockholm Conference on Environment. This was further modified in 1988. This Act has given elaborate powers to central government for the protection and conservation of forests including biodiversity as well as also for the establishment of national parks in consultation with state governments. In order to make this Act more effective, six regional centres at Bangalore, Bhopal, Bhubaneswar, Lucknow, Shillong and Chandigarh have been established. At present, governments (both at centre and in states) are very particular about the forest conservation and for this the National Forest Policy was also declared in 1988.

Laws Relating to Hazardous Wastes Management

There were various laws, which directly or indirectly dealt with hazardous wastes and toxic substances, but they were not effective under the changing modern conditions. Therefore, the central government has passed important rules in exercise of powers conferred by the Environmental (Protection) Act, 1986. These rules are as follows:

1. Hazardous Wastes (Management and Handling) Rules, 1989
2. Manufacture, Storage and Import of Hazardous Chemical Rules, 1989
3. Hazardous Micro-Organisms Rules, 1989
4. National Environment Tribunal Act, 1995
5. National Environment Appellate Authority Act, 1997
6. Bio-Medical Wastes (Management and Handling) Rules, 1998
7. Recycled Plastics Manufacture and Uses Rules, 1999
8. Municipal Solid Wastes (Management and Handling) Rules, 2000

A brief review of the above rules is presented as under:

Hazardous Wastes (Management and Handling) Rules, 1989

These rules aim to deal with the problem of hazardous wastes comprehensively.

Although, the term 'hazardous wastes' has not been defined in the rules, but Rule 3(i) provides that 'hazardous wastes' means waste substances, which are generated in the processes as indicated in the schedule.

Rule 4 fixes the responsibility of the occupier and operator of the facility for proper collection, reception, treatment, storage and disposal of hazardous wastes without any adverse effect on the environment.

Rule 4A describes the duties of the occupier and operator of a facility as follows:

(a) contain contaminants and prevent accidents and limit their consequences on humans and the environment; and

(b) provide persons working on the site with information, training and equipment necessary to ensure their safety.

'Proper authorization' by the State Pollution Control Board is really the control mechanism. This authorization letter or permit is issued to a man who is well versed in this technique and possesses proper and adequate facilities, technical capabilities and equipment to handle hazardous wastes safely (Rule 5).

Import and export of hazardous wastes have been completely prohibited for dumping and disposal. However, as an exception, such wastes may be permitted to be imported only as raw material for recycling or reuse (Rule 12). Such wastes can be used for processing and reuse as raw material only after procuring a proper permit from the State Pollution Control Board. In such a case, the exporting country should also inform and seek permission from the central government, which may be granted or refused by it. The occupier exporting or importing hazardous wastes from or to India shall comply with the Articles of the Basel Convention to which India is a signatory. Further, the Ministry of Environment and Forests shall be the nodal agency to deal with transboundary movement of hazardous wastes.

Manufacture, Storage and Import of Hazardous Chemical Rules, 1989

Hazardous chemicals have been dealt with separately under the rules of 1989. The following are the requirements which a chemical industry shall be required to fulfil before it starts working or in case of an existing industry within a period of ninety days of coming into operation of these rules, i.e., November 27 1989. Following are the main provisions of these rules:

1. *Notification of sites*: No one can undertake any industrial activity which would produce a threshold quantity or more of an additional hazardous chemical unless he submits a written detailed report about the industry in accordance with Schedule 7 at least three months before commencing the activity (Rule 7). Rules of 1989 have provided a list of 684 such

hazardous chemicals. Therefore, an industry before its commencement is required to give the above notice.

2. *Safety report*: Before a chemical industry starts functioning, it has to prepare a safety report containing information specified in Schedule 8 at least ninety days before commencing that activity and in case of an existing industry within a period of six months after coming into operation of these rules (Rule 10). The report should be prepared with the help of experts not associated with such industrial activity.
3. *Preparation of on-site emergency plan by the occupier*: Under Rule 13, the occupier is required to prepare and keep up-to-date on-site emergency plan furnishing the details of how major accidents will be dealt with. This plan shall include the name of person responsible for safety and who can take action according to the plan. A mock drill based on the on-site emergency plan shall be conducted every six months.
4. *Preparation of off-site emergency plans*: Rule 14 makes it obligatory on the authorities concerned to prepare and keep up-to-date and adequate off-site emergency plan detailing how emergencies relating to a possible major accident on that site will be dealt with. Further, such plans should be prepared by the authority before a new industry starts its activity or in case of an existing industrial activity within six month of coming into operation of these rules (Rule 14). The authority concerned shall ensure the rehearsal of the off-site emergency plan at least once in a calendar year.
5. *Information to the persons liable to be affected*: One of the important features of the rules is to impose a mandatory duty on the occupier of the industry to take appropriate steps to inform persons outside the site who are likely to be affected by a major accident (Rule 15).

Bio-Medical Wastes (Management and Handling) Rules, 1989

These rules are applicable to all those persons who generate, collect, receive, store, transport, treat, dispose, or handle bio-medical wastes in any form. Bio-medical waste has been defined as "any waste, which is generated during the diagnosis, treatment or immunization of human beings or animals or in research activities pertaining thereto or in the production or testing of biologicals and including categories mentioned in Schedule I". Schedule I has mentioned 10 categories of bio-medical wastes, which include human anatomical waste, animal waste, microbiology and biotechnology waste, waste scraps, discarded medicines and cytotoxic drugs, solid waste, chemical waste, incineration ash, etc.

Municipal Solid Wastes (Management and Handling) Rules, 2000

It consists of nine rules and four schedules. Rule 3 (xv) defines 'municipal solid waste' as follows:

> "Municipal solid waste includes commercial and residential wastes generated in a municipal or notified area in either solid or semi-solid form including industrial hazardous wastes *but* excluding treated bio-medical wastes."

Rule 3 has also defined various terms used in the rules such as anaerobic digestion, bio-degradable substance, bio-methanation, disposal, land filling, recycling, leachate segregation, vadose water, vermicomposing, etc.

Rule 4 declares that every municipal authority shall be responsible for the implementation of the rules and for any infrastructural development for collection, storage, segregation, transportation, processing and disposal of municipal solid wastes. Overall responsibility has to be given to the Secretary of the Department of Urban Development of a state/union territory and the District Collector/Deputy Commissioner in particular to implement the provisions of the rules.

The Central Pollution Control Board and the State Pollution Control Boards have the responsibility of monitoring compliance with standards regarding groundwater, ambient air quality, leachates and compost quality including incineration standards as provided in Schedules II, III and IV of the rules of 2000. Further, the municipal authority will apply for the setting up of waste processing and disposal facility including landfills, to the State

Pollution Control Board, which shall issue the authorization within forty-five days for a given period. Such authorization shall be valid for one year only.

The municipal solid wastes shall be managed and handled with the compliance criteria and procedures laid down in Schedule II, which provides parameters of (i) collection of municipal solid wastes, (ii) segregation, (iii) storage, (iv) transportation, (v) processing, and (vi) disposal of municipal solid wastes, and their compliance criteria. Schedule III provides for specifications for landfill sites and Schedule IV lays down the standards for composting, treated leachates and incineration.

Enforcement of Environmental Legislations

National Environment Tribunal Act, 1995

The Act has been passed with a view to provide for 'strict liability' for damages arising out of any accident occurring while handling any hazardous substances, and to dispose of such cases expediously. It has also recognized the principle of 'no-fault liability' in accidents occurring due to hazardous substances. It also provides heads under which compensation for damage may be claimed in such accidents.

Section 3 enunciates the principle of 'no-fault' of the owner to pay compensation for death, injury or damage to human beings and environment. Further, the claimant shall not be required to plead and establish that the death, injury or damage was due to any wrongful act, neglect or default of any person.

The National Environment Tribunal will hear the applicant and would be guided by the principles of natural justice and shall also have the power of the civil court as provided under the Civil Procedure Code of 1908 (Section 5). Both the parties shall be heard before an injunction is issued by the tribunal.

The central government shall establish the National Environment Tribunal consisting of one chairperson, vice-chairperson, judicial members and technical members; and the bench shall consist of one judicial member and one technical member each (Section 9). The chairperson either must be or has been a judge of the Supreme Court or a High Court; or has for at least two years held the office of vice-chairperson, who will also be a judicial person (Section 10).

National Environment Appellate Authority Act, 1997

The Government of India has also established a National Environment Appellate Authority, which is chaired by a retired Supreme Court judge. It is aimed to hear appeals with respect to restriction of areas in which any industry process/operation of industry shall not be carried out, subject to safeguards provided by the Environment (Protection) Act, 1986. It is a type of check on the establishment of the industries and their likely fall-outs.

Apart from above-mentioned legislations directly related with environment, there are other Acts and rules also, which are applicable in certain cases. These are:

1. Atomic Energy Act, 1962
2. Radiation (Protection) Rules, 1971
3. Insecticides Act, 1968
4. Indian Fisheries Act, 1897

Ozone Depletion

Ozone is a form of oxygen with three atoms, instead of the normal two, and forms a fragile shield scattered in the stratosphere absorbing the sun's ultraviolet radiation, away from the earth's surface. It forms simply a three millimetre thick layer, but if it disappears or thins, all terrestrial life will be annihilated. Near the earth's surface, ozone is an increasingly troublesome pollutant, but safely up at a height of 20 to 30 kilometres from the earth in the atmosphere, it is as important to life as oxygen itself.

The thinning of ozone layer has generated global concern during the last few years. This is due to several chemical pollutants discharged by industries or produced through other chemical reactions. Chlorofluorocarbons (CFCs) are substances that are inert, inexpensive, stable, non-inflammable, non-toxic, easy to store and produce. The population explosion is one of the causes of the increase of CFCs due to use of airconditioners, insulation, solvents and fire-killers. In 1986, three US agencies, viz., National Aeronautics and Space Administration (NASA), National Oceanic and Atmospheric Administration (NOAA) and Federal Aviation Administration (FAA) started reporting on ground and satellite-based data on ozone depletion in stratosphere by the use of chemicals like halon 1301, methyl the chloroform, carbon tetrachloride, solvents-FC-113, aerosols, foams and refrigeration CFC-11, and air conditioning CFC-12 that are depleting the layer 4, 5, 8, 12 and 26 per cent, respectively, on global scale, because of human activities. As far as CFC regional consumption is concerned, USA is on top consuming 29 per cent, followed by Russia and Europe 14 per cent, while in China and India it is merely 2 per cent. The total ozone amounts in the northern hemisphere, middle and high latitudes have decreased, and sudden and unexpected decreases in the amount of spring time Antarctic zone is confirmed on 15 to 20 kilometres in the stratosphere ozone layer.

The increase in ozone layer depletion will invite the lethal ultraviolet rays from the sun which will increase cancer, eye damage, injure plants and marine life and even reduce our immunity to diseases. The UV-B damages the genetic material DNA and also causes skin cancer. The ultraviolet radiation even reduces the efficiency of the immune system, thus impairing the body's resistance. Experts are of the opinion that animal and plant world would face a grim challenge if radiations are not checked. Certain crops have been found vulnerable to such radiations. Under impacts of radiations proteins in plants, microbes and animals would be affected and such changes in spatial orientation would be critical in the formed part of the reaction centre of an enzyme. Near cities, where population concentration is more, ozone could be formed near the earth's surface having disastrous effects on human health, crops and ecosystems. It would also increase the incidence of smog in areas of industrial concentration. Ozone has had its effect on the earth's climate by adding to the greenhouse effect.

The world has now started paying serious thought to the most dramatic evidence of ozone depletion, which has come in the form of a 'hole' in the ozone layer, and appears every spring over the Antarctica. This hole has grown over the last ten years. Till now, no clear explanation has been found to explain this phenomenon and scientific research in this field is in progress. But, the general opinion regarding the cause of this depletion is the CFC. In fact, this is the duty of the developed countries, which have both technology and infrastructure, to check the ozone depletion. Since this problem is not a problem of individual nations, therefore, combined efforts can prove more fruitful.

The concern about ozone layer protection began in the late 1970s and early 1980s. In 1978, while the United States banned the principal CFCs for most uses, in 1980 European Community countries placed a limit on the production of CFCs and cut their use in aerosol products by 30 per cent. Sweden, Norway and Canada also put limits on CFC use. In 1975, the UNEP has also expressed serious concern about ozone depletion and also developed a World Plan of Action on the Ozone Layer.

The European Community (EC) accounted for 45 per cent of world CFC output, and by the mid-1980s it was exporting a third of its production to developing states. Because of the major producer states' interests in continuing production, the EC member-states constituted a veto coalition. Since participation of these states was necessary for a strong ozone protection regime, their cooperation was important. The large developing nations, such as India, China, Indonesia, Brazil and Mexico, also appear to have had some potential as a veto coalition. Their bargaining leverage was based not on their consumption of CFCs but on their potential as producer and consumers of CFCs. These countries were already producing on a small scale; although they were providing less than 5 per cent of the world's CFC production, their production was increasing by 7 to 10 per cent each year. However, in the negotiations on the Vienna Convention, these countries did not take advantage of their veto power. At this stage, no Third World country played an active role.

The Montreal Protocol began the process of strengthening the ozone layer protection regime. Because of new findings, most nations accepted the idea of some controls. However, the extent and the timing of the controls were contentious issues. Lead states argued for a freeze, followed by a gradual reduction in the production of ozone-depleting substances over a period of 10 to 14 years, whereas the veto coalition wanted a production cap. The Toronto Group still pressed for a cut, but as a compromise its members suggested a 50 per cent cut. As late as April 1987, the EC insisted it would agree to a reduction of no more than 20 per cent, but at the Montreal Conference later that year the EC representative agreed to a 50 per cent reduction.

Developing countries successfully pressed for some concessions; they obtained a derogation that would allow them to increase their CFC use for the first decade of the agreement. They were also to receive technical assistance as well as information and advice on CFC recycling and conservation. The fear was that without some concessions Third World countries would set up their own CFC production plants.

Scientific revelations about ozone depletion continued to unfold, and they spurred the regime strengthening process. The Montreal Protocol came into force on January 1, 1989, and the negotiations on its amendment began promptly. At a meeting to amend the protocol in Helsinki in May 1989, the veto coalition began to shift its position dramatically. The EC members were among 80 nations voting for a complete CFC phaseout by the year 2000.

At the London meeting in June 1990, a new coalition of 13 industrialized states pushed for a 1997 deadline for the final elimination of CFCs. However, the four leading CFC-producing nations—the United States, the United Kingdom, France and Italy—joined by the Soviet Union, offered an alternate phaseout date of the year 2000. The push by some industrialized states for a 1997 deadline caused the United States to change from a lead to a veto role.

Developing countries were usually at a disadvantage with respect to the size and make-up of their delegations. A developing country was likely to be represented by a single generalist, whereas the industrialized countries were more likely to have a team of specialists. Countries that had a strong economic interest in the process were usually represented by large delegations. But, most delegations feel between these two extremes. They had, on average, two to four members, usually representing scientific, industrial economic, legal, and political disciplines. The delegations that had specialists had an advantage since these people usually had special knowledge of, or experience regarding, the ozone issue.

The potential for further regime transformation still exists. With the developing countries now on board, the regime can be further strengthened by speeding up the timetable for phaseout. Transformation can also take the form of regime weakening, and the developing countries or any other large country or group of countries can render the regime ineffective by forcing the countries to delay the final phaseout date.

Greenhouse Effect and Global Warming

The phenomenon, commonly known as 'greenhouse effect', occurs due to emission of certain gaseous pollutants in the air which, after the heating of the atmosphere, causes the average global temperature to rise. In other words, the effect produced by certain gases, such as carbon dioxide or water vapour, causes a warming of the earth's atmosphere by absorption of infra-red radiation. The atmosphere protects us by serving as a light scattering and heat mediating blanket. A large portion of heat emitted from the earth is re-absorbed by the atmosphere and is, in effect, conserved, with the result that the surface of the earth is warmer than it otherwise would be. In simple words, this warming is called the greenhouse effect, by analogy with the ability of a greenhouse to keep its inside warmer than the outside during the day time (Figure 6.1).

The atmospheric concentration of these gases has relatively increased since the advent of the industrial era. There has emerged a growing consensus in the scientific community that the anthropogenic greenhouse gas emission of carbon dioxide, nitrous

Figure 6.1
Greenhouse Effect

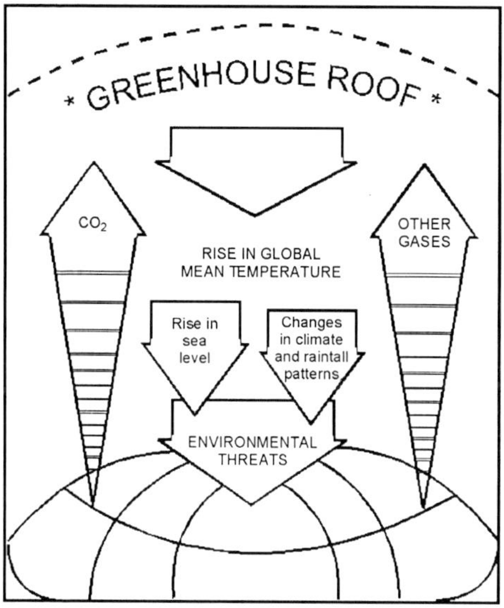

oxide, CFCs, methane and low level ozone threatens to disrupt human societies and natural ecosystems.

The developed world accounted for nearly 80 per cent of the total industrial carbon dioxide emissions and the rest of 20 per cent originated in the developing world. On the other hand, 98 per cent CFCs are produced in developed world and only 2 per cent in developing world. With the current trend of emissions a WHO study speculates that the combined effect of the six most important greenhouse gases could by the early years of 2030s commits the global warming equivalent to doubling of pre-industrial concentrations of carbon dioxide. The scientists are of the opinion that the earth will be hotter by 2° to 4°C by the middle of the 21st century.

The atmospheric blanket keeps the earth habitable and protects living forms from fatal radiations of the sun. The atmosphere intercepts solar radiation, reflecting a third of it, while the rest is absorbed by the atmosphere, ocean, ice, land and biosphere. The energy absorbed is balanced by the outgoing radiation from the atmosphere and the earth. This vital balance will be altered with infringement of greenhouse effect resulting in an overall rise in the average global temperature.

Amongst the most dramatic consequences of the greenhouse climatic disruption is an unprecedented rise in global sea levels to the extent of 8 to 25.5 inches by the end of the century if gas emissions continue at the present rate. Melting of polar ice and glaciers, thermal expansion of seas would cause worldwide coastal flooding and rise in sea level will result in submergence of many coastal areas. It will not only affect the ecological balance but will be a threat to the people and economy of the countries like Bangladesh, Netherlands, as well as to many coastal and island countries. In fact, the impact of worldwide climatic disruption could have hazardous consequences for the survival of the planet both biologically and economically. The Montreal Protocol was a step in this direction but an overall solution requires a combined efforts of all nations and international bodies. Apart from this, scientific and technological research in this field can also reduce the risk to a great extent, provided it reaches all nations specially to the developing nations.

Per Capita Greenhouse Index

National rankings reflect the contributions of individual countries to the atmosphere's growing store of greenhouse gases. But it is also of interest to compare countries by per capita contributions of these gases, since the citizens of our planet vary widely in their relative responsibility for these emissions.

Per capita figures also can be looked at as an indication of how much greenhouse gas emissions and global warming potential might grow if developing countries, in the process of development, significantly increase their per capita emissions. If just China and India, for example, raised their per capita emissions to the current world average, 1.1 metric tonnes of carbon dioxide heating equivalent per annum, total worldwide additions to the atmosphere would increase 28 per cent; if raised per capita emissions to the level of France, worldwide additions to the atmosphere would increase 68 per cent.

Figure 6.2-A compares the per capita emissions for the 10 countries of the Organization for Economic Cooperation and Development (OECD) with the highest national Greenhouse Index Rank. Similarly, Figures 6.2-B and 6.2-C compare per capita emissions for the 10 planned economies and 10 developing countries, respectively, with the highest national emissions. The large ranges among per capita emissions in each economic group suggest that national policies can make a significant difference in a country's contributions to atmospheric warming potential, although, clearly, geography also plays a role. Both the United States and Canada, for example, emit more than twice the per capita greenhouse gases that Japan does – a difference attributable to both geography and policy. Mexico emits about half the per capita emissions of Colombia and about one quarter those of Brazil. At the same time, differences between economic groups are a reminder that any agreement to limit greenhouse gas emissions will have to take into account questions of individual equity and the legitimate aspirations of nations to develop.

The increase and atmospheric concentration of greenhouse gases are responsible for climatic change, especially in rise of temperature. or in other word, responsible for global warming. Changes in greenhouse gas concentrations are closely correlated with changes in the earth's surface temperature. It has been established that warming of global climate and rise in CO_2 and CH_4 levels coincide. Some evidence exists that predicted warming has begun to manifest itself already, but this evidence is controversial. Temperature records taken around the world since 1860 suggest that a global warming of 0.5°–0.7° C has occurred since this year, with nearly half this rise occurring since 1965. Table 6.1 shows the contributions to global warming by greenhouse gases and human activity:

Figure 6.2

Per Capita Net Greenhouse Gas Emissions

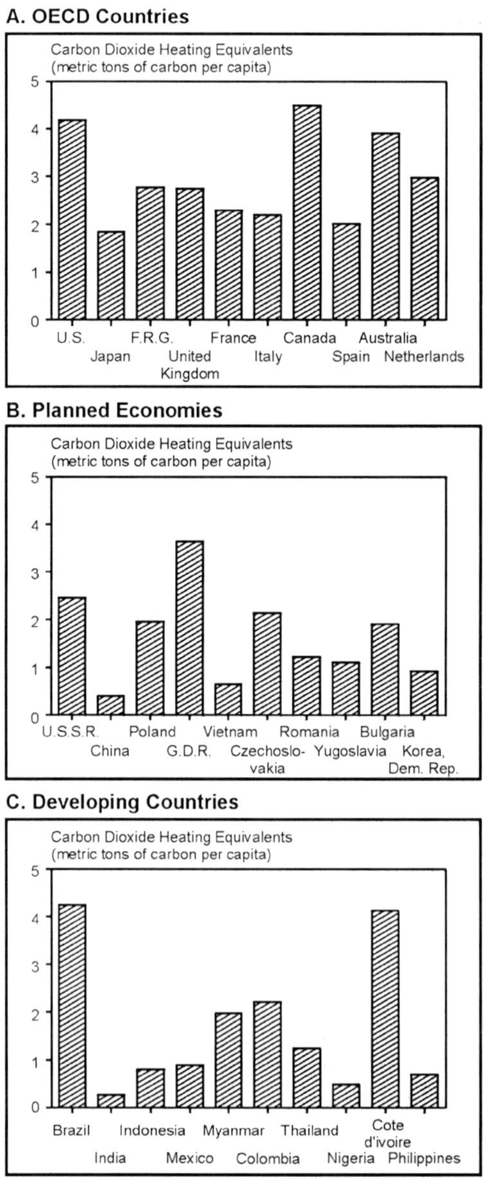

Source: World Resources, 1991, Oxford University Press, p. 18.

Table 6.1

Contributions to Global Warming by Greenhouse Gases and Human Activity

(per cent of global warming)

Sector	*Carbon Dioxide*	*Methane*	*Ozone*	*Nitrous Oxide*	*Chloro-fluoro-carbons (and others)*	*Per cent Warming by Sector*
Energy						
Direct	35	3	X	4	X	49
Indirect	X	1	6	X	X	
Deforestation	10	4	X	X	X	14
Agriculture	3	8	X	2	X	13
Industry	2	X	2	X	20	24
Per cent Warming by Gas	50	16	8	6	20	100

Note: X = not available.

Sources: V. Ramanathan, R.J. Cicerone, H.B. Singh *et al.*, "Trace Gas Trends and their Potential Role in Climate Change", *Journal of Geophysical Research*, Vol. 90, No. D3 (1985) pp. 5547-5566.

Policy Options Available to Address Global Warming

The responses of human societies to global warming can take several approaches. First, prevention strategies can be employed to reduce the quantities of greenhouse gases being emitted. Mitigation mechanism strategies can attempt to compensate for emissions that do occur; for example, through reforestation policies that increase the uptake of CO_2 from the air by trees and other plants. Lastly, strategies can be employed that help communities and nations adapt to changes in climate and their consequences. In practice, all three types of policies are likely to be important. Here, we discuss a range of prevention and mitigation policies.

It is worth noting that the problem of global warming is intimately linked to other serious environmental problems involving the atmosphere, in particular those of acid precipitation, urban smog, and depletion of the stratospheric ozone layer. The problems are linked chemically because, once released, many of the pollutants that cause trouble interact in complex and synergistic ways within the atmosphere or play a role in more the one problem. They are linked economically because it is often the same human activities that release the pollutants responsible for all three problems. And, they are linked in a policy sense because policies designed to attack one problem—by altering an economic activity to reduce emission of the pollutant responsible, for example—inevitably will affect other problems as well. A policy designed to produce automobile that use less fuel, for example, would reduce not only CO_2 emissions, but may also reduce the oxides of nitrogen (NO_2) emissions that contribute to acid precipitations, urban smog and global warming.

While work should proceed simultaneously on mitigation and adaptation strategies, prevention deserves the highest priority. Preventing the emission of greenhouse gases that would be released into the atmosphere not only delays the onset of significant global warming, but also slows its advance and reduces its ultimate magnitude.

To reduce greenhouse gas emissions or even to slow their rate of growth on a global scale will require an extraordinary degree of political consensus. As the greenhouse gas indicators discussed earlier in this chapter make clear, only one country or even one region can prevent the build-up of greenhouse gases by itself, although leadership by individual countries will be important in achieving global consensus. To be broadly acceptable, ideally, prevention policies should confer other local benefits on their adopting countries in addition to the worldwide benefit of reducing the risk of a global warming.

Many policies have been proposed and are under study. It seems clear, however, that any successful prevention strategy will include five key elements:

- increasing the efficiency of energy production and use;
- switching from carbon-intensive fuels such as coal to hydrogen-intensive fuels such as natural gas, where possible;
- encouraging the rapid development and use of solar and other carbon-free energy sources;
- elimination the production of most CFCs and developing the means to recapture those now in use; and
- reducing the rate of deforestation.

Acid Rain

Acid rain is a matter of great global concern and has become one of the major environmental problems. The term 'acid rain', used first by Robert Angus Smith, the Chief Alkali Inspector of UK in 1872, described the acidic nature of rain falling around Manchester. Acid rain is commonly defined as "a condition in which natural precipitation becomes acidic after reacting chemically with pollutants in the air".

Among air pollutants sulphur and nitrogen are significant compounds. In particular, sulphur dioxide (SO_2) and oxides of nitrogen (NO and NO_2) are released from a variety of sources. Sulphur dioxide reacts in air to form sulphur trioxide. In turn, sulphur trioxide reacts rapidly with atmospheric moisture to produce sulphuric acid.

Sulphur trioxide + Water $\rightarrow$ Sulphuric acid.

Similarly, the oxides of nitrogen react in air to produce nitric acid. Both these acids are very strong acids. These materials, when present in the atmosphere, dissolve in water droplets and fall to earth as acid rain. A pictorial representation of acid rain from a thermal plant is shown in Figure 6.3.

Under normal conditions, rain water is slightly acidic because carbon dioxide dissolves in it and reacts to form a weak acid, which is not harmful. But man's contribution through fossil fuel, power plants, industries, automobiles has disturbed this natural acidic balance and converted natural rain into precipitated acid rain with several environmental implications.

The adverse effects of acid rain can be seen on vegetation, soil, marine resources, monuments as well as on man. Air pollutants and acids generated by industrial activities are now entering forests at an unprecedented scale. Many forests in Europe and North America now receive as much as 30 times more acidity than they would if rain and snow fell without pollutants. Its reaction includes change in colour of leaves, premature drops of leaves and flowers, tree crowns progressively thin, and, ultimately, trees die. Marine resources can be totally devastated with loss of aquatic life,

Figure 6.3

Acid Rain from a Thermal Plant

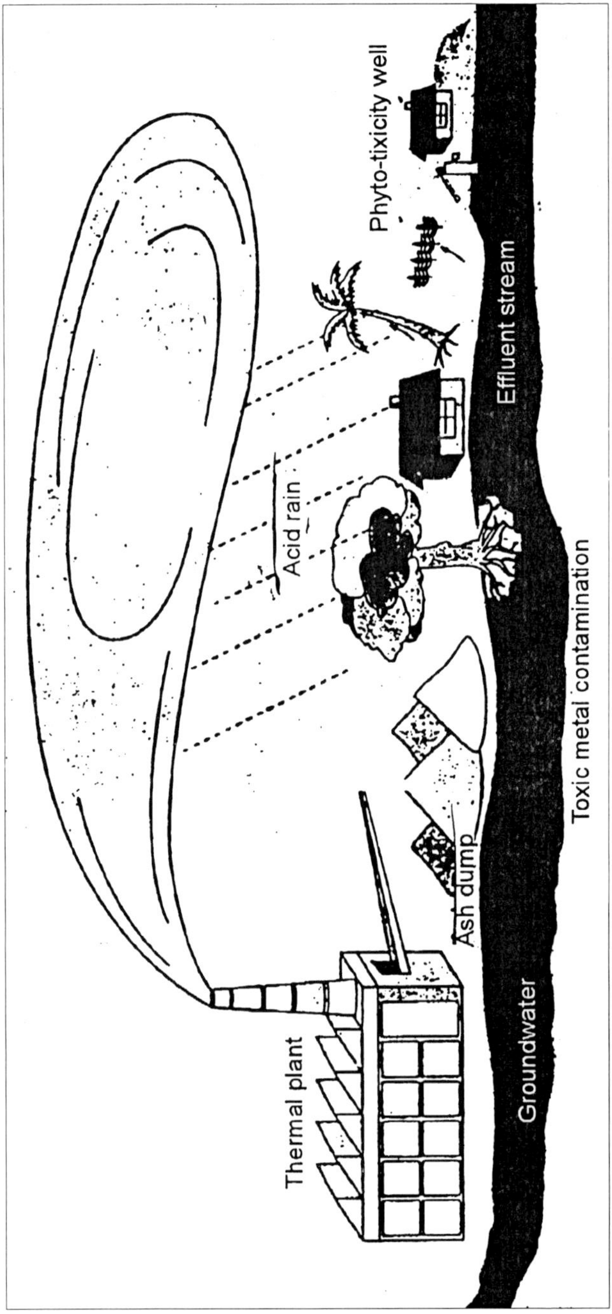

fishes can die and entire lakes and streams can be destroyed. The affected fishes, if consumed by humans and birds, cause dangerous effects. In soil, the rate of decomposition of organic matter and formation of nitrogen fixing organisms is reduced by acids. Human health may also be affected increasing respiratory and skin problems.

Acid rain is an increasing problem in industrial areas of America, Europe and Asia, where large amount of fossil fuels are burned. The ill-effects of acid rains have no national limits as nature knows no geographical boundaries. Only developed technology can save the world from this.

7

Human Population and the Environment

According to ecologists, population has been defined as a "collective group of organisms of the same species or other groups within which individuals may exchange genetic information occupying a particular space". Thus, each and every organism is an integral part of the ecosystem and has its impact over it. In the present context, population means 'human population', which not only uses the environment as habitat but through its multifarious activities also changes certain natural processes in the ecosystem, thus becoming a cause of the ecological crisis. The situation becomes more alarming due to the population pressure and overexploitation of environment.

The interaction between population and environment is very complex and dynamic. This complicated interrelationship is not yet fully understood or spelt out at micro level, nor are the spatio-temporal variations over the nation or the globe understood in their entirety. But, there are no two opinions about the fact that the environment is constantly changing due to human activities, which leads to problems like soil erosion, devastating floods, acute droughts, unforeseen climatic changes, desertification and general degradation of the environment. Figure 7.1 indicates the relationship between population and eco-crisis.

The environment—natural, economic and cultural—acts and reacts in a composite manner and determines the growth and

Figure 7.1
Population and Eco-Crisis

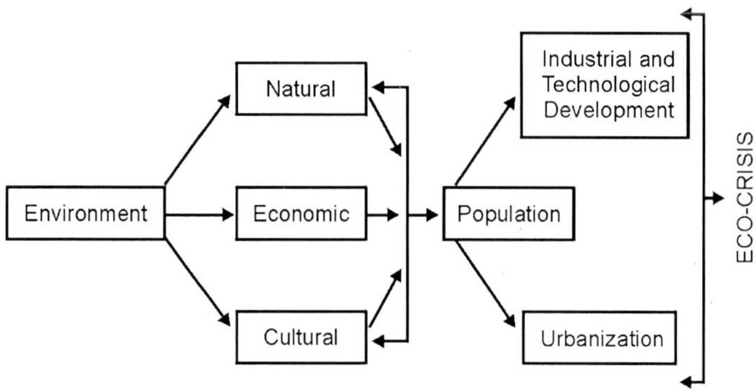

spatial pattern of the population. On the other hand, human activities create chain reaction in the ecosystem. These reactions, pollution and disturbances are now evoking great concern. All these aspects of the population and their impact over the environment need analysis so that the problem can be understood more clearly and steps be suggested for future planning.

Population Growth and Distribution

The growth in human population is a continuous process and in the last 10,000 years the population of the world has increased over a thousand-fold, to about 4.5 billion, and much of that change actually has occurred in the last few hundred years. The current population of the world is estimated to be over 5.7 billion. Table 7.1 indicates the growth of population.

According to the United Nations estimates, the population growth rate at present hangs around 2.5 per cent annually. The rate of increase is staggering. Every 30 seconds, about 117 live babies are born and some 46 people die—a net increase of 71 new inhabitants. This means, over 2,00,000 new mouths to be fed each day or nearly 75 million a year. In spite of the implementation of population control programmes, in the next few decades, there will be high growth rate, because of the effects of declining fertility. After that, if current programmes of family limitations succeed, there are reasons to believe that growth rate will slacken

Table 7.1
Growth of World's Population

Year	Population (in millions)	Average Annual Growth Rate (in millions)	(in percentage)
1650	545	1.8	0.29
1750	728	3.5	0.44
1800	906	5.3	0.51
1900	1,171	8.7	0.64
1920	1,810	21.8	1.11
1940	2,246	24.7	1.05
1950	2,493	49.1	1.81
1960	2,984	64.8	2.15
1969	3,788	145.8	2.23
1981	4,492	70.4	1.7
1990	5,293	80.1	1.76
2000	6,134		

and the population will stabilize in the distant future. The growth rate is much higher in developing countries than in developed nations as shown in Figure 7.2.

Figure 7.2
Trends in Growth of World Population

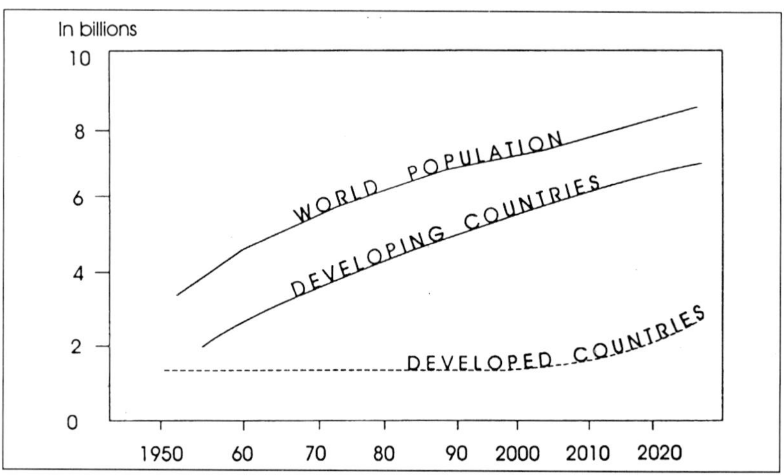

Another aspect of the population, which is considered to be effective in terms of its impact over the ecosystem, is its spatial patterns, both at macro and micro levels. The characteristic feature of the distribution pattern of world population is the concentration of population in limited areas.

Asia is having about 61 per cent of the world population (3.34 billion), followed by Europe having population of 742,400,000. While Africa is having 656,108,000 population, which is about 12 per cent of the world population. On the other hand, North and South Americas are having 442,115,000 and 308,770,000 population respectively. Australia is having a population of 18,287,000—the lowest among continents.

This unequal distribution of population is the main cause of several environmental problems. On the one hand, there are countries like China and India, where population pressure is maximum and resources are limited, and on the other hand, in countries like USA and Canada, where population is less and resources are more. In fact, the positive correlation between population and resources is a key component for sustainable development.

The Demographic Transition

Generally, nations go through a four-stage change process over time, known as the 'demographic transition' as depicted in Figure 7.3.

Stage I (no growth): Both birth and death rates are high, resulting in little or no population increase. There are no clear examples of such nations in present times.

Stage II (rapid growth): The birth rate is still high, but the death rate is falling due to advancement in public health. Many developing countries, such as China, India, Bolivia and Saudi Arabia are in this category.

Stage III (slow growth): The death rate is relatively low and the birth rate is declining such as in China and Indonesia.

Stage IV (stagnation): Birth and death rates are both low, giving a very low rate of increase. Most of the European countries are in this category.

Figure 7.3
Demographic Transition Model

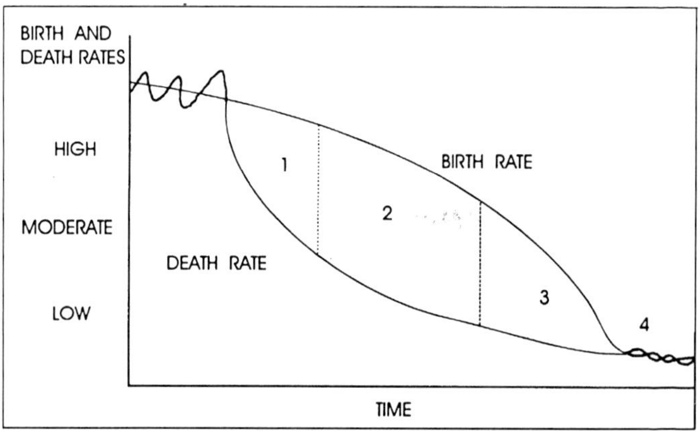

In fact, the rapid growth of population leads to chronic problems like malnutrition, unemployment, disease and, of course, degradation of environment.

Ecological Checks on Growth of Population and Carrying Capacity of Environment

Although growth of population is an ongoing process, there are certain natural checks, which have limiting effects over unlimited growth. The famous demographer, Thomas Robert Malthus, in his writing *Principles of Population* (1798), had pointed out the dire ecological consequences in the continuing growth of population. He claimed that population has a tendency to increase geometrically (in series 1,2,4,8,16 ...), while the food resources for that population, even with improving agricultural methods, increase only arithmetically (in series 10,20,30,40,50,...). When growth reaches that point, it can be kept in check, according to Malthus, only by "war, vice and misery". But, in 1817, Malthus paid more attention to the curtailment of population increase through birth control than to the gloomy devices of war, vice and human misery.

The carrying capacity of environment means the maximum number that the local environment can afford; or the biological capacity to provide food to them. This is represented in Figure 7.4 by three graphs illustrating hypothetical relations.

Figure 7.4
Environmental Constraints on Growth of Population (Three Hypothetical Relations)

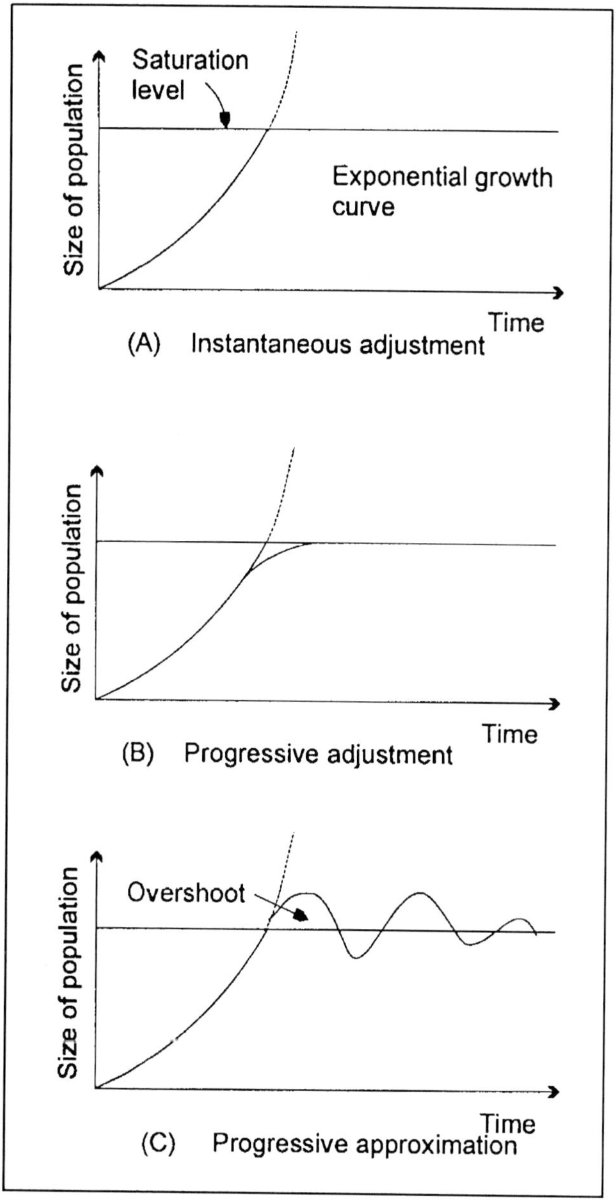

When population growth approaches a point of ceiling, the three situations are: first, the rate of increase may be unchanged until the ceiling is reached, and then abruptly drop to zero; secondly, the rate of increase may decline; and thirdly, the population may overshoot the ceiling.

The three possible adjustments are instantaneous adjustment, progressive adjustment and progressive approximation. In fact, the carrying capacity of the environment also changes with time due to technological and scientific developments.

The gist of Malthus' thoughts is that if the growth of population is beyond the level of saturation, then nature makes adjustments in its own way. We can say that growth of population will be steady and smooth only when there is an adjustment between environment and growth. Increase in population leads to overexploitation of environment and becomes a cause of eco-crisis, ultimately leading to large-scale deaths due to famines, floods, earthquakes, landslides, etc., and also sometimes due to epidemics. The wars and other conflicts between nations also sometimes take place due to overpopulation.

In the history of mankind, there are several instances when the population has been reduced due to natural calamities. The death toll in India due to famines of 1837, 1863 and 1876-78 was 8, 10 and 50 lakh respectively. In China, during the 1877-79 famine, 90 lakh lives were lost and another 30 lakh were lost in 1928-29. Even in Soviet Union, in 1932-34, 40 lakh people died due to famines. According to Malthus, "famine seems to be the first, the most dreadful resource of nature. The power of population is so superior to the power in the earth to produce subsistence for man that premature death must in some shape or other visit the human race".

Similarly, floods, earthquakes, volcanic eruptions, landslides, storms, etc., have claimed thousands (even lakhs) of lives every year. Apart from natural hazards man himself acts as a destroyer either for his selfish motives or for political and economic superiority. The First World War (1914-18) claimed 72 lakh lives and in the Second World War (1939-45) the number was 73 lakh. In the Spanish civil war (1936-39) 63 lakh people died. While in India communal riots of 1946-48 have claimed 59 lakh deaths, American civil war (1861-65) 58 lakhs, Russian revolution (1918-20) 57 lakh, etc. The Vietnam war, Arab-Israel conflict, India-Pakistan wars, India-China war, Gulf wars, etc., are so many examples in which thousands of lives have been lost. The growth of population may not be a direct cause of it, but it is certain that population pressure resulted in the social and economic tensions and became a cause of environmental degradation.

Urban Ecology

Rapid urbanization is a worldwide phenomenon. According to an estimate, in 1935, the number of 'million cities' was 56, which has now crossed the number 125. In year 1800, only 1.7 per cent population was living in cities, which became 5.5 per cent in 1900 and 25.8 per cent in 1975 and by the end of this century it was 39.27 per cent. Trends in the rate of urbanization vary from country to country. For example, the United States has more than 70 per cent urban population, while in India, its percentage in 2001 was 27.78. The pattern of urban population growth in developed and developing countries has been shown in Figure 7.5.

Urbanization continues to increase because the benefits gained from high density crowding are the so-called 'agglomeration economies'. While having a positive impact on income levels, employment, production and market economics, urbanization has brought with it many problems, including a shortage of housing, inadequate water supply, sanitation and waste disposal facilities, congestion, traffic problems, air, water and noise pollution, as well as unsafe social environment. The overall quality of urban environment has deteriorated over the years with the largest cities reaching saturation points and being unable to cope with the increasing pressure on their infrastructures. While cities are considered 'engines of economic growth' given the fact that they contribute nearly 60 per cent of the national income, they are also inherently unsustainable in environmental terms. The situation has become worse in developing countries where cities are growing at a very fast rate and very little efforts are being done

Figure 7.5

Actual and Projected Urban Population Growth (1950-2025)

Actual and Projected Percentage Urban Population Growth in Developing Regions

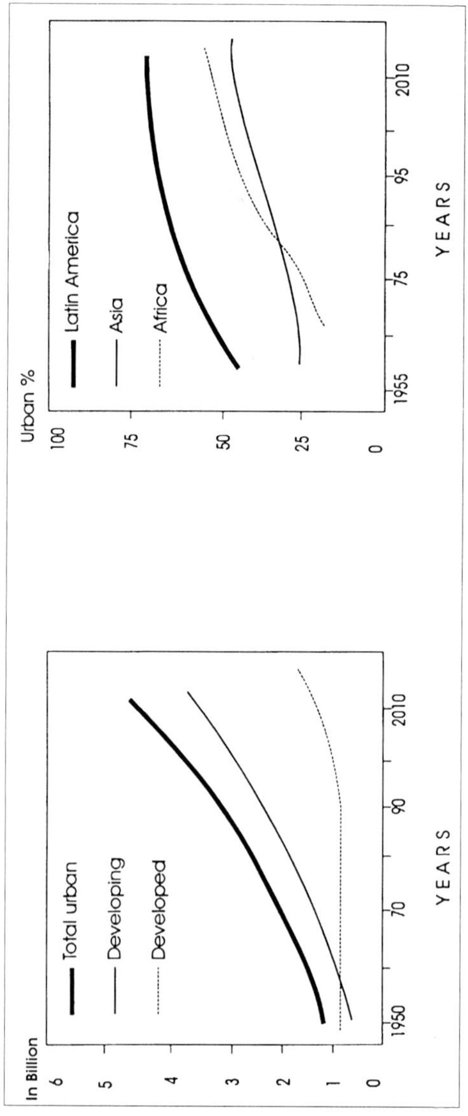

Source: Prospects of World Urbanization (UN, 1989).

to safeguard the urban ecology. In brief, it can be stated that nearly four-fifths of the total investment is cornered for the development of the urban habitat, yet it has not been able to meet even the basic needs of its dwellers. About 30 to 60 per cent people are bound to live in clumsy houses and slums. Now, urbanization is posing a big threat to environment. The process of urbanization, coupled with industrialization, has caused urban atrophy, urban congestion, growth of stinking slums, and impurification of air and water. The urban slum people are denied minimum shelter space and even minimum amount of water, sanitation and electricity. There is thus need to develop new kinds of technology to reconstruct industries in order to protect urban ecology. The process of urbanization should be channelized in such a way that the entire urban area will remain pollution-free and become an environment-friendly zone.

Critical Issues

Some of the critical issues related with the problem of population and eco-crisis are as follows:

(i) Both the population and environment are complex systems and their interactions are also dynamic, complex and inconstant with time and space, therefore, planning for each country/region should be based on realistic research.

(ii) The production systems should be taken into consideration as interaction between population and environment varies with production system, i.e., capitalistic, socialistic or mixed.

(iii) The high population growth and high fertility among the poor masses leads to more pressure upon the world's resources and deterioration of the environment.

(iv) The migration of population from one natural environment to another or from rural to urban areas is responsible for rapid environmental degradation.

(v) Along with environmental issues, proper attention should be given to relieving hunger, poverty and malnutrition. Only then, the quality of environment can be improved in developing countries.

(vi) For growing population a three-fold development policy should be adopted:
  (a) social welfare (food, water, shelter, health and literacy);
  (b) self-reliance (technological, economic and strategic); and
  (c) advanced science and technology (frontier level areas).

  This can be achieved through:
  (a) strategy for resource allocation,
  (b) manpower development,
  (c) extension and transfer facilities, and
  (d) technological management.

Indian Scenario

India is the best example of the relationship between population and environment. Right from ancient times too much importance has been given to nature or environment. The environment not only directs but also determines the growth of population, its distribution and functional structure. There was complete coordination and co-existence between man and nature but with the rapid growth of population this balance has not only been disturbed but has also become a threat to the ecosystem and is now responsible for the degradation of the environment.

India's population has very rapidly grown since the demographic watershed of 1921, when medical treatment, sanitary improvement, etc., started reducing mortality drastically and led to concomitant population explosion. In 1941, there were about 319 million Indians, which rose to 683 million in 1981, 846 million in 1991 and 1,027 million in 2001, as shown in Table 7.2.

Over the past few decades, the average rate of population growth has roughly been about two per cent (in 2001 it was 1.95 per cent) annually. If current high levels of fertility are drastically reduced to half (which is not possible), even then, India's total population was 1,02,87,37,436 in 2001. To provide food, clothing, shelter, education, employment and health care to this colossal mass of humanity would be a herculean task. The impact of such a growing population on the environment is also a cause of great concern to all of us and all efforts should be taken for the harmonious relationship between population and environment.

Table 7.2

Growth of Population in India

Census Year	*Population (in millions)*	*Percentage of Decadal Variation*
1901	238.39	-
1911	252.09	+5.75
1921	251.32	-0.31
1931	278.97	+11.00
1941	318.66	+14.22
1951	361.08	+13.31
1961	439.24	+21.51
1971	548.15	+24.80
1981	683.32	+24.66
1991	846.30	+23.85
2001	1,028.73	+21.34

The growth of population in India has created several environmental problems, some of which are:

(i) overall reduction in agricultural land,
(ii) lower productivity,
(iii) deforestation,
(iv) soil erosion, landslides and expansion of wasteland,
(v) shortage of drinking water,
(vi) malnutrition,
(vii) gradual change in climatic conditions,
(viii) increasing frequency of floods and droughts,
(ix) increasing level of pollution, and
(x) adverse effects on human health and quality of life.

In 1901, only 5.81 per cent population was living in cities, which increased to 18.92 per cent in 1951 and 25.63 per cent in 1971. In 1981, the percentage of urban population was 26.91, while in 1991 census 25.7 per cent population was urban, residing in

4,689 cities and towns. Similarly, the number of 'million cities' in India in 1991 was 23, which increased to 27 in 2001. The process of migration from rural to urban areas has also created several socio-economic problems. The overall quality of urban environment has deteriorated over the years and has now reached a point where immediate attention is needed not only by the government but people also. The situation in metropolises like Mumbai, Kolkata, Delhi, Chennai, Bangalore, Hyderabad, Ahmedabad, Kanpur, etc., is becoming worse year by year, where even minimum shelter for a large section of population is not available.

Due to uncontrolled urbanization in India, environmental degradation has been occurring very rapidly and causing shortages of housing, worsening water quality, excessive air pollution, noise, dust and heat, and the problems of disposal of solid wastes and hazardous wastes. Urbanization, associated with industrialization, has created several environmental problems, such as:

(i) growth of slums;
(ii) industrial pollution (air, water, soil);
(iii) air and noise pollution by vehicular traffic;
(iv) problem of solid waste disposal;
(v) sub-standard and unhygenic residential conditions;
(vi) problem of safe drinking water;
(vii) destruction of natural sites, vegetation, etc.; and
(viii) problem of waste water, etc.

Environment policies for cities in 1990s outline some basic principles for innovative policies, which are also applicable to India. These are:

1. There is need to intensify cooperation between different levels of government—local, regional and national—and each should be made responsible to protect the urban environment.
2. Cooperation between the public sector and the private sector must grow in designing solutions to environmental problems.
3. Minimum environmental standards must be established and enforced.

4. The local community must take part in devising and implementing environmental policies. Local initiatives stimulate greater awareness of local problems and potential.
5. Prices must incorporate environmental and social costs. Local taxes and user fees are most appropriate for demand management and lead to resource conservation.
6. Synergies that can contribute to environmental protection must be identified. In a synergetic relationship, mutually enhancing activities are more productive when they are coordinated.
7. Short-term decisions must be taken within the framework of long-term strategies. Environmental strategy-based urban planning can provide a long-term strategy within which short run decisions should be taken.

There is also need to develop the environment-friendly city. With systematic efforts by the government and communities including NGOs each city can be developed as a model environmental city.

Tasks Ahead

We have discussed above some measures for the improvement of urban environment. Apart from these, there is also need to plan strategy to limit population as well as for a balanced friendly ecosystem. Such measures are urgently required not only for countries having larger populations but also for all the developing countries. Some measures or action programmes may be as follows:

(i) Fertility reduction programmes should be intensified to limit population growth.

(ii) Population welfare programmes like child care, immunization, malnutrition control, safe drinking water, etc., and also programmes to relieve poverty, hunger and to raise socio-economic status of women should be implemented properly.

(iii) Rural development programmes related to massive employment in rural non-agricultural sectors, to conserve rivers, ponds, forests and grazing land in villages, to enhance the quality of life in rural areas by innovative technology for making cheap but durable housing, sanitation, drainage, water supply systems, etc.

(iv) Agriculture improvement programmes should be started along with horticulture, fishing, dairy and poultry.

(v) Knowledge of land-soil water management should be given to villagers so that they can adopt soil conservation measures and can use available water resources.

(vi) The use of alternative sources of power such as biogas as well as alternative technology for bio-fertilizers be should popularized so that quality of environment can be improved.

(vii) Widespread social forestry and agro-forestry programmes should be implemented.

(viii) Conservation of forests and massive afforestation programmes should be part and parcel of a national programme.

(ix) For urban areas, apart from the above suggested measures, new urban land use policy, new mode of urban transport and rapid transit systems and urban slum development programmes should be formulated for the improvement of quality of life in cities.

(x) Strict pollution control measures should be adopted without any political interference.

The above programmes can be fruitful only if there is political will, economic discipline, distributive justice and true commitment to ensure planning for balanced ecosystem.

Environment and Human Health

The growth, survival and health of mankind are directly linked with environment. The components of the environment, i.e., relief, climate, soil, natural vegetation and water bodies not only affect the human health but determined its overall status also. With the degradation of environment and due to its negative impact on health, it becomes necessary not only to study the environmental impact assessment on human health but also develop awareness about their consequences. This is also necessary because health is the primary concern for "quality of life" and a good environment is required for quality of life. A good environment is the environment, which is pollution-free, having proper drinking water, parks, playgrounds and good sanitation facility. The development of green belt around habitation and industrial areas will also help in developing proper environment. Similarly, proper waste management system should be adopted because solid and other wastes are the main cause of several diseases not only in urban areas but also in rural areas.

The changes in our environment induced by human activities have had a influence on our health pattern. Urbanization and industrialization, though symbols of development, also lead to diseases related to overcrowding and poor quality of drinking water resulting in an increase in water-borne diseases like diarrhoea and air-borne bacterial diseases like tuberculosis, etc.

Pollution has become a great threat to human health today. Air pollution mainly affects the respiratory system. Bronchitis, emphysema, asthma and lung cancer are some of the chronic diseases caused due to exposure to polluted air. It is feared that lung cancer is caused mainly due to polluted air because carcinogens are found in the polluted air. Its mortality rate is higher in urban areas. Likewise, sulphur dioxide is the most serious and widespread air pollutant. Its lower concentration is a cause of spasms in the smooth muscle of bronchioles and its higher concentration induces increased mucus production. Sulphur dioxide is also considered to cause cough, shortness of breath, spasm of the larynx and acute irritation to the membranes of the eyes. It also acts as an allergenic agent. When it reacts with some compounds, sulphuric acid is formed, which may damage lungs.

Carbon monoxide often affects the oxygen-carrying capacity of blood. Nitric oxide is reported to be a pulmonary haemorrhage.

Water pollution is probably responsible for more human illness than any other environmental influence. The diseases so transmitted are chiefly caused by micro-organisms and parasites. Sewage and polluted water are responsible for several water-borne diseases. Some of the diseases caused by polluted water are cholera, typhoid, infantile diarrhoea, dysentery, infectious hepatitis, polio, giardiasis, amoebic dysentery, jaundice, zondic, etc. Cholerais, an illness caused by ingestion of the bacterium *Vibriocholeral*, results rapidly in massive fluid depletion and death in a very large percentage of patients. It is transmitted by drinking water contaminated with the faces of infected individuals. In developing countries, deaths by cholera are still common. Guineaworm is another disease caused by polluted drinking water. In India alone, about 18 lakh people suffer from this disease. *Schistosomiasis* is a group of diseases caused by infection through worms in water. There are certain chemicals present in polluted water, which may cause diseases like nepurities, wrist drop, foot drop, etc.

Similarly, other forms of pollution like noise, land, radioactive and thermal are also responsible for several diseases and have had adverse effect on human health. In India, access to safe drinking water remains an urgent need as only 72 per cent of the population in urban area receives well-treated water supply. The situation in rural areas is much worse. In India, almost all surface water sources are contaminated and unfit for human consumption. The diseases commonly caused due to contaminated water are diarrhoea, trachoma intestinal worms, hepatitis, etc. In 2002 WHO report shows that about 21 per cent of all communicable diseases in India are water-borne diseases. Epidemiological studies have also shown that diarrhoea and intestinal worm infections account for an estimated 10 per cent of the total burden of disease.

An uncontrolled disposal of urban wastes into water bodies, open dumps and poorly designed landfills also causes surface water and ground water contamination. Industrial wastes containing heavy metals such as mercury, chromium, lead and arsenic can threaten or destroy marine life. Health hazards such as malaria, filariasis, hepatitis and cholera can also spread. The epidemic of jaundice is also a result of contaminated water supply. In 1955-56, in Delhi, about 29,300 persons developed jaundice, following contamination of the drinking water supply from contents of a severed drain from Najafgarh in West Delhi. Similarly, epidemic of Hepatitis-E has been caused due to drinking of polluted water. In India, major incidences of hepatitis epidemics have occurred in various urban centres as shown in Figure 7.6.

Figure 7.6

Hepatitis Epidemics in India

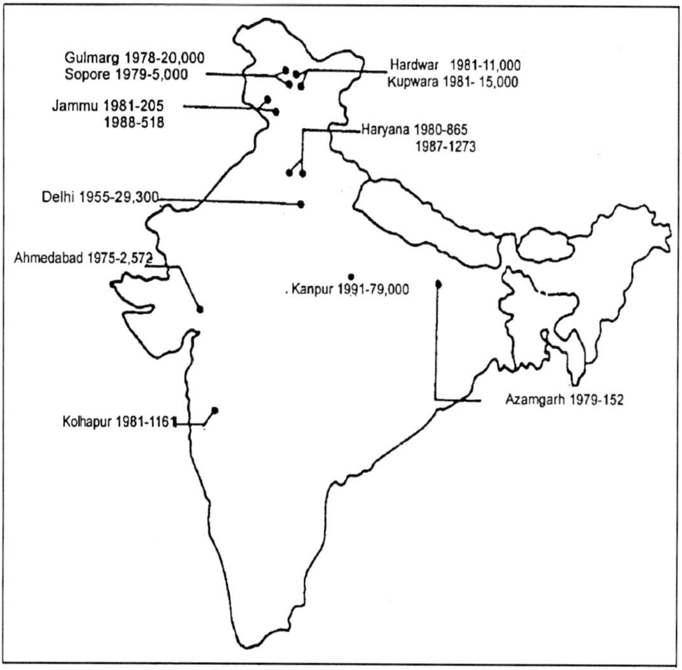

A few remedies to control the water pollution are:

- industries should enforce standards for water effluents;
- the Pollution Control Boards must enforce the laws;
- adequate sewage disposal facilities should be developed, so that sewage is not directly released into the water stream;
- the sewage and water treatment plant should be established by every municipal body;
- for small- and medium-sized industries, which cannot afford effluent plants, combined treatment plants be established;
- a pollution tax be imposed, especially on industries responsible for water pollution;
- more and more *Sulabh* type of toilets be built;
- action plans concerning water pollution should be completed within specified period; and

— above all, awareness among people about sanitation and its related impact on their health should be promoted.

Environmental health, as defined by WHO, comprises those aspects of human health, including the quality of life, that are determined by physical, chemical, biological, social and phychosocial factors in the environment. It also refers to the theory and practice of assessing, correcting, controlling and preventing those factors in the environment that adversely affect the health of present and future generations. The sustainable development is possible through healthy environment and healthy people through healthy environment and healthy people. Therefore, master plans for each micro region should not only be prepared but also implemented properly to protect environment and human health.

8

Fieldwork

Fieldwork is an essential component of environmental studies and as such the University Grants Commission (UGC) has prescribed this in the syllabus for various postgraduate courses. The syllabus for fieldwork is as follows:

— Visit to a local area to document environmental assets—river, forest, grassland, hill and mountain.
— Visit to a local polluted site—urban, rural, industrial and agricultural.
— Study of common plants, insects, birds, etc.
— Study of simple ecosystems—pond, river, hill slopes, etc.

Environment can be studied properly only through field study. It is a subject of theoretical as well as of applied nature. Therefore, after theoretical study, one should go to the field and study the various aspects of environment. Through such field studies students can be able to understand the local environment and its problems. They are also in a position to suggest measures to solve environmental problems. In other words, they will not only play a vital role in protecting environment but also able to develop awareness among other people.

Preparation for Fieldwork

Prior to fieldwork, necessary preparations are essential, otherwise it will be a futile exercise. The fieldwork should be done under the supervision of an experienced teacher or a group of teachers, having some experience of such fieldwork. If possible, it should be conducted by subject teachers, specially of botany, geography, zoology and environmental science. Some of the guidelines for fieldwork preparations are as follows:

(i) Selection of the Subject/Topic

Before fieldwork, this is necessary to select specific subject for the study. Environment is a vast subject, therefore, for each group of students, a specific topic should be given, and if required, sub-topics may also be given. Some of the topics as per syllabus are as follows:

1. *Local environment:* Study of geographical environment, such as relief (mountain, hills, plateau), forest, river, grassland, soils, water resources, minerals resources, climate, etc.
2. *Pollution:* Air, water, noise, land pollution. Areas of pollution and their causes and effects.
3. Solid waste disposal problem.
4. Slums.
5. Industries and their impact on environment.
6. Soil erosion, deforestation.
7. Study of common plants, insects and birds.
8. Ecosystem study – selected according to local environment such as river, pond, hill slope, grassland, etc.

The selection of topic should be made by the teacher and its importance should be explained to students before fieldwork.

(ii) Selection of Area

This should be local so that students can easily able to conduct fieldwork without any extra expenditure.

(iii) Time Schedule

The fieldwork may be completed in three days' time and in next two days completion of data be done.

(iv) Study Groups

The group formation should be done according to the number of students. In each group, 10 to 15 students can be included so that proper communication is possible among students and between students and teachers.

(v) Necessary Material

Each student should carry his own notebook, pen/sketch pen, recording schedule/proforma and a common camera, etc.

After above preparation, students will be ready to go into the field.

Empirical/Visual Survey

Empirical survey is an important aspect of fieldwork. Each student should record according to his or her own visual inspiration about various environmental aspects such as hills, rivers, ponds, grass-lands, trees, birds, animals, etc. Similarly, in habitation, types of houses, roads, drinking water, source of water, waste disposal, human occupation, health, etc., should be recorded. Both physical and man-made structures be noted.

Data Collection

Two types of data are required: (i) secondary, and (ii) primary.

Secondary data will be obtained from Census, Statistics Department, Municipal Board, Panchayat, Industries office, PWD, PHED, etc. The topographical sheets published by Survey of India will be very useful for fieldwork.

Primary data will be collected during field study. This data collection should be done through well-designed questionnaire. This questionnaire should be prepared by the subject teacher and given to the students during fieldwork for data collection.

Recording of Informations/Data

(a) General Informations

1. City/Town/Village Tehsil, District
2. Location Latitude and Longitude

3.	Population	(year . . . .) Total Population Male/Female Population Literacy Percentage – Male, Female SC Population ST Population

(b) Geographical Characteristics

Mountain/Hill	Location, height, nature of slope covered by vegetation or not.
Rivers	Name of the river, origin place, nature – perennial or non-perennial, use of river water, water pollution – source and nature.
Forests	Location, type, name of trees, use, deforestation, aforestation, wildlife.
Grassland	If any, its nature and use.
Desert	If any, its topography, nature of sand dunes, land use.
Agricultural Land	Land use patterns, crops grown, irrigated or non-irrigated, use of fertilizers and pesticides, etc.

These infomations can be collected by the whole team and not by individuals.

Study of Local Polluted Area

It will be a useful field study in towns and cities, where pollution is a common environmental problem. For this study, city should be divided in several study areas or specific problem can be selected and given to a group or groups. Some of the topics are:

1. Water Pollution
2. Air Pollution
3. Noise Pollution
4. Land Pollution

5. Problem of Waste Disposal
6. Industrial Pollution
7. River Pollution
8. Slums
9. Pollution by Transportation
10. Pollution.

One should collect informations about causes, sources and effects, and also try to suggest measures of control.

Study of Common Plants, Insects and Birds

This study may be of more importance to the students of botany and zoology, because they have basic knowledge about plants, birds, etc. On the basis of observation, students may be asked to list the name of local birds, insects, plants, etc., and afterwards find out their characteristics. This type of study can also be done for gardens, parks – botanical and zoological, etc.

Study of Simple Ecosystems

First of all, selection of a particular ecosystem, i.e., river, pond, mountain, grassland, desert, etc., should be done. Documentation of general features is to be done during fieldwork. The fieldwork is to be done to record:

(i) Identity of ecosystem – its site and characteristics – biotic aspects, habitats, food chains, foodweb, etc.
(ii) Ecosystem goods and services (resources).
(iii) Who use them and how?
(iv) Is the utilization sustainable or unsustainable (signs of degradation)?
(v) How can the ecosystem be used sustainably?
(vi) Role of producers, decomposers and consumers in selected ecosystem.

Methodology

(i) Observation of ecosystem
(ii) Questioning with local people
(iii) Discussion with users and scientific officers
(iv) Findings

And finally, a brief report stating findings and results should be prepared with conclusions.

Preparation of Report

Preparation of report is the most important aspect of field study. After data collection, tabulation and representation of data by graphics, etc., is done. The final report is prepared under the supervision of teacher concerned.

The report should be prepared under the following heads:

(i) Importance of the study.
(ii) Objectives.
(iii) Basis of selection of field area.
(iv) Methodology – field observations, data collection, tabulation and statistical methods used, maps and diagrams and analysis.
(v) Analysis of each point studied during fieldwork.
(vi) Problems.
(vii) Suggestions.
(viii) Conclusions.

This report will then be evaluated by examiners. But, at the same time, this type of study will definitely develop awareness among students about local environment and associated problems, or in other words, it will generate a general awareness in society about environmental problems.

Glossary

acid rain A condition in which natural precipitation becomes acidic after reacting chemically with pollutants in the air.

aerosol A substance consisting of small particles, typically having diameters that range from 1/100 micrometer to 1 micrometer.

air pollution The deterioration of the quality of air that results from the addition of impurities.

albedo A measure of the reflectivity of a surface, measured as the ratio of light reflected to light received. A mirror or bright snowy surface has a high albedo, whereas a rough, flat road surface has a low albedo.

arithmetic growth In population studies, growth characterized by the addition of a constant number of individuals during a unit interval of time. For instance, if there are x individuals in year 0 and x + a in year 1, arithmetic growth implies x + na in year n.

atmosphere The predominantly gaseous envelope that surrounds the earth.

atom The fundamental unit of an element.

atomic nucleus The small positive central portion of the atom that contains its protons and neutrons.

atomic number The number of protons in an atomic nucleus.

autotroph An organism that obtains its energy from the sun, as opposed to a heterotroph, which is an organism that obtains its energy from the tissue of other organisms. Most plants are autotrophs.

background radiation The level of radiation on earth from natural sources.

benthic organism A plant or animal that lives at or near the bottom of a body of water.

biodegradable Refers to substances that can readily be decomposed by living organisms.

biogas Methane produced by fermentation of organic waste. Biogas is chemically identical to methane produced in any other manner.

biogeochemical cycles The transport of elements between rock, water, air and living organism in an circular fashion that periodically returns them to each stage.

biomass The total weight of all the living organisms in a given system.

biome A group of ecosystems characterized by similar vegetation and climate that are collectively recognizable as a single large community unit. Examples include the Arctic Tundra, the North American prairie, and the tropical rain forest.

biosphere That part of the earth and its atmosphere that can support life.

birth cohort A group of individuals born in a given period, such as in a particular year.

birth rate The number of individuals born during some period, usually a year, divided by an appropriate population. For example, the crude birth rate in human populations is the number of live children born during a given year divided by the mid-year population of that year.

black lung disease A series of debilitating and often fatal diseases that affect the lungs of miners who work in underground coal mines.

bloom A rapid and often unpredictable growth of a single species in an ecosystem.

branching chain reaction A chain reaction in which each step produces more than one succeeding step.

breeder reactor A nuclear reactor that produces more fissionable material than it consumes.

cancer An abnormal, unorganized, and unregulated growth of cells in an organism.

carnivore An animal that eats the flesh of other animals.

carrying capacity The maximum number of individuals of a given species that can be supported by a particular environment.

chain reaction A reaction that proceeds in a series of steps, each step being made possible by the preceding one. See also branching chain reaction.

chemical bond A linkage that holds atoms together to form molecules.

chemical energy The energy that is absorbed when chemical bonds are broken or released when they are formed.

clear-cutting The practice of cutting all the trees in a designated area. Clear-cutting leaves behind barren, open regions but is sometimes the cheapest way to harvest timber if only short-term economic evaluation is used. See selective cutting.

climate The composite pattern of weather conditions that can be expected in a given region. Climate refers to yearly cycles of temperature, wind, rainfall, and so on and not to daily variations.

climax community A natural system that represents the end, or apex, of an ecological succession.

common mode failure An accident in which a single event causes multiple failures and thereby knocks out redundant systems. See redundancy.

competition An interaction in which two or more organisms try to gain control of a limited resource.

composting The controlled, accelerated biodegradation of moist organic matter to form a humus-like product that can be used as a fertilizer or soil conditioner.

cooling pond A lake or pond used to cool water from an electric generating station or any other industrial facility.

cooling tower A large tower-like structure used to cool water from an electric generating station or any other industrial facility.

critical condition In nuclear science, a critical condition is said to exist when a chain reaction continues at a steady rate, neither accelerating nor slowing down.

critical minimum size In general, a critical condition relates to a point at which some property changes very abruptly in response to a small change in some other property of the system. In ecology, a population is said to be reduced to its critical minimum size when its numbers are so few that it is in acute danger of extinction.

crude rate A vital rate with the entire population of some area as the denominator.

death rate The number of individuals dying during some period, usually a year, divided by an appropriate populations. For example, the crude death rate in human populations is the number of deaths during a given year divided by the mid-year population of that year.

decibel (*dB*) A unit of sound intensity equal to 1/10 of a bel. The decibel scale is a logarithmic scale used in measuring sound intensities relative to the intensity of the faintest audible sound.

demographic transition The pattern of change in vital rates typical of a developing society. The process can be outlined briefly as follows. Birth and death rates in a pre-industrial society are typically very high; consequently, population growth is very slow. Introduction or development of modern medicine causes a decline in death rates and hence a rapid increase in population growth. Finally, birth rates fall, and the population grows slowly once more.

demography The branch of sociology or anthropology that deals with the statistical characteristics of human populations, with reference to total size, density, number of deaths, births, migrations, marriages, prevalence of disease, and so forth.

desert A climate system in which rainfall is less than 25 centimetres per year. These systems are barren and support relatively little plant or animal life.

desertification The diminution or destruction of the biological potential of the land, which can ultimately lead to desert-like conditions.

doubling time The time a population takes to double in size, or the time it would take to double if its annual growth rate were to remain constant.

ecological niche The description of the unique functions and habitats of an organism in an ecosystem.

ecology The study of the interrelationships among plants and animals and the interaction between living organisms and their physical environment.

economic externality That portion of the cost of a product that is not accounted for by the manufacturer but is borne by some other sector of society.

ecology the science of all the relations of all organism and their environment.

ecosystem A group of plants and animals occurring together plus that part of the physical environment with which they interact. An ecosystem is defined to be nearly self-contained, so that the matter that flows into and out of it is small compared with the quantities that are internally recycled in a continuous exchange of the essentials of life.

ecosystem homeostasis The control mechanisms within an ecosystem that act to maintain constancy by opposing externals.

entropy A thermodynamic measure of disorder. It has been observed that the entropy of an undisturbed system always increases during any spontaneous process; that is, the degree of disorder always increases.

environment The sum total of all conditions, agencies and influences which affect the development, growth, life and death of an organism, species or race.

environmental resistance The sum of various pressures, such as prediction, competition, adverse weather, and so on, that collectively inhibit the potential growth of every species.

epidemiology The study of the distribution and determination of health and its disorders.

estuary A partially enclosed shallow body of water with access to the open sea and usually a supply of freshwater from the land. Estuaries are less salty than the open ocean but are affected by tides and, to a lesser extent, by wave action of the sea.

euphotic zone The surface volume of water in the ocean or a deep lake that receives sufficient light to support photosynthesis.

eutrophication The enrichment of a body of water with nutrients, with the consequent deterioration of its quality for human purposes.

expectation of life The number of years an infant can be expected to live under a specified schedule of death rates.

extrapolation The prediction of points on a graph outside the range of observation.

evolution, theory of A theory that states that species are not unchangeable but arise by descent and modification from pre-existing species.

fire climax A condition in which the continuance of a given ecosystem is maintained by fire.

fission (*of atomic nuclei*) The splitting of atomic nuclei into approximately equal fragments.

food chain An idealized pattern of flow of energy in a natural ecosystem. In the classic food chain, plants are eaten only by primary consumers, primary consumers are eaten only by secondary consumers, secondary consumers only by tertiary consumers, and so forth.

food web The actual pattern of food consumption in a natural ecosystem. A given organism may obtain nourishment from many different trophic levels and thus give rise to a complex, interwoven series of energy transfers.

fusion (*of atomic nuclei*) The combination of nuclei of light elements (particularly hydrogen) to form heavier nuclei.

Gaia The ancient Greek goddess of the earth. This word has recently been used to describe the biosphere and to emphasize the interdependence of the earth's ecosystems by likening the entire biosphere to a single living organism.

gas A state of matter that consists of molecules that are moving independently of each other in random patterns.

gasohol A motor fuel consisting of approximately 90 per cent gasoline and 10 per cent ethyl alcohol.

genetic engineering The process of artificially removing specific genes from one organism and replacing them with genetic information from another.

geo-metric growth In population studies, growth such that in each unit of time, the population increases by a constant proportion. Also called exponential growth.

geothermal energy Energy derived from the heat of the earth's interior.

Gloger's rule A rule, proposed by C.W.L. Gloger, stating that animals living in warm climates are more darkly coloured than closely related animals living in cold climates.

green revolution The realization of increased crop yields in many areas due to the development of new high-yielding strains of wheat, rice, and other gains in the 1960s.

green-house effect The effect produced by certain gases, such as carbon dioxide or water vapour, that cause a warming of the earth's atmosphere by absorption of infra-red radiation. The term is an inappropriate analogy to green-houses, which were once thought to keep themselves warm by admitting sunlight but retaining infra-red radiation. However, it has been shown that most of the heat retention in green-houses results from the conservation of warm air. The atmosphere, of course, is open, so the mechanism is not the same.

gross national product (*GNP*) The total value of all goods and services produced by the economy in a given year.

half-life (*of a radioactive substance*) The time required for half of a sample of radioactive matter to decompose.

hard energy system An energy system based on large centralized electric-generating facilities. See also soft energy system.

hazardous waste The material that poses a threat to human health and the environment.

heat A form of energy. Every object contains heat energy in an amount that depends on its mass, its temperature, and the specific heat of the materials of which it consists. Heat can also be generated by chemical reactions such as combustion.

heat engine A mechanical device that converts heat to work.

heavy oil Natural petroleum deposits that are too thick to be extracted by conventional pumping techniques. Heavy oils are found in "dry" conventional wells and also in oil shales and tarsands.

hectare A metric measure of surface area. One hectare is equal to 10,000 square metres or 2.47 acres.

herbicide A chemical used to control unwanted plants.

herbivore An animal that eats only plant matter.

heterotroph An organism that obtains its energy by consuming the tissue of other organisms. See also autotroph.

home range The area in which an animal generally travels and gathers its foods.

hormones These compounds can be used as insecticides, for if sprayed properly they will disrupt the life cycle of specific insect larvae and kill them.

humus The complex mixture of decayed organic matter that is an integral part of healthy soil.

hydroelectric power Power derived from the energy of falling water.

hydrological cycle (*water cycle*) The cycling of water, in all its forms, on the earth.

injunction A legal order requiring a defendant to stop doing a wrongful act.

innate capacity for increase The maximum rate of growth of a population as determined by the reproductive capacity of the organism.

inversion A meteorological condition in which the lower layers of air are cooler than those at higher altitudes. This cool air remains relatively stagnant and causes a concentration of air pollutants and unhealthy conditions in congested urban regions.

isotopes Atoms of the same element that have different mass numbers.

joule A fundamental unit of energy, 4.184 joules = 1 calorie.

kinetic energy Energy of motion.

krill Small, shrimp-like crustacean that grow in large numbers in the cold waters of the southern oceans. Krill represent a primary food supply for many species of whales.

legume Any plant of the family Leguminosae, such as peas, beans, or alfalfa. Bacteria living on the roots of legumes change atmospheric nitrogen, N_2, to nitrogen-containing salts that can be readily assimilated by most plants.

mass number The sum of the number of protons and neutrons in an atomic nucleus.

megalopolis An agglomeration of several smaller cities and towns into a single expanded urban area.

meteorology The science of the earth's atmosphere.

mine spoil The earth and rock removed from a mine and discarded because the mineral or fuel content is too low to warrant extraction.

mineral reserves The estimated supply of ore in the ground.

molecule The fundamental particle that characterizes a compound. It consists of a group of atoms held together by chemical bonds.

mutagen A substance that causes mutations. An inheritable change in the genetic material of an individual.

mutation A change in the structure or amount of gerietic material.

mutualism An interaction beneficial and necessary to both interacting species.

natural selection A series of events occurring in natural ecosystems that eliminate some members of a population and spares those individuals endowed with certain characteristics that are favourable for reproduction.

neutron A fundamental particle of the atom, that is, electrically neutral.

nodules Small pieces of rock, typically having a mass of about 1 kg, that are found on the floor of the ocean. These nodules are rich in manganese and also contain several other minerals such as copper, iron, aluminum and cobalt.

noise Unwanted sound.

nuclear reactor A device that utilizes nuclear reactions to produce useful energy.

omnivore An organism that eats both plant and animal tissue. Common omnivores include bears, pigs, rats, chickens and people.

open dump A site where solid waste is deposited on a land surface with little or no treatment.

ore A rock mixture that contains enough valuable minerals to be mined profitably with currently available technology.

organic farming A set of farming practices that uses no synthetic fertilizers or chemicals.

organochlorides A class of organic chemicals that contain chlorine bonded within the molecule. Some organochlorides, such as DDT, are effective pesticides. They are generally broad-spectrum and long-lived in the environment.

organophosphates A class of organic compounds that contain phosphorus and oxygen bonded within the molecule. Some organophosphates, used as pesticides, are broad-spectrum and extremely poisonous, although they are not long-lasting in the environment.

Ozone Triatomic oxygen, O_3.

Ozone layer A region of the stratosphere, at 20-25 km, where the concentration of Ozone (O_3) is higher than elsewhere.

parasitism A special case of predation in which the predator is much smaller than the victim and obtains its nourishment by consuming the tissue or food supply of a larger living organism.

photosynthesis The process by which chlorophyll bearing plants use energy from the sun to convert carbon dioxide and water to sugars.

phytoplankton Any microscopic, or nearly microscopic, free-floating autotrophic plant in a body of water. There are a great many different species that exist in a community of phytoplankton; these plants occur in large numbers and account for most of the primary production in deep bodies of water.

plankton Any small, free-floating organism living in a body of water.

pollution The impairment of the quality of some portion of the environment by the addition of harmful impurities.

polychlorinated biphenyl (*PCB*) A class of organochloride chemicals that are structurally related to DDT. They were used widely in the plastics and electrical industries until they were found to be potent environmental poisons.

population The breeding group to which an organism belongs in practice. A population is generally very much smaller than an entire species, for all the members of a species are seldom in close proximity to each other.

population distribution The composition of a population categorized by several variables, often age and sex.

population ecology The branch of ecology dealing with the size, growth, and distribution of populations of organisms.

power The amount of energy delivered in a given time interval. Power = energy/time.

prairie An extensive area of fairly level, predominantly treeless land. Prairies are characterized by an abundance of various types of grasses.

predation An interaction in which some individuals eat others.

predator An animal that attacks, kills and eats other animals.

primary consumer An animal that eats plants.

radioactivity The emission of radiation by atomic nuclei.

radioisotope A radioactive isotope.

radiolysis A chemical change initiated by radiation.

rate of natural increase The difference between the crude birth and crude death rates. Also called the crude reproductive rate.

rate of population growth The increase in population over a given time divided by the initial population.

recycling The process whereby waste materials are re-used for the manufacture of new materials and goods.

redundancy Superabundance. In the context of safety systems, redundancy refers to the provision of a series of devices that duplicate each other's functions and that are programmed to go into operation in sequence if a preceding device in the series fails.

rendering The cooking of animal wastes such as fat, bones, feathers, and blood to yield tallow (used in the manufacture of soap) and high-protein animal feed.

replacement level The level of the total fertility rate that, if continued unchanged for at least a generation, would result in an eventual population growth of zero.

resource Any source of wealth or means of producing wealth.

respiration The process by which plants and animals release energy by the step-wise oxidation of organic molecules.

saltwater intrusion The movement of salt water from the ocean to terrestrial groundwater supplies that occurs when the water table in coastal areas is reduced.

sanitary landfill A site where solid waste is deposited on a land surface, compacted, and covered with dirt to reduce odours and prevent disease and fire.

savannah A type of tropical or sub-tropical prairie that is subject to seasonal patterns of rainfall. Savannahs are common in central Africa.

secondary consumer A predator that eats an animal that eats plants.

selective cutting The process of cutting selected trees in a stand of timber. See clear-cutting.

smog Smoky fog. The word is used loosely to describe visible air pollution.

soft energy system An energy system based on the use of small, home-sized, decentralized devices using renewable resources.

solar cell A semi-conductor device that converts sunlight directly into electrical energy.

solar collector A device designed to concentrate solar energy for a useful purpose.

solar design active systems: Heating systems that use a controlled flow of some substance; usually air or water, to collect, store, and transmit heat from the sun. *passive systems*: Construction systems that use the structure of a building itself to collect, store, and transmit heat from the sun.

solar energy Energy derived from the sun.

species A group of organisms that interbreed with other members of the group, but not with individuals outside the group.

species diversity The number of species present in a particular area or community.

strip mining Any mining operation that operates by removing the surface layers of soil and rock, thereby exposing the deposits of ore to be removed.

subsidence The settling of the surface of the ground as deep ground water or minerals are removed.

subsidies Economic incentives to induce polluters not to despoil the environment.

succession The sequence of changes through which an ecosystem passes during the course of time. *Primary succession* is a sequence that occurs when the terrain is initially lifeless, or almost so. *Secondary succession* is the series of community changes that takes place in disturbed areas previously occupied by a biological community synfuels An abbreviation for synthetic fuels, liquid fuels produced from oil shales, tar sands, or coal.

sustainable development The development that meets the needs of the present without compromising the ability of future generations to meet to meet their own needs.

synthetic chemicals Compounds produced by chemical reactions performed in a laboratory, as opposed to those formed naturally.

technological fix An approach to solving a social problem, such as environmental degradation, by technical or engineering methods.

thermal pollution A change in the quality of an environment (usually an aquatic environment) caused by raising its temperature.

thermodynamics The science concerned with heat and work and the relationships between them. *First Law of Thermodynamics*: Energy cannot be created or destroyed. *Second Law of Thermodynamics*: It is impossible to derive mechanical work from any portion of matter by cooling it below the temperature of the coldest surrounding object.

threshold level The minimum dose of a toxic substance that causes harmful effects.

tidal energy Energy derived from the movement of the tides.

total fertility rate (*TFR*) The total number of infants a woman can be expected to bear during the course of her life if birth rates remain constant for at least one generation.

toxic substance Any substance whose physiological action is harmful to health.

trespass An illegal intrusion or invasion of other people's property.

trophic Pertaining to nourishment.

tropical rain forest A biome that occurs when high, fairly constant rainfall and temperature permit plants to grew rapidly throughout the year.

tumour An abnormal growth of unregulated cells.

tundra Arctic or mountainous areas that are too cold to support trees and are characterized by low mosses and grasses.

urban sprawl The growth of suburban areas and the expansion of cities to pre-empt increasingly large areas of land.

urbanization A demographic process characterized by movement of people from rural to urban settlements, from small towns to large cities, and from large cities to their suburbs.

vital event In demography, a birth, a death, a marriage, a termination of marriage, or a migration.

water pollution The deterioration of the quality of water that results from the addition of impurities.

water table The upper level of water in the zone of saturated subsurface soil and rock.

weathering The breaking down of rocks into smaller particles by physical and chemical processes.

Xerophite A plant adopted to arid conditions.

zero population growth A condition in which the birth and death rates in a population are equal therefore, the size of the population remains constant.

Bibliography

Adasdair, Blai and David, H. (1995) *Environment and Business*, Routledge, London.

Arvill, R. (1967) *Man and Environment: Crisis and the Strategy of Choice*, Penguin.

Bach and Wilfried (1972) *Atmospheric Pollution*, McGraw Hill, New York.

Bahuguna, S. (1990) Tehri: The Dam of Discontent, *Yojana*, Vol. 34 (10), pp. 9-12.

Brown, E.H. (1970) Man Shapes the Earth, *Geographical Journal*, Vol. 136, pp. 74-85.

Brij Gopal and N. Bhardwaj (1979) *Elements of Ecology*, Vikas Publications, N. Delhi.

Burton, Robert, W.K. and Gilbert, F.W.(1978) *The Environment as Hazard*, Oxford University Press, New York.

Billihgs, W.D. (1971) *Plant, Man and the Ecosystem*, Macmillan.

Clapham, W.B. (1973) *Natural Ecosystems*, Macmillan, London.

Colinvaux, Paul. A. (1973) *Introduction to Ecology*, John Wiley and Sons, New York.

Darlingten, P.J., (1957) *Zoogeography*, John Wiley, New York.

Dasseman, R.F. (1976) *Environmental Conservation*, John Wiley, New York.

Detwyler, T.R. (1971) *Man's Impact on Environment*, McGraw-Hill, New York.

Dikshit, R.D. (1984) *Geography and the Teaching of the Environment*, Department of Geography, Poona University, pp. 68-83.

Dogra, Bharat (1980) *Forest and People*, Himalaya Darshan Prakashan Samiti, Rishikesh.

Dowdeswell, W.H. (1984) *Ecology: Principles and Practice*, Heinemann, Oxford.

Flanagan, D. (1970) *The Biosphere*, W.H. Freeman and Co., San Francisco.

Furley, P.A. and Newey, W.W. (1983) *Man and the Biosphere*, Butterworths, London.

Futehally, I. (1988) *Our Environment*, NBT, New Delhi.

Gerasimov, I.P. (1983) *Geography and Ecology*, Progress Publishers Moscow.

Glan, L. A. and Rhoda, L.M. (eds.) (1970) *Ecological Crisis Readings for Survival*, Harcourt Brace Jovanovich, New York.

Goudie, Andrew (1986) *The Human Impact on the Natural Environment*, Basil Blackwell, Oxford.

Haggett, P. (1972) *Geography: A Modern Synthesis*, Harper and Row, London.

Irving, R.M. and Priddle, G.B. (1971) *Crisis-Reading in Environmental Issues and Strategies*, Macmillan, London.

Jackas, G.V. and White, R.O.(1939) *The Rape of the Earth*, Fabev, London.

Keith, Smith (1996) *Environmental Hazards*, Routledge, New York.

Kumar, V.K. (1982) *Kanpur City: A Study in Environmental Pollution*, Tara Book Agency, Varanasi.

Maddox, J. (1972) *The Doomsday Syndrome*, McGraw-Hill, New York.

Manivasakam, N. (1992) *Environmental Pollution*, N.B.T., New Delhi.

Mash, G. P. (1964) Man and Nature (*Physical Geography as Modified by Human Action*, Charles Scriber, New York.

Maxwell, K.E. (1973) *Environment of Life*, Dickenson Publishers, Co., California.

Nicholson and Max (1970) *The Environmental Revolution*, McGraw-Hill, New York.

Odum, Eugene P. (1971) *Fundamentals of Ecology*, W. B. Saunders Co., London.

Park, C. C. (1980) *Ecology and Environmental Management*, Butterworths, London.

Peter, C. and Susan, C. (1998) *The South, The North and the Environment*, Printer, London.

Pfajjlin, J. R. and Ziegler, E.N. (eds.) (1976) *Encyclopedia of Environmental Science and Engineering*, Vol. I and II, Gordon and Breach Science Publishers, New York.

Rao, K. L. (1975) *India's Water Wealth*, Orient Longman, New Delhi.

Raven, P.H., Berg, L.R. and Johnson, G.B. (1993) *Environment*, Sounders College Publications, Orlando.

Saraf, R.K. (eds.) (1973) *Proceedings of Symposium on Environmental Pollution*. CEPHERI, Nagpur.

Seshadri, B. (1969) *The Twilight of India's Wildlife*, Oxford, London.

Singh, H. H. and Others (eds.) (1986) *Geography and Environment*, Concept, N. Delhi.

Sharma, H. S. (eds.) (1988) *Environmental Design and Development*, Scientific Pub., Jodhpur.

Sharma, P. D. (1988) *Elements of Ecology*, Rastogi, Meerut.

Singh, L. R. and Other (eds.) (1983) *Environmental Management*, Allahabad Geographical Society, Allahabad.

Singh, Savindra and Tiwari, R.C. (eds.) (1989) *Geomorphology and Environment*, Allahabad Geographical Society, Allahabad.

Singh, S. P. (1990) Tehri Dam: An Assessment and Vision, *Yojana*, Vol. 34 (10), pp. 5-8

Smith, G.H. (ed.) (1965) *Conservation of Natural Resources*, New York.

Stephen, T. (1996) *Environmental Management Plans Demystified*, Spon Press, London.

Stoddard, D. R. (1965) *Geography and the Ecological Approach*, Geography, Vol. 50, pp. 242-51.

Strahler, A. N. and Strahler, A.H. (1976) *Geography and Man's Environment*, John Wiley, New York.

Thomas, W. L. (1965) *Man's Role in Changing the Face of the Earth*, University of Chicago Press.

Taylor, G. (1967) *Geography in the 20th Century*, Methuen, London.

Turk, J. (1985) *Introduction to Environmental Studies*, C.B.S. College Publishers, Chicago.

UNESCO (1981) *M.B.A. Information System Biosphere Reserves*, Publishers, No. 2.

UNESCO (1970) *Use and Conservation of Biosphere*, Natural Resources Research 10, Paris.

World Commission on Environment and Development (1987) *Our Common Future*, Oxford University Press.

Zimmermann, E.W. (1951) *World Resources and Industries*, Harper and Row, London.

Index